W9-CCX-118

Customer WinBack

Jill Griffin

Michael W. Lowenstein

Foreword by Don Peppers and Martha Rogers

Customer WinBack

How to Recapture Lost Customers— And Keep Them Loyal

 JOSSEY-BASS
A Wiley Company
San Francisco

Copyright © 2001 by Jossey-Bass Inc., 350 Sansome Street, San Francisco, California 94104.

Jossey-Bass is a registered trademark of Jossey-Bass Inc., A Wiley Company.

No part of this publication may be reproduced, stored in a retrieval system, or transmitted
in any form or by any means, electronic, mechanical, photocopying, recording, scanning,
or otherwise, except as permitted under Sections 107 or 108 of the 1976 United States
Copyright Act, without either the prior written permission of the Publisher or authorization
through payment of the appropriate per-copy fee to the Copyright Clearance Center,
222 Rosewood Drive, Danvers, MA 01923, (978) 750-8400, fax (978) 750-4744. Requests
to the Publisher for permission should be addressed to the Permissions Department,
John Wiley & Sons, Inc., 605 Third Avenue, New York, NY 10158-0012, (212) 850-6011,
fax (212) 850-6008, e-mail: permreq@wiley.com.

Jossey-Bass books and products are available through most bookstores. To contact
Jossey-Bass directly, call (888) 378-2537, fax to (800) 605-2665, or visit our website
at www.josseybass.com.

Substantial discounts on bulk quantities of Jossey-Bass books are available to corporations,
professional associations, and other organizations. For details and discount information,
contact the special sales department at Jossey-Bass.

TCF Manufactured in the United States of America on Lyons Falls Turin Book.
This paper is acid-free and 100 percent totally chlorine-free.

Library of Congress Cataloging-in-Publication Data
Griffin, Jill.
    Customer winback : how to recapture lost customers and keep them
loyal / by Jill Griffin and Michael W. Lowenstein.
        p. cm. — (The Jossey-Bass business & management series)
    Includes bibliographical references and index.
    ISBN 0-7879-4667-2
    1. Customer loyalty. 2. Customer services. 3. Customer relations.
I. Lowenstein, Michael W., 1942- . II. Title. III. Series.
HF5415.5 .G753 2001
658.8'12—dc21

                                                                    00-011080

FIRST EDITION
HB Printing 10 9 8 7 6 5 4 3 2 1

The Jossey-Bass
Business & Management Series

Contents

It's a fact—most companies don't track customer loss and lack strong win-back programs and systems • Three key reasons why customer defection goes unmanaged • The short- and long-term substantive rewards of customer win-back • How companies like First Union and Doubleday Direct are saving high-value customers

The interconnectivity of acquisition, retention, and win-back • How you can turn your firm into a customer loyalty laboratory • Six customer groups you want to track • Practical ways to slice and dice purchase data and uncover important trends • Why you need to know customer lifetime value and how to estimate it • The win-back decision map—your direction finder for recovering lost customers and saving at-risk customers

Different ways customers say good-bye • How to determine whether a customer is worth winning back • How to estimate the second lifetime value of a win-back prospect—even with little

—ᴡᴡ— Foreword

No matter what business you're in, customers are the central mission of your enterprise. A business, to stay in business, must be able to get, keep, and grow customers. And if for some reason you don't manage to keep a customer, then by all means figure out how to get the customer back. Getting customers to return, once they have terminated their relationship with you, is what *Customer WinBack* is about.

In subscription-based consumer service businesses, such as credit cards and long-distance phone services, customer "win-back" is a widely known and closely watched practice. It is firmly rooted in the discipline and economics of direct marketing. Populations of ex-customers are divided carefully into test cells and control groups, with marketing analysts constantly applying new offers to try to increase the win-back rate, or to lower the win-back cost.

In business-to-business situations, a good salesperson knows that one reliable source for new prospects consists of former customers who have left the franchise long enough to become disillusioned with a competitor's offering.

But in many businesses, customers leave in droves every day, with no exit interview, no understanding of why they left, *and no effort, ever, to keep them or win them back.* A single consumer customer often costs from $10 to as much as $400, or even more, to replace with a new customer; yet many companies today spend nothing on getting these customers back into the fold. Lots of companies allocate budget to customer acquisition when the real problem is retention and win-back.

As a result, the companies that make a real effort to win customers back enjoy dramatic results:

• American Airlines recognizes the importance of valuable customers. The company monitors these customers so that in the event their business trails off, American can initiate a phone call to them through its WinBAAck program. Relationship managers talk to customers about why their business has declined and occasionally offer "treatments," or enticements, to return to American based on profile data and the reasons for the decline in flight activity. What American learned is that approximately 50 percent of customers called were flying less due to reasons such as a job change or retirement; the other 50 percent cited service-related reasons, which American can address internally as a result of the feedback loop. According to Elizabeth Crandall, American's managing director of personalized marketing, most customers appreciate the calls and the fact that American recognizes them as valuable customers. A recent investment in E.piphany software will help the company identify the next round of WinBAAck customers.

• An insurance agent won his company's sales award for the year. When he was asked how he made such spectacular numbers, he admitted he dug into his records for the past seven years and turned up a lot of customers he'd lost but wished he hadn't. He simply called each one and asked why they'd left. Many couldn't remember why, some had moved, and many were happy to hear from the agent—and of course were already familiar with his products. It was the most productive sales year he ever had, and the benefits paid off in successive years through renewals.

Getting a customer to return can be accomplished in many different ways, using a variety of tactics and offers. However, what all successful win-back programs have in common is that they are proactive, strategically sound initiatives rather than occasional hit-and-run tactics. A win-back program may be based on promotional offers or it could be based on service-oriented customer coddling, but all successful programs are deliberate. They are measurable. And they are well thought out.

Thinking carefully about how to win customers back is what this book is all about.

December 2000   DON PEPPERS AND MARTHA ROGERS
PARTNERS, PEPPERS AND ROGERS GROUP

⚊ᴂᴂⵀ Preface

When it comes to protecting customer relationships you had better be ready to win back customers you thought you would never lose. Just ask United Parcel Service (UPS), which suffered staggering customer defection as a consequence of a fifteen-day Teamsters work stoppage in 1997. Suddenly, much of the firm's rock-solid base of 1.5 million customers was turning to Federal Express, Airborne, RPS, and the United States Postal Service. The strike made UPS customers see the dangers of using a single delivery company to handle their packages and parcels. FedEx, for example, delivered 850,000 additional packages each day of the strike and reported expecting to keep as much as 25 percent of that new business.

Reclaiming these lost customers was of paramount importance to UPS. Both profits and jobs depended on it. Even after the 80,000 drivers were back behind the wheels of their delivery trucks or tractor-trailers, many thousands of UPS workers were laid off. A UPS manager in Arkansas was quoted as saying, "the degree that our customers come back will dictate whether those jobs come back."

Lost jobs and lost profits propelled UPS into an aggressive win-back mode as soon as the strike was settled. Customers began receiving telephone calls from UPS officials assuring them that UPS was back in business, apologizing for the inconvenience of the strike, and pledging that UPS's former reliability had been restored. Drivers dropping by for pickups were cheerful and confident, and they reinforced the idea that things were back to normal. UPS issued letters of apology and discount certificates to customers to further help heal the wounds and rebuild trust. And it initiated face-to-face meetings with customers large and small—all with the goal of getting lost business back.

These win-back initiatives worked. They built an important bridge of recovery back to the customer. The actions, coupled with the company's cost-effective services, the continuing advances in shipping technology, and the dramatic growth in on-line shopping, enabled UPS to reinstate many laid-off workers and at the same time increase its profits a remarkable 87 percent in the year following the devastating strike.

The experience of UPS is not an isolated case. Protecting customer relationships in these uncertain times is a fact of life for every business. It has been determined that most companies lose between 10 and 40 percent of their customers each year. The economic impact of this customer loss can be found in downsizings, rightsizings, plant closings, and layoffs, all with crushing effects on employees and their communities. Left unchecked, customer turnover results in a *multiplier* effect, creating alienation among the remaining customers, negative company growth, and the erosion of employee trust.

Nowhere are the consequences of customer defection more visible than in the world of Internet commerce, where the opportunities for customer loss occur at warp speed. E-tailers and Web service companies are spending incredible sums of money to draw customers to their sites, but they are not turning enough of those customers into repeat customers. As a result relatively few of these companies, including many well-established sites, have turned a profit. E-customers have proven to be a demanding lot—they want value, and they want it fast. These customers show little tolerance for poor Web architecture and navigation, outdated information, and insufficient customer service. One study we've seen showed that most Internet e-commerce sites will lose 60 percent of their new customers within six weeks.

What's more, the Internet also serves as a high-speed pathway for negative customer opinion. Unhappy customers in the bricks-and-mortar world usually express their displeasure to between two and twenty people; on the Internet, angry former customers have the opportunity to tell thousands.

Without question, we've entered a new era of customer defection in which customer turnover is reaching epidemic proportions and wrecking businesses and lives along the way. It's time to truly understand the consequences of customer loss and then apply proven winback strategies to regain these valuable customers. That's why we've written this book.

How does a company defend itself against the perils of customer loss in the first place? The best plan, of course, is a proactive one that anticipates customer defection and works hard to lessen the risk.

That's why we devote the second half of this book to key strategies you can use to defection proof your company, such as gathering and applying the right customer data, using customer teams, creating staff loyalty, and targeting the right kind of customers in the first place.

But in today's hypercompetitive marketplace, no retention program can be 100 percent foolproof, so customer win-back programs are a necessary part of any loyalty plan. The good news is the mounting evidence that the rewards from win-back success and the benefits surrounding it far outweigh the investment costs. The bad news is that most companies are still largely unprepared to address this opportunity. We discovered this firsthand when we interviewed scores of marketing executives and consultants and when we conducted our original defection and recovery research in 1999 among purchasing agents, sales managers, and marketing managers. In our national study, conducted among a cross section of business-to-business and consumer product and service industries, we found that most firms are largely uninformed about the reasons for customer loss.

Worse still, purchasing agents generally saw suppliers' efforts at recovery as less than effective. Sales managers and marketing managers reported investing a meager percentage of their marketing dollars to win back lost customers. Alarmingly high percentages didn't know customers' lifetime value, rates of customer loss, or rates of recovery. In the light of findings like these, it's no wonder that customer turnover is a disease at epidemic levels.

Building and sustaining customer loyalty is harder than ever before. Now's the time to put in place specific strategies and tools for winning back lost customers, saving customers on the brink of defection, and making your company defection proof. Our book will help you do just that.

Austin, Texas   JILL GRIFFIN
Collingswood, New Jersey   MICHAEL LOWENSTEIN
December 2000

⤳ Acknowledgments

We are deeply grateful to the many clients, colleagues, and friends whose contributions helped make this book a reality. Cambridge Technology Partners sponsored our nationwide win-back research study. Barbara Rodgers, Greg Furman, Jean Reilly, and Lisa Boone opened their Rolodexes and provided us valuable contacts for interviews. Victor Hunter, Nick Poulos, Christine Foschetti, Peter Dresch, Kathy O'Neal, Bonnie Martinez, Fernando Roman, Catherine Sheeran, Bill McCausland, and Margaret Sheridan provided us with important insights into win-back and save strategies.

We also offer our special thanks to our agent, Jeff Herman, for his encouragement; to our editor, Cedric Crocker, for his patient and collaborative style; to Judy Barrett and Cheryl Rae for their feedback and suggestions; and to Marshall Segal, Elizabeth Peck, and Mary Birnbaum for their ace research skills.

We also wish to thank Bernd Stauss (Catholic University of Eichstaett, Germany), Adrian Payne (Cranfield University, United Kingdom), Peggy Sheehan (Horizon Research), Joene Grissom (Grissom & Associates), Susan Clark (The Phineus Company), John Titus (*Inc.* magazine), David Pilgrim (Cambridge Technology Partners), Bill Underwood (American Honda), Julie Anderson (Cellular One), Terry Varva (Marketing Metrics), Stuart Schaeffer (ClubCorp), Mary Jo Walker (Wachovia Bank), Gerald Evans (Sara Lee), Joe Udell (Addressing Your Needs), Peter Wayman (Associates Relocation Management Company), Patrick Asbra (*Austin Business Journal*), Bob Allen (Aegis), Judy Kearney (Holiday Inn/Orlando), Bill Cone (Wells Fargo), Mike Booth (SLP), Kirk Trantham (*Philadelphia Inquirer/Daily News*), Doug Rose (QVC Network), Clyde Boyce (*Time* magazine), Robert Paisner (ScrubaDub Car Wash), Corie Raben (Dell Computer), Amy Van Court (Fast Company), Shari Altman (Sara Lee Direct), Brian Wolfe (*Sports Illustrated*), Pat McMahan (VISA), Susanna Hagg (Cap Gemini, France), Michael Price (Price Automotive Group), James Di Costanzo

(PNC Bank), John Hubich (Wachovia Bank), Tom Cox (IKEA), Dorothy Simmons (American Cancer Society), Elizabeth Haight (The Math Works), François Clemenceau (SLP InfoWare, France), Dave Manchee (*Newsweek* magazine), Mike Duffy (*Wall Street Journal*), Frank Britt (Streamline), Pam Bilbrey (Baptist Healthcare), Renee Corapi (Hanna Andersson), and Olivier Willi (Swissair, Switzerland).

Above all, we owe extraordinary gratitude to our spouses, Mack Nunn and Susan Lowenstein, for their unwavering encouragement and support throughout the two years we have spent on this project.

J.G.
M.L.

~~~ The Authors

Jill Griffin is author of the business best-seller, *Customer Loyalty: How to Earn It, How to Keep It* (Lexington, 1995; Jossey-Bass, 1997). She has been helping organizations build fiercely loyal customers for over twenty years. At RJR/Nabisco, she served as senior brand manager for the corporation's largest brand. In the service sector, Griffin served as director of sales and marketing for AmeriSuites Hotels and was responsible for launching and expanding the new chain nationwide.

Griffin has served on the marketing faculty at the University of Texas and holds M.B.A. and B.S. degrees, magna cum laude, from the University of South Carolina. In 1989 she founded the Austin, Texas–based firm The Griffin Group, specializing in loyalty and win-back solutions. Services include loyalty and win-back program development, customer and staff loyalty research, and keynote speaking and training (www.loyaltysolutions.com). Clients include Microsoft, Sun Microsystems, Ford, Hewlett Packard, Arthur Andersen, Sprint, Wells Fargo, Dell, Toyota, Cendant, IBM, Advanced Micro Devices, and Marriott Hotels.

Michael W. Lowenstein, CPCM, is managing director of Customer Retention Associates, a customer and staff loyalty program development and research firm located in Collingswood, New Jersey (www.customerloyalty.org). With over thirty years' experience in customer and staff loyalty research, CRM, loyalty program development, customer win-back, service quality, customer-driven corporate culture, and strategic marketing and planning to draw on, he is an active speaker and trainer, regular contributor to two customer loyalty newsletters, and author of two well-regarded books: *Customer Retention: An Integrated Process for Keeping Your Best Customers* (1995) and *The Customer Loyalty Pyramid* (1997).

Lowenstein has been an instructor for Pennsylvania State University and the American Management Association, and he holds an

M.B.A. degree in marketing from the University of Pittsburgh and a B.S. degree in economics and marketing from Villanova University. His clients include First Union, Toyota, Prudential, Westvaco, Cigna, Charles Schwab, Borg-Warner, Sygma, Metropolitan Life, Microsoft, and Georgia-Pacific.

PART ONE

How to Win Back Lost Customers

In the next five chapters we explore the major aspects of winning back lost customers. In Chapter One we look at the facts and findings that prove win-back is critical to your company's success. In Chapter Two we look closely at one firm's customer *loyalty laboratory* and how win-back plays a vital role in acquiring and retaining high-value customers. We also introduce the win-back decision tree, a blueprint for in-depth planning. Chapter Three examines the specific strategies you can use to win back lost customers. Chapter Four focuses on how you can save customers on the brink of defection. And the last chapter in this section, Chapter Five, guides you in mobilizing and managing a win-back team.

CHAPTER ONE

Why Customer Win-Back Is Critical to Your Success

B y any standards, Toni Neal was a high-value customer that any credit-card company would want to keep. This hard-charging founder and CEO of a highly successful Austin, Texas–based consulting firm with a staff of twenty-plus held three credit cards (we'll call them Super Deluxe, Deluxe, and Regular) from a leading credit-card provider. A ten-year customer, Toni consistently used these cards for business and personal purchases, charging on average $10,000 to $15,000 a month. Most Christmases, she took some much needed rest from her business and vacationed for three weeks in Hawaii, charging her entire holiday (typically $15,000 to $20,000) on these cards. All was well, or so she thought, until she attempted to pay the bill for an important client lunch and was informed by the waiter that her Deluxe card charges had not been approved. Perplexed, Toni gave the waiter a competitive card for the lunch bill and, on returning to her office, immediately called the card company to inquire about the refusal. She was informed by the service representative that her Deluxe card was rejected because her account was overdue by about $200. "No," corrected Toni. "I'm current on my bill, but I have a $200 charge that's in dispute and I'm still waiting on correspondence from your company regarding resolution."

Unmoved, the rep insisted that the $200 payment was due and that no additional charges would be accepted on the card until Toni "paid her bill." As both a long-time card holder with an excellent credit history and a meticulous record keeper in her own right, Toni felt there had to be a simple solution, and so she asked to speak to a supervisor. Again the rep refused. Angry and exasperated, Toni instructed the rep to immediately cancel two of her three cards and promised that her next call would be to another credit-card company to sign up as a new card member. True to her word, Toni made the call and set up her new account that very day.

With the exception of statements that arrived in the mail showing her accounts had been closed and the disputed $200 had been reconciled, Toni heard nothing from her former credit card company right away. Finally, about a month later, Toni received a call from a service rep inviting her to become a Deluxe card member. The rep turned out to be unaware Toni had canceled the card just weeks earlier. Toni eagerly explained to the rep why she had canceled two of her cards and why the remaining card in her wallet went unused. The rep's response? Nothing. Rather than saying, "we're so sorry," or, "what can we do to reinstate you as a valued customer?" or, "let me transfer you to my supervisor," the rep simply stated that Toni didn't sound like she was very interested in using this company anymore and ended the call.

At the time of this writing, Toni has again departed for her annual three-week Christmas holiday in Hawaii, where her credit cards will be used extensively. This caps another year of annual business and personal credit-card purchases of roughly $200,000. But this year, unlike previous years, there are no longer Super Deluxe or Deluxe cards in Toni's wallet. She counts herself as an official former customer, one with more questions than answers.[1]

When Toni told us about her experience, key questions came to mind:

- Why was the service rep so rigid over a $200 "past due" amount with a high-value customer with an excellent payment history?

- Why didn't the card issuer's customer information system consolidate all of Toni's card information into one centralized computer file so customer representatives could recognize Toni's three-card value?

- Why didn't the card issuer's system flag Toni as a high-value defector as soon as she canceled her cards?

- Why was the card issuer's database of prospect names not coordinated with the database of recently lost customers?

- Why did the second rep not pursue reactivation with Toni after hearing about Toni's unhappy experience?

Before you write off Toni's experience as something that could not happen to one of your customers, think again. If your company is like most, you have labored hard to sharpen and improve your customer acquisition and retention programs, but you have done very little to recover those customers who, for various reasons, fell through the cracks and stopped buying from you.

You're not alone. Every year, the average firm loses 20 to 40 percent of its customers (see Figure 1.1). What's more, customer defection is likely the least recognized and most misunderstood dynamic in any organization (Figure 1.2). Left unmanaged, it adversely affects profits and growth, hinders the opportunities for attracting new customers, and damages employee morale—all of which jeopardizes a firm's overall success.

Figure 1.1. Annual Customer Defection Rates, by Industry.

Industry	Defection Rate
Internet Service Providers	22%*
U.S. long distance (mainstream)	30*
U.S. long distance (high usage)	35*
German mobile phone market	25
Clothing catalogs	25
Residential tree and lawn care	32
Newspaper subscription	66

*Percentage of U.S. households that reported switching between Internet service providers (ISPs) or telephone carriers within the last twelve months (reported to the authors by Peter Dresh at J. D. Power & Associates, January 2000). Moreover, 59 percent of households surveyed said they definitely, probably, or might switch their local phone service carrier in the coming year, and 34 percent of those with ISPs said they definitely, probably, or might switch carriers in the coming year.

Figure 1.2. It's a Fact: Most Firms Don't Focus on Customer Loss.

In 1999, we asked sales managers, marketing managers, and purchasing agents from 350 randomly selected companies, representing a cross section of industries, about their firms' customer loss and win-back practices. The answers, outlined here, show that most companies are not informed about customer loss and do not have strong win-back policies, programs, and monitoring systems.

1. Do you know how many customers you lose per year?

Marketing managers	Sales managers
Yes: 52%	Yes: 70%
No: 48%	No: 30%

   Close to 50% of the marketing managers and 30% of the sales managers could not identify their company's percentage of annual customer loss. Those who did know their firm's defection rate said it averaged about 7 to 8% when in fact, the average company loses 20%, or more, of its customers every year.

2. Do you identify a customer as lost?

Marketing managers	Sales managers
Yes: 80%	Yes: 94%
No: 20%	No: 6%

   Generally speaking, sales managers were more able to determine when customers had defected than marketing managers were. Over 20% of marketing managers said they did not identify customers as "defectors," versus 6% of sales managers.

3. Do you conduct defection interviews among lost customers?

Marketing managers	Sales managers
Yes: 53%	Yes: 57%
No: 47%	No: 43%

   Forty-three percent of sales managers and 47% of marketing managers said they did not conduct defection interviews among lost customers, thus depriving their companies of insight about root causes of defection.

4. Does your company have a system for identifying customers who are at high risk of defection?

Marketing managers	Sales managers
Yes: 44%	Yes: 31%
No: 56%	No: 69%

   Sixty-nine percent of sales managers and 56% of marketing managers did not have a system for identifying high-risk customers. This creates high vulnerability to customer loss as well as inability to counter attrition. (Similarly, a recent KPMG study among telephone companies found 50% could not identify customers on the brink of defection.)

5. Do you know what percentage of your customers you are able to win back?

Marketing managers	Sales managers
Know: 50%	Know: 84%
Don't know: 50%	Don't know: 16%

(continued)

Fifty percent of marketing managers and 16% of sales managers did not know their company's win-back success rates. So, especially among marketing managers, there is a knowledge void about their company's win-back processes.

Few companies are aware of their true customer defection rates, and fewer still know the profit impact associated with this loss. For example, when the wireless telephone industry talks about customer churn, the issue doesn't sound very consequential. After all, with losses estimated at 1 percent to 3 percent a month, how big a problem can losing these few subscribers be?

Very big, as Bill McCausland found when he did the math. The average carrier's current churn rate of around 2.5 percent a month works out to a whopping 30 percent a year. "Over a three-year period, you're turning over your customer base. That's a huge loss of customers," says McCausland, a former GTE executive.[2]

What makes the problem critical are the costs represented by those lost subscribers. The average carrier spends $300 to $700 to acquire one customer, including such costs as sales commissions, advertising, and promotion. Lost customers cost the company an average of $57 a month in lost revenues. If you have a customer base of one million subscribers, McCausland says, and "you are losing three hundred thousand customers [30 percent] at $500 per customer a year, that's $150 million a year."[3]

The loss of money is not all that's important; when a customer defects, you are also losing goodwill and a valuable source of information about your business. If a happy customer is good advertising, a lost customer is often bad advertising. Each one of those lost customers is a potential *ambassador of bad news*. People share their stories of discontent with others, and that is harmful to your business reputation (see Figure 1.3).

If, however, you follow up with lost customers and identify the reason for their defection, you can learn important information about your own business practices. Are your customer service representatives uninformed? Are they brusque with customers? Are there steps you can take to make sure that other customers are not lost? A loyal customer is a valuable asset, and one you should not let go of without a fight.

Figure 1.3. What One Lost Customer *Really* Costs.

Lost customer

1 unhappy customer spending $200/month defects	$2400 revenue lost/year

Lost business due to negative word of mouth

The unhappy customer tells on average 11 other people	11*
These 11 people tell 5 others	55*
Total people 1 lost customer influences	66
Assume 25% of those 66 people will not do business with you	17
Amount of lost opportunity from 17 people who would likely spend $200/month	$40,800 revenue lost/year

Total business forfeited

Due to 1 lost customer and associated negative word-of-mouth	$43,200 revenue lost/year
	$432,000 lost over 10 years

*Research by Technical Assistance Research Programs has found that an upset customer tells an average of eleven people about an unhappy experience and that those eleven people tell five others.[4]

WHY DEFECTION GOES UNMANAGED

Without a doubt, the first critical step in reducing customer churn is to constantly examine your acquisition and retention programs and look for ways to improve your ability to attract and keep high-value customers. The many books and articles written and seminars presented about selling, retention, and loyalty attest to the importance of these programs. But until now, most companies have limited their focus to acquisition and retention initiatives. Why don't they take the additional steps needed to recover lost revenue and learn from defections? Three reasons drive defection blindness and win-back apathy.

1. *Retention rates can mislead.* Defection rates of 50 percent may masquerade as 80 percent retention rates. A defection problem can disguise itself in seemingly healthy retention numbers. For example, think of a college that retains 80 percent of the students in each class from one year to the next. This retention rate sounds pretty healthy

until you consider that if the college starts with 1,000 freshmen, 80 percent retention means a sophomore class of 800, a junior class of 640, and a senior class of just 512. Only when you monitor the fallout or churn among an original group of recruits over time and compare the end result with the starting numbers does the real defection picture emerge. This same analysis can be applied to customer retention rates. Assume in that year one, you recruited one hundred new customers and your annual retention rate averages 80 percent. By the end of only four years, only 51 percent of these 100 customers will still remain ($100 \times .8 \times .8 \times .8$). In other words, even with a steady and respectable retention level of 80 percent, the *half-life* of your customer base, the amount of time it takes for one-half of the customer base to be lost, is only four years. Yikes! That's a huge profit drain that cannot be counteracted simply by recruiting new customers as replacements.

2. *Firms are unaware of both the substantial loss associated with customer defection and the substantial profit recovery potential associated with win-back.* In his groundbreaking book *The Loyalty Effect*, Frederick Reichheld[5] was the first to examine why the profit contribution of a mature customer who has bought from a firm for a number of years is dramatically higher than that of a customer who has been buying from the same firm for only one or two years. He identified and isolated six important economic effects of customer loyalty and their impact on annual customer profitability.

- *Acquisition cost.* Once the customer is acquired, acquisition costs are no longer incurred.

- *Base profit.* Base profit is the difference between the price a customer pays and the company's costs. The longer a company retains a customer the longer it earns base profit, and the better its initial customer acquisition investment looks over time.

- *Revenue growth.* As customers mature and become more and more familiar with the company's array of products and services, their spending tends to accelerate as they increasingly buy a greater cross section of company offerings.

- *Cost savings.* As customers get to know a business, they tend to be less costly to service. Mature customers don't waste time requesting services the company doesn't provide, and they are less dependent on employees for information and advice.

- *Referrals.* Loyal customers recommend the business to others. In many industries, such as insurance, home building, car sales, and software, referrals are a major driver of new business.

- *Price premium.* Customers who have been around long enough to learn a company's procedures and acquaint themselves with its full product line will invariably get greater value from the business relationship. This generally makes them less price sensitive on individual items than new customers.

What Reichheld's work has taught companies around the world is this: when a long-term customer leaves, his defection adversely affects the firm's bottom-line profitability, and for the reasons just outlined, this profitability deficit is not offset simply by recruiting a new customer. Therefore, using win-back measures to extend the profit contribution of a mature, high-value customer who has defected or is on the brink of defection is crucial to any firm's profit management success.

3. *Companies see lapsed customers as dead opportunities.* For many firms the words *lost customer* immediately evoke an image of a group of disgruntled former buyers who, at the first suggestion of returning to the firm as a customer, would immediately say, "No way!" and bolster the refusal with some heartfelt "been there, done that" sentiment. Yet growing evidence suggests the probability of win-back success and that the profits and other benefits resulting from win-back initiatives far outweigh the investment costs.

THE FINANCIAL PAYBACK ON WIN-BACK

A study by Marketing Metrics has found firms have a much better chance of winning business from lost customers than from new prospects. The research found the average firm has a 60 to 70 percent probability of successfully selling again to "active" customers, a 20 to 40 percent probability of successfully selling to lost customers, and only a 5 to 20 percent probability of making a successful sale to prospects.[6]

Industry Experience

The experience with win-back programs of MCI sales director Catherine Sheeran reinforces Marketing Metric's research findings. Comparing win-back to acquisition success, Sheeran reports, "Our success rates with win-back were three to four times better than with prospecting. For example, if you have a 5 percent rate in converting prospects, you can expect a 15 to 20 percent success rate in reactivating inactive customers."[7]

In the retail industry, reactivation promotions also typically out pull prospect promotions. Retail Resources vice president Christine Foschetti reports this happens 95 percent of the time. "There are those few exceptions with incredible incentives that will drive in higher prospect results; however, generally it is by far more cost effective to communicate with your own customers—even the inactive ones—than prospects."[8]

There are several reasons why customer win-back has a higher success probability than acquisition. You have advantages with lost customers that you don't have with prospects—you have information about them. Because of their past purchase history, you typically know where and how to reach a lapsed customer, whereas potential customers are much harder to find. For example, if past behavior tells you a customer doesn't respond to telemarketing calls, you will know to send mail and e-mails instead. If the director of engineering signed all past equipment orders, you will want to investigate starting your reactivation efforts with him or her. Consider this win-back experience:

> An agent told us recently that he got to thinking about the problem of lost customers about a year ago and dug back into his records for the past seven years. He turned up a number of customers that he had lost, but wished he hadn't. Without doing any formal research, he simply got on the phone and called these customers. What he discovered was that in many cases the individual contacts who stopped buying from him were no longer working for the company. And when they were, they remembered buying from him, but couldn't recall why they had discontinued buying. "It was just like opening new doors," the agent said, "except that they were already familiar with the products. In most cases, I was able to schedule meetings with them and to at least get some trial orders started. Soon, the trial orders turned into regular orders and we had the business back."[9]

Having customer information increases the probability of winning at win-back and can lower your reacquisition costs as well.

How Doubleday Direct Saves a Member

Perhaps the most compelling evidence that win-back pays comes from the book club business. Book clubs offer membership services. The extensive customer data obtained in this type of direct-mail business make a profitability comparison between winning back expired members and acquiring new members relatively easy.

Doubleday Direct has a seventy-year history of operating book clubs worldwide. With thirty book clubs under its management, recruiting new members is the biggest single cost of the business. Because acquisition is very costly, Doubleday Direct has taken steps to "save a member" wherever possible. Its save-a-member programs have two phases: (1) the termination phase, when the member contacts Doubleday with the intention of leaving the relationship, and (2) the revitalization phase, in which expired members are contacted about reactivating their book club membership.

MANAGING THE TERMINATION PHASE. When members call in to cancel their memberships, telephone representatives ask them why they want to terminate. The representatives have on-line access to all relevant data about the member, and they are empowered to offer solutions to high-value members and trained to diplomatically say good-bye to members identified as unprofitable. Approximately 60 percent of the cancellations can be prevented in this way. Most of these customers say they are not happy with the automatic shipment of the main selection, which occurs when the reply postcard is not returned on time, or they are displeased with the frequency of the mailings. With this feedback, the telephone representatives convert these members to either a positive option plan (books are shipped only when explicitly ordered by the member) or the member is suspended from all mailings for a designated time. Other problems are mainly product or service issues that can be solved through offering a toll-free customer support telephone number or coupons for free books. Even though the profit margin for the latter customers is smaller than for others, they still represent higher profits than are achieved by recruiting new members. Mail-in cancellations are treated in a similar way. Either a solution to the problem is offered through a follow-up letter or the customer is called by a telephone marketing representative.

LEVERAGING THE REVITALIZATION PHASE. Doubleday has done considerable analysis of the economics behind winning back lost members in comparison to acquiring new members. One particular test was very revealing. Two separate mailings were compared, one to a list of externally acquired addresses and one to a list of expired members. For both mailings, the same creative treatment and offers were used. (Six books were offered for $1 and a premium or a seventh book for $4.98.) The only difference between the mailings was a variation in the letter in the package: the external prospects were introduced to the club, while the expired members were "invited to come back."[10]

As Figure 1.4 illustrates, across every profit variable the return on winning back expired members exceeded the return on acquiring new members. From cost per order to gross and net contribution per order, profitability of expired members was greater than profitability of the external list. Moreover, the net return on investment from the expired member list was almost ten times (214 percent) larger than the return from the external list (23 percent).

Every company is unique, of course, but the Doubleday Direct side-by-side comparisons provide strong evidence that winning back lost customers can be a profit-making strategy for any firm.

WIN-BACK BENEFITS BEYOND THE BOTTOM LINE

As we've seen, the bottom-line financial rewards from win-back can be significant. But equally valuable are those rewards that are not as immediately definable in terms of dollars and cents: discovering ways customers think you could improve, detecting other at-risk customers, and controlling negative word of mouth.

Figure 1.4. Response of External List Versus Response of Expired Members.

Mailing	Total Cost per Order	Gross Contribution per Order	Net Contribution per Order	Net Return on Investment
External list	$57	$70	$13	23%
Expired members	$28	$88	$60	214%

Source: B. Stauss and C. Friege, "Regaining Service Customers," *Journal of Service Research,* May 1999, p. 359.

Uncover Improvement Opportunities

Dialogue with customers who are on the brink of leaving or who have already defected can help you pinpoint opportunities to improve product and service delivery, correct miscommunications, and identify new product opportunities. Just ask Bruce Grench, who knows firsthand the value of lost customers. As a young sales executive for Procter & Gamble, Grench saw the growing market for incontinent supplies and also saw how limited retail shelf space curtailed consumer choice. These insights spurred Grench to launch his own company, Home Delivery of Incontinent Supplies (HDIS), with the concept of making bladder control products convenient, affordable, and less embarrassing to purchase. By delivering the products to customers' doorsteps in discreet packages, HDIS has become the "L. L. Bean of adult diapers" in ten short years.

Ever mindful of leveraging customer switching dynamics, Grench and his staff keep a careful watch on lost customers and have a process for interviewing defectors to understand why they left. Says Grench, "The hope is that we can find something we're not doing right, because it offers us an opportunity." Two customer tracking processes help HDIS flag defectors. When a customer calls in to cancel regular delivery, the service representative inquires why the customer is canceling and enters a code for the reason in the database. In addition, the HDIS computer system tracks customer repurchase rates and flags inconsistencies. For example, when a customer who typically reorders every sixty days has not reordered in seventy-five, an HDIS rep calls to ask the reason.

Understanding lost customer dynamics has helped HDIS strengthen customer loyalty. For example, HDIS discovered that some customers were being lured away by competitors' coupons even though HDIS had a long-standing policy to honor these coupons on HDIS purchases. In interviewing defectors, HDIS discovered many didn't know about the coupon policy. This information helped HDIS sharpen its coupon acceptance message.

Lost customer surveys also showed some customers were leaving HDIS and jumping to store brands. Yet this research also showed these defectors liked and trusted HDIS as a company and would be receptive to HDIS-branded products if they were available. This led Grench and his team to launch HDIS's own brand, Reassure. Reassure has been a real success, now representing 30 percent of all HDIS revenues.[11]

The lessons here are these: lost customers are not all the same, and it's a mistake to assume they are all a lost cause. Many can be profitably won back. Customers who switch do so for varying reasons and circumstances. This fact makes many of your former customers, especially those who jumped from your product to another product, strong win-back candidates.

Develop an At-Risk Profile

By analyzing lost customers, you can develop a profile for detecting at-risk customers. When banking consultant Paul Lukin worked with a large southern bank to increase customer retention, he and his team found that a significant proportion of defectors were the affluent and older customers who had been with the bank for ten years or longer. This was a surprise, because it was assumed that younger and less tenured customers were the most likely to leave. Furthermore, almost all the defectors had at one time considered this bank their primary bank and most took all their accounts and services away. Hence the revenue loss was not limited to the loss on checking accounts but included the loss on other products as well. The bank recognized that attrition in this customer segment was a considerable revenue drain because it left behind a younger and less profitable customer base. The bank quickly put retention processes in place that identified and targeted older customers who had not yet left the bank and that helped protect against further leakage of this vital customer segment.[12]

Limit Negative Word of Mouth

A lost customer recovery program can help you limit negative word of mouth from unhappy customers who defect and encourage positive word of mouth from the customers who are regained. If their concerns are left unaddressed, defecting customers can be a deadly source of informal negative publicity. In examining defections at the large bank mentioned earlier, Paul Lukin found that most customers visited a branch to close their account, yet bank staff did not attempt to keep the business. Bank executives were disturbed to hear that about eight in ten defectors said no one tried to convince them to stay with the bank. Reports Lukin, "my banking clients learned that their lack of attempt had a serious effect on the defecting customer since it communicated a lack of caring on the part of the bank. This lack of attempt added 'insult' to the already 'injured' departing customer."[13]

Even when the lost customer is so unhappy that she will never come back, you need to look for ways to neutralize some of the anger. Keeping a positive image in the marketplace is highly important. Indeed, according to 63 percent of the 650 CEOs responding to a poll conducted by *The Chief Executive* and Hill & Knowlton, corporate reputation is more important now than it was five years ago. Here are the percentages of executives who found corporate reputation important in each of these seven key areas:[14]

Helps sell products and services	77%
Makes it easier to attract top employees	61
Increases credibility in time of crisis	53
Encourages lower employee turnover	41
Allows greater pricing power	28
Tends to raise valuation and stock price	23
Leads to preferred merger and joint venture partners	12

Even though keeping a positive marketplace image is key for any company, not doing so is more perilous than ever. Never before has it been easier for a customer to spread good and bad tidings about a company. With the advent of the Internet, more and more buyers have in essence a giant megaphone through which they can tell others everywhere in the world (literally) about their buying experiences. Given customers' real-time communication ability, customer feedback on a business can balloon to extreme proportions in a remarkably short period of time. Biologists tell the parable of a lily leaf that doubles in size every day. The day before it completely covers its pond, it covers only half the water, and the day before that only a quarter, and the day before that only a measly eighth. So, although the lily is growing all summer long, it is only in the last week of the cycle that most bystanders would notice the proportions of that growth. But by then, it is far past the tipping point. The pond has been strangled, cut off from the light, and is no longer alive. The lily leaf offers a rich analogy to the Internet and its power to influence public opinion about your products and services.

Want a quick lesson in how the voice of the customer is growing? Using any search engine, go on the Web and search under the word *complaints*. Soon you will download a list of thousands of complaint Web sites. For example, thegripe.com is a Web site where you can leave your "gripes, grumblings, moans, brickbats and criticisms" about a host of topics ranging from work, the Web, money, your city, and so on. This site offers a "gripe of the week" competition, and at the time of this writing, the winning gripe was about Microsoft mice. Planet-feedback.com and Epinions.com are other places for consumers to discuss products and services, along with comments.com, complaints.com, problems.com, defective.com, concerns.com, failures.com, criticisms.com—you get the picture.

In addition to the Web sites that serve as complaint clearing houses, you'll see company-specific sites established by frustrated yet enterprising customers. For example, The Bally Total Fitness Complaint Guestbook, launched by a disgruntled former customer a few years back, allows surfers to read what others have to say about Bally and share their own stories. Contributor comments are categorized into five areas: Bally employee confessions, credit and collections, facilities and sanitation, rude behavior, and sales tactics.

The double whammy of customer defection and negative word of Web seems a particular threat for e-commerce companies. A recent poll of Web shoppers by Cogitative Inc. found only 55 percent of shoppers declared allegiance to a particular Web site and had no interest in switching to another site to perform the same activity. That means a whopping 45 percent of e-shoppers reported a likelihood of switching. Poor technical performance—such as frequent downtime and slow turnaround speed, outdated content, and poor customer service—is the leading reason given when Web shoppers defect to other sites. In addition, Cogitative research found 30 percent of respondents expect the same selection of products they find when shopping in the analog world, and 50 percent expect a better range and selection. With Web site capability still in its infancy and more and more dot-coms and traditional retailers scrambling to get on-line, customer loss and win-back will be increasingly important dynamics requiring careful management by all retailers.

With word of Web an increasingly awesome power in the marketplace and corporate reputations more important to success than ever, customer defection and win-back initiatives can be pivotal in reducing negative word of mouth.

WHY NOW'S THE TIME TO FOCUS ON CUSTOMER LOSS AND WIN-BACK

If all the benefits we have described for your company's finances, reputation, and customer information system have not completely convinced you that you need customer recovery programs and now, hold on! There are at least three more good reasons why the time is right for your firm to establish customer loss and win-back initiatives alongside your acquisition and retention programs.

1. *Never before have technological tools for winning back lost customers been more available or affordable.* We all know the ease with which e-mail can be sent. But can technology really help you launch a direct-mail campaign to lost customers? Consider ELetter Inc., the on-line direct-mail service that allows you to launch an entire direct-mail campaign in minutes. Using the ELetter Web site, you upload your address list and document file. Next you select a format for your mailing (letter, postcard, or booklet). In one to four business days your mailing will be on its way. ELetter prints, folds, seals, addresses, adds postage, sorts, and then delivers your entire campaign to the post office. Sound expensive? Colored booklets can be printed and mailed for around $2.60 each, a letter for $.70, and a postcard for $.49.

2. *In any market space, there is a limited number of best customers, so you need to keep yours close.* Win-back is one more tool to do this. In *All Customers Are Not Created Equal,* Garth Hallberg points out that "for most categories [of business], one-third of the buyers account for at least two-thirds of the volume. This 'high-profit segment' generally delivers six to ten times as much profit as the low-profit segment. Moreover, they are critical, not only because of their profit contribution, but also because of their relatively small number."[15] Bottom line, this small segment of profit-producing consumers deserves a high priority in your marketing plan. That's why you need to back up your retention efforts with win-back and save programs that return that high-value customer to your business as quickly and efficiently as possible.

3. *Win-back programs can give you a real competitive edge.* A combination of strong acquisition, retention, and win-back programs can help you bullet proof your firm against competitive attacks. Conversely, if your competitor gets strong win-back programs in place

before you do, your chances for recapturing and keeping the best customers are reduced considerably. In many things in life, there is true advantage to being first. Win-back programs are no exception.

Let's take a look at how one company is masterfully leveraging these three factors—using technology, protecting its best customers, and being first to market with state-of-the-art service systems—in a highly volatile, rapidly changing marketplace.

Like many businesses, banks are under attack from all sides. Brokerage firms and mutual funds are out to grab traditional bank customers and the highly profitable ones are the most sought after. The 80/20 rule is often applied to various forms of economic distribution. Applied to profits it states that 80 percent of a firm's profits are generally produced by roughly 20 percent of its customers. This rule is alive and well in banking today and perhaps even an understatement. According to Market Line Associates, an Atlanta bank consulting firm, the top 20 percent of a typical bank's customers contribute as much as 150 percent of overall profit, while the bottom 20 percent of customers siphon off about 50 percent of profits from the bank's bottom line. It is this profit awareness that has awakened banks to the reality that they should fight harder to keep some customers and not others.

That's precisely the motivation propelling First Union Corporation, the nation's sixth largest bank, to find ways to help its reps provide effective but tiered customer service, with a keen eye toward saving those customers with highest value. Customer service rep Amy Hathcock is one of hundreds of frontliners fielding phone calls at the company's huge customer service center in Charlotte, North Carolina. They handle forty-five million customer calls a year, and first-class customer service is a critical priority. In her call center cubicle, Hathcock is surrounded by an array of reminders to deliver the personal touch to callers. A "practice random kindness" bumper sticker is posted near her phone and a television carrying the weather channel hangs from the ceiling so she can take a quick glance and know if her current caller is in a rainstorm.

But when deciding to say yes or no to a caller who requests a lower interest rate on a credit card or wants to avoid a $28 bounced check penalty, the answer is anything but random. All of it depends on the color of the tiny square that pops up on the screen alongside the customer's name. For customers who get a green pop-up, waivers are granted because these customers generate hefty profits for the bank. Not so the red pop-ups. These customers lose money for the bank, and so Hathcock stands firm. Yellow is for the borderline customers, whose profitability provides some space for negotiation. Einstein, the bank's computer system, takes a quick fifteen seconds to pull up the ranking on a customer, using a formula of variables including such items as minimum balances, account activity, and branch visits.

First Union has seen evidence of the 80/20 rule in numerous ways. During a recent focus group with customers, First Union bankers spoke with a woman who had kept as little as $18 in a savings account for more than twenty years. Most of her money was held by another financial institution. She kept the account because of sentiment: her mother had opened it for her when she was thirteen.

Recognizing that the 80/20 rule is profoundly at work in their customer base, visionary banks like First Union are separating the profitable from the nonprofitable customers and servicing them accordingly. Nonprofitable customers make frequent branch visits, keep less than $1,000 in the bank, and call often to check on balances. These nonprofitable behaviors are in stark contrast to those of the most profitable customers, who keep two thousand dollars or more in their accounts, use a teller no more than once a month, and almost never use the call center. The bank's worst customers often cost the bank a minimum of $500 apiece each year, while favored customers each generate more than $1,000 in profits each year.

First Union estimates its Einstein system added at least $100 million in annual revenue to its 1997 total revenues of about $12 billion. But these gains have not come without a real commitment to finding out which customers to service and save through extraordinary service. "Everyone isn't all the same anymore," says Steven G. Boehm, general manager of the bank's customer information center.[16]

Whether you're a small mom 'n' pop company or a Fortune 100 corporation, the time is now to put workable plans in place for saving at-risk customers and winning them back if they leave. Technology and know-how are converging to make this possible for any company, regardless of size. It's the next frontier for companies who are truly committed to leveraging the loyalty and profits from their customers. Get there first, and you'll enjoy a big advantage over your lagging competitors.

SUMMARY

- Losing customers costs your business thousands (or even hundreds of thousands) of dollars a year.
- Lost customers mean lost reputation and lost opportunities.
- Recapturing customers is easier than you think.
- Knowledge is essential—learn who you are losing and why you are losing them.
- Now is the time to start recovering lost customers—the time and technology are right.

CHAPTER TWO

Managing the Big Three

Acquisition, Retention, and Win-Back

A national hotel company we know was fighting hard for customer loyalty and the profits it produces. As a leader in its market space, the chain, with four hundred-plus hotels, invested heavily in high-profile advertising and loyalty reward programs—all in the name of getting and keeping the highly coveted frequent business traveler.

The chain's method of segmenting its reward program members was simple: guests were in the gold category when they stayed fifty or more nights a year; guests staying fewer than fifty nights were classified as average. On the suspicion that customer defection among some of the top travelers was reducing revenue, the company analyzed loyalty reward customers by time periods, number of stays, frequency of stays, room rates, and so forth. Using a set of rules adjusted for seasonality and cyclical usage, the company identified those gold customers who had stopped staying with the chain in the past year or were staying less than before.

Next, these gold customers, most of whom were business travelers, were called by hotel representatives and tactfully queried about their lack of visits to find out whether they had stopped working, changed jobs, were traveling to markets where the chain had no hotels, or had been disappointed in the service they received. Callers also tried to learn what hotels these travellers were currently using. This information enabled the chain to remove low-need customers from the lost customer file and soothe high-value customers who felt forgotten or underserved. The callers had a fair amount of autonomy in offering a free night or a cash reward, depending on a lapsed customer's circumstances and future value.

The average customers were sent postcards in lieu of calls. These postcards said, "We miss you," and offered to add credit points to customers' reward accounts on their next stay.

What were the results of these win-back efforts? Nothing short of spectacular: 85 percent of the lapsed gold members contacted were reactivated, and reactivation among the average customers contacted by mail averaged an impressive 40 percent. A total of $4.5 million dollars in incremental revenue was generated over the sixteen weeks the win-back program was offered. Moreover, the recovered customers were tracked for an additional four months after the win-back promotion period. During this time, room usage among the reactivated gold customers was sustained at higher average levels than the customers' best usage levels prior to defection.

The lesson here is simple: the most effective acquisition and retention programs will never eliminate or prevent all customer defection. If you are truly committed to long-term customer loyalty, you need a plan that provides hard-working strategies for not only acquisition and retention but also win-back.

LINKING LOYALTY TO THE BIG THREE

Loyal customers exhibit five distinct purchasing behaviors that are critical to your bottom line. A loyal customer is one who

1. Makes regular repeat purchases

2. Purchases across product and service lines

3. Refers others

4. Demonstrates an immunity to the pull of the competition

5. Can tolerate an occasional lapse in the company's support without defecting, owing to the goodwill established through regular, consistent service and provision of value

When you earn a customer's loyalty, you are also maximizing that customer's revenue contribution to your firm. But in today's hyper-competitive marketplace, a customer's loyalty is challenged at every turn. Every day your best customers are inundated with more choices than ever before. So how can you ensure your profitable customers will remain loyal against ever-increasing competition and the threat of defection? Without a doubt, your first defense is strong acquisition and retention programs. *There is absolutely no substitute for attracting high-potential customers and retaining them.* (Our previous three books on loyalty strategies are proof of our devotion to these initiatives. Chapter Eight of this book also examines effective targeting strategies.)

But the truth is no acquisition or retention program offers 100 percent protection. To maximize customer loyalty and profits, you need a fully equipped marketing arsenal, complete with acquisition, retention, and win-back programs. We call these programs the Big Three. Figure 2.1 compares and contrasts the Big Three in terms of overall focus, target and the target's product experience, customer segmentation, and customer communication opportunities.

Your Company as a Loyalty Lab

For years we have observed firms taking an assembly line approach to producing loyal customers that looks something like this: the sales and marketing departments are stationed at the beginning of the assembly line, and as new prospects roll along the conveyor belt, these departments do their assigned tasks to turn prospects into new buyers. Once these tasks are complete and the prospects are turned into buyers, the conveyor belt continues to roll along, this time moving the new buyers to the operations and customer service stations where the orders are filled and service is provided. Next, the new buyers travel along on the conveyor belt to shipping and billing. Finally, if all goes well, the buyers remain on the conveyor belt and come around again and again for more marketing and selling and order fulfillment. The objective is to keep the customers on the conveyor belt, because every time a customer goes around, your company is spending less to make more.

Experience has taught us that this assembly line approach to developing customer loyalty has two fatal flaws. First, most firms have few or no resources on their assembly line devoted to win-back. Indeed,

Figure 2.1. Comparing the Big Three.

Key Focus	Targets and Their Product Experience	Customer Segmentation	Customer Communication
Acquisition management Encompasses all the efforts directed at attracting high-value prospects and turning them into first-time buyers.	Prospects: these potential customers lack experience with your product or service.	Segmentation is based mainly on externally acquired data.	Mainly directed one way, toward the prospect.
Retention management Focuses on two areas: (1) strengthening the relationship with existing customers by increasing value of services, and (2) identifying at-risk customers and stabilizing the endangered relationship through active programs.	Current customers: they've had product or service experience with you.	Segmentation is based on database information reflecting past purchasing behavior and lifetime value.	Two-way communication opportunities available.
Win-back management All the efforts associated with recovering and rebuilding the relationship with the lost customer.	Lost customers: they've had experience with your product or service and a purchasing history with you.	Segmentation is based on database information reflecting past purchasing behavior and future purchasing potential as a result of win-back.	Communication is often two-way.

the win-back function may not even exist. Second, there is little coordination on the assembly line between acquisition, retention, and (if it exists) win-back. Although each function may be very efficient as an independent unit, unless these three functions share information and pool their reservoirs of knowledge, they cannot produce maximum loyalty. If your company thinks of customers as being on an assembly line, you'll notice that people at the beginning of the line may not even know when a customer falls off in the middle or at the end of the line—unless there is a system for constantly collecting and sharing information. This lack of information robs sales and marketing staff of valuable insights on how to sharpen acquisition programs for maximum loyalty and retention.

Rather than the assembly line approach to loyalty development, we propose a new model we call the *loyalty laboratory*. Think of your firm as a scientific loyalty lab in which you and your staff look for and gather insights about the best practices for customer acquisition, retention, and win-back. Every initiative taken by your firm in acquiring new customers, retaining customers, or winning back lost customers is an experiment of sorts, with an outcome that deserves assessment and analysis. The ongoing question is this: *What effect will this initiative or program have on customer loyalty?* The better you are at uncovering and leveraging this cause and effect, the closer your acquisition, retention, and win-back programs can get to achieving maximum loyalty. Ideally, every staff member in your firm should be a scientist of sorts, constantly looking for the cause-and-effect factors affecting the Big Three. This search for understanding can pay surprising rewards.

Just ask George Renaudin, vice president of government programs at Oshsner Health Plan, which serves 185,000 commercial and 50,000 Medicare members in Louisiana. When Oshsner expanded its Medicare plan from its Baton Rouge and New Orleans hubs into surrounding markets in 1997, Renaudin was shocked to find Medicare members leaving the Oshsner plan at a rate of 20 percent, almost three times higher than defection rates in other markets (7 percent). To get to the bottom of why so many people were leaving the plan, Renaudin immediately conducted lost member research and the answers came quickly.

Says Renaudin, "We were the first health plan to offer Medicare risk in these towns. We found that people left us mostly because they were unfamiliar with the workings of Medicare risk. They didn't like the primary-care provider structure. Also, our provider network cut some people off from their preferred hospital or doctor." The lost member research also found that during a two-month period, many new members were canceling their applications within the first ninety days. Says Renaudin, "They were having serious buyer's remorse. This indicated dysfunction in our sales process."

Lost member research findings have driven important changes at Oshsner companywide. "We changed our sales process to focus on more information, and we've beefed up our new-member orientation," says Renaudin. "We want to make sure that new enrollees understand the system up front, to avoid the surprises and misunderstanding that contribute to disenrollment." And Oshsner didn't stop there. It redesigned its sales incentive system so that commissions and bonuses were linked to ninety-day cancellations and first-year disenrollments. Oshsner now takes back the sales commission if a new member leaves the plan in the first three months. This encourages the sales staff to be sure customers know what they need to know about the plan before they become customers so they will later remain customers. The results? In the first six months of 1998, ninety-day cancellations dropped by 34 percent and Oshsner enjoys a disenrollment rate of less than 10 percent, among the best in the region. And it is hoping, says Renaudin, "to get that down to five."

Having a firm understanding of member defection rates has added a strong dose of realism to Oshsner's acquisition goals. In 1998, Oshsner budgeted for 2,500 new Medicare members that year to add to its base of 45,000 members, but the plan was projected to lose 2,000 members the same year as well. Reports Renaudin, "At that rate, in order to gain 2,500 members, we had to add 4,500. That's a pretty compelling reason to hold onto the folks you already have."[1]

The more you understand and manage the cause and effect between acquisition, retention, and win-back, the better your probability of consistently sustaining high levels of loyalty. Ignoring any one of the Big Three and their cause-and-effect influences can rob you of critical insights on ways to maximize the long-term loyalty and revenue from your customer base. The Big Three management matrix illustrated in Figure 2.2 summarizes some of the causes and effects among acquisition, retention, and win-back.

Big Three Interdependence

Acquisition, retention and win-back may appear to be separate functions on the surface, but as the matrix shows, they must be operationally correlated if you are to achieve the overall goal of developing and maintaining customer loyalty. The Big Three are interdependent and mutually supportive when you have a system in place that shares customer information and knowledge and insight among the functions.

Big Three management is essential in virtually any industry in any country. For example, managers at MTN, a mobile telecom company in South Africa, were investigating whether a *churn buster* model made economic sense for the company. Their first step was to quantify the churn problem in detail. They analyzed closely the number of handsets MTN sold and compared that number to the number of connected customers. There was a big gap. Given the number of handsets

Figure 2.2. Big Three Management Matrix.

What Retention Can Teach You About Acquisition.	What Acquisition Can Teach You About Retention.	What Win-Back Can Teach You About Acquisition.
Knowing which of your existing customers become loyal can help you sharpen your prospect targeting thereby attracting more high-potential customers.	Knowing new customer needs enables you to better customize products and services to provide increasing value to customers.	Knowing which customers have defected and why can help you sharpen your prospect targeting to avoid attracting prospects that are prone to defection.
What Retention Can Teach You About Win-Back.	What Acquisition Can Teach You About Win-Back.	What Win-Back Can Teach You About Retention.
Knowing the customers' past purchasing patterns and habits can help you more effectively segment lost customers according to future value potential.	Comparing the profiles of high-value prospects against lost customers can be helpful for identifying those lost customers most worthy of win-back.	Knowing which customers have defected and why can help with early detection of at-risk customers.

distributed, the number of new connections should have been much higher. At the time, MTN was offering "sexy" new handsets (they were smaller and had a longer talk time, cool colors, and the like), and everyone wanted one. MTN did not have a handset upgrade policy so the only way existing customers could get a new handset was to cancel their present contract and give up their phone number, sign a new contract, and be assigned a new phone number. Could it be that a lot of the churn was from existing customers canceling and then signing up again as new customers so they could get the upgraded handsets?

MTN pulled the names of disconnects over the last four years (the life of its network). The data showed that only about 35 percent of the customers who disconnected had left the network. About half of these had gone to competitors to get a different pricing plan or better network coverage, and the other half, for the most part, could no longer afford or no longer needed a cell phone.

The surprising finding was that the remaining 65 percent of disconnected consumers had never actually left the network. Instead, these supposedly disconnected customers had canceled their contracts with MTN but then signed up again. Explains Margaret Sheraton, MTN's group marketing executive at the time, "When we sat back and looked, the situation was very clear: our salesforce and the consumer had a sweet deal. We compensated our salesforce based only on new connections, so they were perfectly happy to sign an existing customer up again. And customers were willing because they got new phones! And our policy of providing new customers with a recording that said, 'That number has changed, the new number is . . .,' made it even more convenient for an existing customer to disconnect and reconnect with a new contract and phone number."

What did this win-back analysis teach MTN about acquisition and retention management? Lots of things, according to Sheridan. "MTN had always believed that keeping the phone number was a big value to consumers and that consumers would resist leaving their network to avoid the hassle of a new number. Boy, were we wrong! People could care less about their cell phone numbers. We now know 80 percent of a user's cell phone calls are made to seven to eight people. It's not hard to let seven to eight people know your new phone number." Sheridan adds that the company soon implemented a handset upgrade policy for current customers. That change alone saved the company a good deal of time and money in sales commissions and paperwork. Longer term, some real changes were required in database management. In South Africa, cell phone bills are generally paid by direct debit of checking accounts, so customers were matched by bank account number rather than name and address. This meant that MTN was not able to relate a canceled account to an actual person's name, but only to their bank account number. And lastly, MTN began looking for better ways to effectively track and compensate sales reps for renewals, not just connections.[2]

The key point to remember is this: if your company is like most, at this very moment it is investing hard-won resources in acquisition and retention programs in an effort to attract and keep high-value customers. To maximize your return on investment, two things are critical: (1) the careful cause-and-effect management of your acquisition and retention programs, and (2) the addition of win-back programs that can return high-value lost customers to your customer pool and provide critical insights for improving the effectiveness of your acquisition and retention programs.

THE HOW'S AND WHY'S OF
BIG THREE MANAGEMENT

By now, we hope you're convinced that a Big Three focus is critical to your business success. It's now time to consider the requirements for managing these three key initiatives.

Keeping an Eye on Six Customer Groups

An important first step to effectively managing retention, acquisition, and win-back, is to recognize the different customer groups that are affected by your Big Three strategies. In acquisition management, the two most critical customer groups are *prospects*, defined as potential buyers who have not yet purchased from you, and *new customers*, defined as customers who have bought from you for the first time.

In retention management, there are three key customer groups to monitor. One group is *retained* customers, defined as customers who have bought from you multiple times and are now showing one or more of the five loyalty behaviors (repeat purchasing on a regular basis, buying a cross section of products and services, referring others, showing immunity to the pull of competition, and having the ability to weather occasional service problems). The second group of customers associated with retention management is *at-risk* customers. Customers are considered at risk when purchase cues and other indicators suggest the relationship is endangered and defection may occur. Identifying at-risk customers and stabilizing the endangered relationship through active recovery programs is a goal of retention management. The third customer group important to retention management is *lost* customers. Customers are considered lost when they have either stopped purchasing or have explicitly terminated the relationship. However, when a customer is at risk but is then retained through adequate recovery measures, this customer is then considered *saved*, and that recovery is considered successful retention management because the customer neither stopped purchasing nor terminated.

Finally, in win-back management, a unique group of customers takes center stage. These customers are called *regained* customers, indicating that they were once customers and then defected but now have emerged from defection to again be active customers.[3]

Using Purchase Data to Help You Manage the Big Three

Analyzed correctly, purchasing data can offer amazing insights on what's working and not working in your acquisition, retention, and win-back programs. The right analyses can also pinpoint yet-to-be-mined opportunity areas among the key customer groups.

Let's examine nine purchase data analyses. Figure 2.3 shows in which of the Big Three programs each analysis is typically performed, which customer group it analyzes, and what you will learn from it. In the following pages we examine these nine analyses (Figures 2.4 through 2.12) in the context of ABC Product Company, a business-to-business widget company with corporate customers nationwide. The company is examining purchase data for the year 2001, with comparisons to 2000.[4] Assume total transactional customers (those who have made purchases, returns, refunds, and so on) for the year 2001 are 44,300, of which 36,445 have made one or more purchases in 2001. Assume 35,934 customers have made one or more purchases in the year 2000.

Figure 2.3. Nine Data Analyses.

Big Three	Customer Groups	Analyses	What You Will Learn
Acquisition	Prospects New customers	New customer analysis	Quality of new customers according to spending patterns
Retention	Retained customers	Revenue decile analysis	Rank of customers in deciles according to past revenue
		Product penetration analysis	Number of products bought
		Recency of purchase analysis	Time lapse since last purchase
		Best customer analysis	Number of customers across 3 decile analyses (revenue, product penetration, recency)
		Retention analysis	Number of customers retained
	At-risk customers	Churn analysis	Revenue decile movement
Win-back	Lost customers	Defection analysis	Defectors by decile
	Regained customers	Win-back analysis	Number of lost customers regained

NEW CUSTOMERS

New Customer Analysis. In this analysis, ABC Product Company defines new customers as ones who generated no revenue in 2000 but generated positive revenue in 2001. The analysis of the buying behavior of these new customers is displayed in Figure 2.4.

Key Learning
- ABC Product Company is attracting a substantial number of new customers, many of whom are producing at high levels. Eight hundred and ninety-four customers, who did not produce revenue in 2000, are among the top 10 percent of customers in 2001.
- Over two-thirds of ABC's new customers fall below the fifth decile revenue level of $1,546.

RETAINED CUSTOMERS

Revenue Decile Analysis. A revenue decile analysis (Figure 2.5) provides a bird's-eye view of customer sales performance, revenue, and order information in increments of 10 percent. This analysis helps identify specific *break points* across a base of customers. (For purposes of this analysis, any customer who was at zero in sales was excluded to prevent skewing of the data.)

Figure 2.4. New Customer Analysis.

Decile	New Customers	Total 2001 Revenue	Average 2001 Revenue	Total 2001 Orders	Average 2001 Orders
1	894	$ 5,370,000	$6,006	8,758	9.8
2	1,389	4,618,845	3,325	6,938	4.9
3	1,660	3,942,378	2,375	6,024	3.6
4	2,252	3,652,134	1,622	6,748	2.9
5	2,274	3,515,000	1,546	5,388	2.3
6	2,464	3,358,000	1,363	5,159	2.0
7	2,372	2,910,956	1,227	4,539	1.9
8	2,424	2,723,798	1,124	4,255	1.7
9	2,049	1,514,085	739	2,895	1.4
10	1,778	155,700	88	2,145	1.2
	19,556	$31,760,896	1,624	52,849	2.7

Figure 2.5. Revenue Decile Analysis.

Decile	Customers	Total 2001 Revenue	% of Total 2001 Revenue	Cumulative 2001 Revenue	Average 2001 Revenue	Total 2001 Orders	Average 2001 Orders
1	3,644	$36,375,000	44.4%	44.4%	$9,982	58,360	16.0
2	3,644	12,081,917	14.7	59.1	3,707	21,781	6.0
3	3,644	8,319,888	10.2	69.3	2,557	15,085	4.1
4	3,644	5,613,206	6.8	76.1	1,725	11,756	3.2
5	3,644	4,854,978	5.9	82.0	1,492	8,253	2.2
6	3,644	4,507,176	5.5	87.5	1,385	7,265	2.0
7	3,644	4,203,179	5.1	92.6	1,292	7,209	2.0
8	3,644	3,843,689	4.7	97.3	1,181	6,538	1.8
9	3,644	1,871,949	2.3	99.6	575	10,194	2.8
10	3,649	293,439	0.4	100.0	90	7,604	2.0
	36,445	$81,964,421	100.0%	100.0%	$2,249	154,045	4.2

Key Learning
  • The average revenue of the top 10 percent of ABC Product
    Company customers is nearly three times greater than that
    of the next 10 percent of customers and represents almost
    half of ABC's customer revenue.

  • Customers in Decile 1 generate an average revenue of close
    to $10,000 and place an average of sixteen orders annually.

  • On average, ABC customers generate $2,249 of revenue from
    4.2 annual orders.

Product Penetration Analysis. A product penetration analysis (Figure
2.6) monitors the different products bought during a specified period,
tracking them by product code. For example, if ABC offers twenty-
five product lines and the top decile buys twelve of them, the company
has 48 percent product penetration in this decile. In Figure 2.6, ABC is
measuring current product code penetration among all customers
who have had transactional activity (purchases, returns, and so on).
So it is looking at product codes purchased in 2001 and averaging
them across all transactional customers in each decile, not just across
those individuals in the decile who have made purchases during 2001.

Figure 2.6. Product Penetration Analysis.

Decile	Customers	Total Product Codes Available	Average Product Codes per Customer	Product Code Penetration
1	4,430	25	11.6	46%
2	4,430	25	6.0	24
3	4,430	25	4.8	19
4	4,430	25	2.8	11
5	4,430	25	2.2	9
6	4,430	25	1.6	6
7	4,430	25	1.5	6
8	4,430	25	1.0	4
9	4,430	25	1.0	4
10	4,430	25	1.0	4
	44,300		3.4	13%

Key Learning
- ABC Product Company customers purchased an average of 3.4 different product codes.
- Half of ABC customers averaged less than 2 different product codes.
- The customers in Decile 1 purchased an average of 11.6 different product codes.

Recency of Purchase Analysis. A recency of purchase analysis examines the time lapsed since an average customer's last purchase. The analysis illustrated in Figure 2.7 measures this time in months. The zero in the final column refers to December 2001, the final month of the analysis. Again, all customers included in this analysis have had transactional activity in 2001.

Key Learning
- The average time lapsed from the last ABC Product Company purchase is 5.3 months.
- Half of ABC's customers haven't purchased in at least six months.

Figure 2.7. Recency of Purchase Analysis.

Decile	Customers	Months Since Last Purchase
1	4,430	0.0
2	4,430	0.8
3	4,430	1.6
4	4,430	2.3
5	4,430	4.4
6	4,430	6.2
7	4,430	7.0
8	4,430	7.5
9	4,430	9.7
10	4,430	13.5
	44,300	5.3

Best Customer Analysis. Best customers are defined as those customers in 2001 who rank in the top decile (Decile 1) across all three decile analyses: revenue, product penetration, and recency of purchase. The analysis of these ranges for ABC is shown in Figure 2.8.

Key Learning
   • ABC finds it has 1,380 customers who match the best customer criteria. They represent 3.8 percent of the total customers (36,445) who have revenue activity in 2001.

   • Their average revenue is $15,545 and their average order is twenty-seven products.

   • They represent $21.5 million in total revenue (1,380 × $15,545) and 37,260 total orders (1,380 × 27). These aggregate figures amount to 26 percent of the revenue from all customers and 24 percent of the orders.

Retention Analysis. The retention analysis (Figure 2.9) tracks retained customers from one period of time to the next: in this case it looks at customers in the database in 2000 who made purchases in 2001. Besides monitoring the purchasing behavior of retained customers from period to period, this analysis also quantifies lost revenue.

Key Learning
   • ABC Product Company is retaining customers at an overall rate of 47 percent.

   • Customers retained from 2000 to 2001 increased their average expenditure on ABC products by 76 percent and their average number of orders by 43 percent.

   • The customer universe in 2000 generated $56.5 million. From those who were retained through 2001, the revenue generation was $46.9 million. This amounts to a reduction of $9.7 million.

Figure 2.8. Best Customer Analysis.

Analysis	Maximum	Minimum
Revenue	$305,775	$4,213
Product code penetration	25	8
Recency of purchase	Previous month	Previous month

Figure 2.9. Retention Analysis.

	Customer Universe in 2000	Retained Customers in 2001	Customer Change	Customer Change (%)
Total customers	35,934 (100%)	16,889 (47%)	−19,045	−53
Average order	3.9	5.6	+1.7	+43
Total orders	140,143	94,578	−45,565	−32
Average revenue per customer	$1,573	$2,776	+$1,203	+76
Total revenue	$56,540,000	$46,883,864	−$9,656,136	−17

AT-RISK CUSTOMERS

Churn Analysis. The churn analysis (Figure 2.10) tracks the activity of customers from one year to the next. The revenue decile assignment of a customer in 2000 is compared to the assignment in 2001. This allows an assessment of customer *migration* across deciles from one year to the next.

In Figure 2.10, the rows (horizontal) represent the customer deciles by revenue for 2000. The columns (vertical) represent the customer deciles by revenue for 2001. So looking at the first decile of 2000, we see that 41 percent of the customers who were in Decile 1 in 2000 were also in Decile 1 in 2001. However, 13 percent of the customers in Decile 1 in 2000 migrated to in Decile 2 in 2001, 9 percent to Decile 3, and so on. Similarly, 15 percent of the customers in Decile 2 in 2000 migrated up to Decile 1 for 2001, 11 percent remained in Decile 2, and 9 percent migrated to Decile 3.

The "defectors" column shows the percentage of customers that had revenue activity in 2000 and no revenue activity in 2001. For example, 32 percent of the customers in Decile 2 in 2000 defected in 2001. Lastly, the "migrated down" and "migrated up" columns present the percentage of customers in each decile that have migrated down or up from 2000 to 2001.

Key Learning
• Nearly half the customers in the top two revenue deciles for 2000 have migrated down into lower deciles for 2001.

Figure 2.10. Churn Analysis.

2000 Decile	Defectors	2001 Decile										Total	Migrated Down	Migrated Up
		1	2	3	4	5	6	7	8	9	10			
		3%	7%	9%	12%	11%	16%	13%	12%	9%	7%	100%		
1	11%	41	13	9	3	3	2	2	2	5	5	100%	48%	0%
2	32%	15	11	9	4	4	3	4	4	5	8	100%	44%	12%
3	44%	8	9	7	4	3	3	4	4	7	7	100%	35%	12%
4	61%	3	5	4	5	3	2	3	2	6	6	100%	20%	11%
5	65%	3	4	4	3	3	3	3	2	4	6	100%	19%	17%
6	71%	2	3	3	2	2	2	2	2	4	5	100%	12%	11%
7	71%	2	3	4	2	2	2	3	3	4	5	100%	10%	14%
8	69%	3	3	4	2	1	2	3	4	4	5	100%	9%	15%
9	50%	4	5	4	5	4	4	3	3	8	8	100%	8%	31%
10	53%	3	4	4	5	4	3	4	3	6	9	100%	0%	33%

• A substantially higher number of the customers in the top five deciles in 2000 are migrating down than are migrating up or remaining stable.

LOST CUSTOMERS

Defection Analysis. The defection analysis examines the revenue and orders lost along with defectors over a certain period. A year is assumed to be an appropriate sales cycle for ABC Product Company, so in Figure 2.11, defectors are defined as customers who produced revenue in 2000 and did not produce any revenue in 2001.

Key Learning
• 350 customers who produced an average of $7,512 in 2000 produced no revenue in 2001. These customers were not "one night stands," as proven by the fact that they purchased an average of ten times in 2000.

• In total, 19,045 customers produced revenue in 2000 and none in 2001, amounting to $24.3 million in lost revenue.

• Customer defection is occurring across the entire customer base, in all deciles.

Figure 2.11. Defection Analysis.

Decile	Defected Customers	% of Customers in 2000	Total Revenue in 2000	Average Revenue in 2000	Total Orders	Average Order
1	350	11%	$2,629,112	$7,512	3,434	9.8
2	1,011	32	3,424,751	3,387	5,691	5.6
3	1,408	44	3,300,326	2,344	5,600	4.0
4	1,946	61	3,124,698	1,606	5,496	2.8
5	2,074	65	2,862,052	1,308	5,072	2.4
6	2,268	71	2,857,650	1,260	4,732	2.1
7	2,259	71	2,597,217	1,150	4,583	2.0
8	2,951	69	2,773,620	770	4,121	1.4
9	2,335	50	624,418	267	4,875	2.0
10	2,443	53	153,309	63	3,920	1.6
	19,045	53%	$24,347,153	$1,278	47,524	2.5

REGAINED CUSTOMERS

Win-Back Analysis. In the win-back analysis, customers who have been won back, or regained, are examined as the number of customers lost in one time period and regained in another. In the case of ABC Product Company, regained customers are defined as customers who were considered defectors in 2001 (because they produced revenue in 2000 but did not produce revenue in 2001) and who came back as customers as the result of a win-back effort. Figure 2.12 shows a win-back analysis of ABC customers from the top three deciles.

Key Learning
• Lost customers represent a substantial revenue opportunity for ABC Product Company if they can be won back. (In Appendix B an analysis of potential profit associated with these regained customers is presented using a number of win-back concepts covered in upcoming chapters.)

Learning Further from Purchase Data Analyses

These nine analyses can teach a company much about its customer groups and managing the Big Three. Here is more of what ABC learned from these and similar analyses and recommendations for further steps it could take.

NEW CUSTOMER ANALYSIS

Key Conclusion. ABC Product Company is acquiring a substantial number of new customers, many of whom are producing at high levels. Eight hundred and ninety-four customers who did not produce

Figure 2.12. Win-Back Analysis.

Decile	Defected Customers in 2001	Defected Customers Qualifying for Win-Back	Lost Customers Regained in 2002	Lost Customers Regained (%)
1	350	300	150	50%
2	1,011	900	360	40
3	1,408	1,200	400	33
	2,769	2,400	910	

revenue in 2000 are among the top 10 percent of customers in 2001. Overall, 19,556 new customers worth $31.8 million were acquired.

Recommendation. Conduct an acquisition analysis. ABC Product Company is acquiring high-revenue producing customers. Analyze the new customers who have established themselves in the top deciles. Determine what is different about those customers, how they were acquired, how they are being serviced, what needs are driving large purchases of ABC products and services, and so forth. Use this learning to target prospects with similar needs through similar vehicles.

RETAINED CUSTOMERS

Key Conclusions
- Customer defection is having a major impact on revenue for the ABC Product Company, so minor increases in retention will also have a major impact.
- ABC has 1,380 customers that match the best customer criteria, defined as those in the top 10 percent of all customers with regard to revenue, product penetration, and recency of purchase. Those 1,380 represented 3.8 percent of the total customers (those who have revenue activity in 2001), and they look like this:

  Average 2001 revenue: $15,545

  Average orders: 27

  Combined, best customers represent 26 percent of total revenue

  Combined, best customers represent 24 percent of total orders

- On average, ABC customers generate $2,249 of revenue from 4.2 annual orders.
- With the exception of Decile 1, ABC customers do not demonstrate high product penetration, with 50 percent of ABC customers averaging purchases of less than three product codes annually.
- The customers that ABC retained during this time period show a significant increase in their average revenue generation, an increase of 76 percent.

- Retention risk appears high, with half of ABC customers not having made a purchase in at least six months.

Recommendations
- Use the information from the acquisition analysis to develop and improve retention strategies. In particular, find out what needs are driving substantial purchases of ABC products by Decile 1 customers. Apply that learning to retaining more ABC customers.

- Improve existing communications and establish ongoing dialogue with customers. ABC customers are averaging 4.2 orders during 2001. This suggests that several opportunities for relationship-building communication exist.

- Invest in customer profiling and dialogue management (customer relationship management) to establish lifetime value estimates for customers. These estimates will enable ABC to better understand and build lifetime value models of its customers. They will also help ABC better define the retention budget that should be apportioned to each customer.

- Conduct a product purchase analysis to determine which products are being purchased together. This analysis could help define a broader or deeper product offering or suggest possible new products. Bundling of complementary products may increase product penetration.

- Implement programs to cross-sell (sell the buyer a different product or service) and up-sell (sell the buyer a higher-priced product or more of what they've already purchased) to existing customers. Look at customers who are buying across product lines to determine their characteristics and what products are being purchased together. Use this learning to explore additional product bundling and up-sell strategies.

AT-RISK CUSTOMERS, LOST CUSTOMERS, AND REGAINED CUSTOMERS

Key Conclusions
- ABC Product Company is experiencing significant customer turnover. In total, 19,045 customers produced revenue in 2000 and zero revenue in 2001, amounting to $24.3 million in lost revenue from defected customers. The defection rate is

53 percent annually. If the entire customer database is considered, as in Figure 2.9, the incremental effect of these changes over several years becomes very clear.

- ABC's win-back efforts have successfully regained a number of high-value customers for the firm. These recovered customers represent significant revenue. (See Appendix B.)

Recommendations
- Conduct a lost customer analysis with particular attention to uncovering the reason why top decile customers are defecting. Use exit interviews and other means for uncovering this information. Use this learning to develop a win-back plan that incorporates lost customer communication programs.
- Establish systems that allow ABC to detect when customers are at risk of defecting and thus immediately implement save strategies.
- Analyze results of win-back initiatives to date. Apply the learning to establish communications and personal contact programs for treating lost customers as high-quality prospects. These programs may include

    On-line and printed newsletters

    Regular sales call patterns in the field

    Off-site training and information events

    Promotional CDs and brochures
- Manage areas about which lost customers complain or are concerned, as identified in exit interviews and formal customer research.

MOVING BEYOND PAST PURCHASE DATA TO LIFETIME VALUE

Past purchase data can give you lots of guidance in how to direct your marketing strategy and effectively manage the Big Three for maximum return on your customer relationships. As you do this, it's important to resist making decisions about acquisition, retention, or win-back in isolation. Instead, the best decision making comes from evaluating these three areas in concert with one another and making the most of the cause-and-effect factors that run between them.

But there's still more to do! If you were to stop here, focusing solely on the customer's past history, you would run the risk of ignoring emerging customer potential and other demographic and lifestyle factors that could influence future purchase activity. After all, it's not a certainty that your best customers today will be your best customers in the future. For example, a young executive may have a lower spent-to-date figure on his credit card than an elderly man has, but demographic data suggest that the young man represents considerably more future purchase potential.

Rather than relying only on past purchase analysis as you make marketing strategy decisions, it's wise to also consider the latest knowledge you can acquire about the customer's future needs. You can get this knowledge by determining *customer lifetime value,* or LTV.

Remember learning to add and subtract fractions in grade school and how you first had to change the base of the fractions to a common denominator? Think about the lifetime value of your customers the same way. Calculating lifetime value creates a common denominator of sorts across your customer set (new, retained, at-risk, saved, lost, and regained customers) that allows you to more fully evaluate customers' future potential and compare one customer's potential to another's. With this insight you can often make better decisions about directing marketing strategy for greatest profit return.

Calculating lifetime value is not a perfect science. It requires the application of facts and reasonable assumptions. Figure 2.13 illustrates a lifetime value estimate for a customer of the ABC Product Company. In this instance, the lifetime is set at three years. Year 1 is the year the customer is acquired. It is estimated that this customer will place an average of three orders in the year of acquisition, with an average order value of $380. The average order value for the new customer in Year 1 is estimated at $576. The number was calculated from data in the New Customer Analysis (Figure 2.4), where average revenue for a new customer was $1,729 and average order size was 2.9. It is assumed that as the customer gains purchase experience, average order value and average orders per year will increase. As customers become more loyal, it is estimated on the basis of past experience that they will place more orders per year and that those orders will increase in size.

Once the total revenue is calculated, the direct costs, acquisition costs, and retention costs must be calculated and subtracted. ABC calculates its direct costs at 70 percent of the revenue for the first year,

Figure 2.13. Customer Lifetime Value Calculation.

	Year 1	Year 2	Year 3
Revenue			
Orders per year	3	5	7
× Average order value	$576	$625	$650
= Total revenue	$1,728	$3,125	$4,550
Costs			
Direct cost	$1,209	$2,031	$3,185
	(70%)	(65%)	(70%)
+ Acquisition cost	$864		
	(50%)		
+ Retention cost		$312	$455
		(10%)	(10%)
= Total costs	$2,073	$2,343	$3,640
Profit			
Gross profit	$(345)	$782	$910
Cumulative lifetime value	$0	$437*	$1,347*

*These figures do not reflect net present value.
Source: Adapted from A. M. Hughes, "Lifetime Value in Business-to-Business Marketing," *CRM Journal*, n.d., *1*(1), 16.

65 percent for the second year, and 70 percent for the third year. It calculates acquisition costs at 50 percent of the first year's revenue. Costs for retention programs are estimated to be 10 percent of revenue for each year after the first year.

This customer's lifetime value over three years and before deductions is $1,347 (−345 + 782 + 910). Lifetime value can be estimated for an unlimited number of years. As real purchase information is collected, the lifetime value estimate should be periodically recalculated and reestimated to reflect the latest learning.

Sometimes LTV includes a customer's referral value. How many orders from other customers might this customer bring in? If you choose to incorporate referral revenue, calculate it as a percentage of sales revenue. Consider, for example, using an escalating percentage beginning with the year of acquisition (that is, Year 1, 5 percent; Year 2, 10 percent; Year 3, 15 percent). This escalation percentage is based on the premise that the longer the relationship with the customer, the more likely the customer is to refer others to you. Then you can adjust the percentages as you learn from new customers how many of them are actually referrals.

Lifetime value recognizes that not all customers are equal in future profit potential. Some represent greater opportunities than others. In directing your marketing spending on the Big Three, you need to invest your greatest resources with high lifetime value customers. Likewise, you need to spend carefully on midlevel to lower-level lifetime value customers and to reprice products or services or otherwise discourage the lowest and the negative lifetime value customers. How do you determine a customer's worthiness for retention resources and win-back resources in relation to all existing customers? One revealing way to address the question is to chart "month of last purchase" data against customer lifetime value, as shown in Figure 2.14, which was shared with us by Lynhurst, New Jersey–based Retail Resources, a full-service relationship marketing arm of Trans Union. (Note that the data that follow are not part of the ABC Product Co. case.) By combining past purchase data with lifetime customer value, marketing priorities reveal themselves, as shown by the shaded areas of the data. The boundaries for these shaded areas are drawn using good old common sense as follows: The shaded area on the left side of the figure represents those customers whose business is most prized and important to the company. In addition to receiving consideration for lifetime value, they have purchased recently and (most likely) on a regular basis, and they purchase at high dollar levels. The company can afford, because of the amounts spent by these customers, to invest more resources to retain them. Likewise, the customers in the middle section have purchased at levels comparable to the company's most valuable customers, but because their purchases have lapsed, reactivation is required.

Finally, at the other end of the spectrum are those customers whose business must be considered highly marginal. They have purchased at very low levels, and even if these customers purchase on an extremely cyclical basis, their dollar expenditures in combination with lifetime value estimates are not sufficient to even merit inexpensive reactivation approaches.

Every company must draw its boundaries according to its specific circumstances. The good news is that by comparing month of last purchase data against customer lifetime value, you will be well on your way to making wise choices regarding spending appropriation.

Figure 2.14. Identifying Priorities for Retention Efforts.

Cumulative Lifetime Value	Month of Last Purchase								Total Customers
	Last Month	2 Months Ago	3 Months Ago	4 to 6 Months Ago	7 to 12 Months Ago	13 to 18 Months Ago	19 to 24 Months Ago	25+ Months Ago	
$4,000+	418	308	457	557	632	487	172	102	3,133
$3,500–4,000	57	72	85	126	139	123	63	42	707
3,000–3,500	66	78	137	179	214	196	76	65	1,011
2,500–3,000	118	142	184	237	385	253	151	103	1,573
2,000–2,500	165	176	271	428	525	436	208	202	2,411
1,500–2,000	243	271	449	690	924	796	441	458	4,272
1,000–1,500	403	542	884	1,256	1,950	1,647	996	1,310	8,958
500–1,000	901	981	2,116	2,791	4,678	5,037	3,256	5,385	25,145
0–500	2,191	2,479	5,354	7,483	14,096	16,894	13,151	34,815	95,463
Total	4,562	5,049	9,937	13,747	23,543	25,869	18,484	42,482	143,673

Work Hardest to Retain These Customers ←

Strive to Reactivate These Customers ←

Do Not Reactivate These Customers ←

Source: Christine Foschetti (vice president of Retail Resources, Lynhurst, N.J.), memorandum, "Reactivating Lost Customers," Aug. 6, 1999.

Losing clients with a high LTV can seriously reduce your profits. Highly valued customers can become at-risk or lost just as others can, so they need particular attention. Thus far in this chapter, we've examined the interdependence between acquisition, retention, and win-back and how the effective management of the key customer groups is essential to long-term customer loyalty and profit maximization.

Even though most firms are accustomed to managing new customers and current (or retained) customers by way of carefully planned and fine-tuned acquisition programs and elaborate loyalty reward programs, it's the rare company that has a plan for effectively capitalizing on the opportunity offered by at-risk and lost customers. Engaging these customers in a successful recovery process through which they become retained customers once more doesn't happen on its own. It requires disciplined, well-planned processes that you fine-tune over time as you gain more and more customer experience. But, as we've demonstrated, the rewards are well worth the efforts. So let's get started.

YOUR DECISION MAP FOR AT-RISK AND LOST CUSTOMERS

The first step in creating a plan for managing at-risk and lost customers is to create a *decision map,* or *decision tree* (see the sample in Figure 2.15). When we use this method with our clients in Big Three brainstorming meetings, key distinctions start to surface. For example, when dealing with at-risk customers, how extensive does the recovery effort need to be? Is the customer simply frustrated and in need of some comfort in order for the relationship to be restabilized, or is the customer so angry and disillusioned that nothing short of aggressive save tactics is in order?

Some often-asked questions about managing at-risk and lost customers that emerge from constructing a decision map are outlined in the following pages. These questions also serve as a quick preview of ideas and skills we present in the upcoming chapters.

• *How should I use the decision map?* Use the decision map as a road map to guide you through Big Three decision points, particularly those related to at-risk and lost customers. With at-risk customers, three options are available: stabilize, save, or retire the relationship. For lost customers, two options exist: make the effort to win them

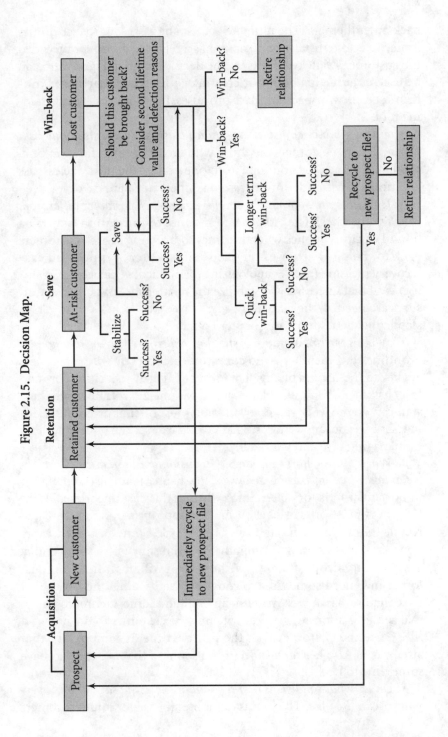

Figure 2.15. Decision Map.

back or let them go. The ultimate goal of any at-risk or lost customer initiative is to reinstate the customer as a retained customer provided the customer's value warrants it. The decision map in Figure 2.15 can be used as a starting point for creating your own blueprint for your firm's specific win-back and save processes. It also makes a great training tool.

• *Under what circumstances should I classify a customer as at risk?* Often, at-risk customers are those who are migrating down in purchases (revenue contribution) from one year to the next. We discuss additional ways to identify at-risk customers in Chapter Four.

• *How does the approach to stabilize an at-risk customer differ from the save approach?* The old adage "An ounce of prevention is worth a pound of cure" applies when it comes to bringing at-risk customers back to the safe harbor of retained status. Often, a quick and easy recovery measure (a letter apologizing for an inconvenience, for example) is all that's necessary to stabilize the relationship. When save measures are needed, they are more aggressive. We discuss saving versus stabilizing tactics more in Chapter Four.

• *What is the role of frontline staff in stabilizing or saving a customer?* Frontline staff members who communicate directly with customers are key to the success of any plan for managing at-risk customers and lost customers. You must plan realistic parameters within which these staff can do the work required, and you must offer appropriate training, supervision, and rewards. That's why we devote all of Chapter Five to managing save and win-back teams.

• *When a save effort fails, does that customer automatically become a candidate for win-back?* Not always. In Chapter Four we outline some important criteria for determining whether this customer deserves the full-court press on win-back. It may be appropriate, for example, to recycle the customer into the new prospect file. Some customers experience so serious a breakdown in their relationship with a supplier that any effort to recover them in the near term will be wasted. The customer may need some time to cool off. This assumes, however, that the company has at least made an apology and some attempt to renormalize the relationship before switching the customer to the prospect file. Once the customer is in the prospect file, it's important that attempts to woo her do not occur too soon, so that her feelings have some time to heal.

• *Under what conditions do I send an unsuccessful save into the permanently retired file?* The litmus test is lifetime value. Some customers are marginal in terms of revenue generation and use of services. Beyond a certain point, such customers may not be worth further recovery efforts. What's more, you probably do not want to send this same low-value customer into the new prospect file because then you will end up investing new acquisition dollars in him. We explore this topic in Chapter Four also.

• *When a customer is lost, what are the criteria for determining whether that customer should be regained, and if she should be regained, how do I determine her priority in relation to other lost customers?* Two key concepts—second lifetime value and reason for defection—are important to answering these questions. We cover these concepts in Chapter Three.

• *For what reasons should I recycle lost customers to the new prospect file?* There are several reasons. For example, it may have been so long since these customer have purchased that they have to be reeducated about the company's products or services, just like prospects in the sales process. Or these lost customers may have defected over a serious breakdown in trust or performance delivery. Rather than begin a formal win-back process, which has a likelihood of failure in the short term in this case, it may be more appropriate to rebuild trust slowly and treat that customer as a high-value prospect. As mentioned earlier, it's important that attempts to woo the lost customer do not occur too soon so that the wounds have some time to heal.

• *When the lost customer is chosen as a win-back prospect, what will the specifics of the win-back plan include?* Win-back success is built on economics and the lifetime value potential of the customer in the postrecovery period (called second lifetime value). The strategic and tactical plan will address the communication medium, message content, frequency of contact, number of win-back attempts, ways to measure win-back success, and the like and will be most successfully developed by trial and error. By testing various elements and tracking responses, your firm can determine what combination of elements applied to what customer segments gives the greatest win-back return. This topic is examined in Chapter Three.

• *If lost customers are not chosen as win-back prospects or do not respond to win-back initiatives, under what conditions should I recycle them to the new prospect file or send them to the permanently retired file?* It all comes down to lifetime value. Take a look at the customer's purchase and service history, demographic and psychographic profile, and lifestyle stage. If these elements indicate there would be no economic value in pursuing win-back, then that customer should be retired. If lifetime value is there, the name should go into the new prospect file. But take care to structure your win-back initiatives in waves. For varying reasons, many customers may not respond to your first win-back attempt. For example, the lost customer may temporarily experiment with another vendor and after comparing services, decide your service is better. In that case, your third or fourth win-back invitation will be right on time. That's why knowing the lifetime value of a win-back candidate is key to your planning. This issue is examined in more detail in Chapter Three.

• *How are lost customers who are sent to the new prospect file assigned to decile rankings so I know who to spend more on and who to spend less on?* Customer lifetime value is again the key. All acquisition dollars should be appropriated to new prospects based on their estimated lifetime value potential. The higher the estimated value, the higher the resources deserved.

• *How are customers successfully stabilized, saved, or regained assigned to decile rankings among the other retained customers?* Customer lifetime value remains the key. All retention dollars should be appropriated to retained customers based on their estimated lifetime value.

SUMMARY

• No program completely prevents customer defection.

• Any company needs the Big Three: acquisition, retention, and win-back strategies.

• You can turn your company into a loyalty lab by helping each employee become a *loyalty scientist,* investigating customer purchase patterns and habits and what drives them.

• Ignoring any one of the Big Three can rob you of critical insights and, consequently, profits.

• Keep an eye on the key six customer groups to really understand what is happening in your Big Three efforts.

• Detailed data analysis is essential in tracking customer behavior and determining customer lifetime value.

• A plan for recovering at-risk and lost customers is essential.

CHAPTER THREE

Winning Back a Lost Customer

We have often listened to stories like this one, which we heard from an advertising account executive for a major news magazine:

> Yesterday, I lost one of my biggest accounts. About a year and a half ago, a large hotel's ad agency—with whom I had a pretty good relationship—came to me and said that they were interested in doing something a little bit different. It amounted to a deal that exceeded $1 million net. It was a very high frequency program for the hotel company and was the first time that they had gotten into large media like our magazine. The program ran great for a year. I found out yesterday that they're not going to renew it.

Losing a valued customer is never fun. It's an unhappy event for all concerned. Learning how to manage that sinking feeling that occurs when a major account says good-bye is a milestone for anyone. You have a choice: you can give in to the disappointment and despair and purge that lost customer from your data files, thereby ensuring that the customer is gone forever. Or you can get focused on the necessary steps to win back that customer.

In Chapter Two we introduced the win-back decision map, or tree. Throughout this chapter, we'll follow the tree's "lost customer" branch step by step and examine the four major decision points one by one.

DECISION POINT: LOST CUSTOMER— DO YOU HAVE ONE?

In some businesses, once customers make a decision to terminate the relationship, they officially communicate their intent to the company. In others, there is never a formal declaration of termination. Instead the customer slips away, either by buying less and less over time or by terminating her purchasing all at once. Figure 3.1 lists some formal and informal ways customers terminate across varying industries.

The end of the customer life cycle is typically characterized by a phase in which the customer is passive and stops purchasing. In many businesses, customers do not typically notify you they are terminating. Instead you must rely on purchase behaviors and other informal signals to tell you that defection is looming. (The customer churn analysis discussed in Chapter Two, which tracks the migration of customers between revenue deciles, helps expose customers in this termination phase.) The quicker you realize that termination is upon you, the better positioned you are to leverage the situation immediately for future opportunity.

Figure 3.1. How Customers Say Good-Bye.

Organization	Formal Termination	Informal Termination
Doctor or dentist	Requests medical records	Periodic visits stop
Insurance	Cancels policy	Policy payments stop
Church	Moves membership to another church	Attendance or tithing stops
Credit card	Cancels credit card	Credit card usage stops
Restaurant	None	Patronizing stops
Magazine	Notifies of nonrenewal	Subscription lapses
Car dealership	None	Periodic servicing stops
Hair dresser	None	Appointments aren't made
Dry cleaners	None	Stops patronizing
Web site	None	Site visits stop
Book club	Cancels membership	None

DECISION POINT: WIN-BACK— YES OR NO?

Not all lost customers make good win-back prospects, nor do you want to win back all lost customers. It's important to segment lost customers by win-back potential, with lost customers who offer the highest probable return on your efforts given greatest priority. Without an effective segmentation strategy, you can waste lots of time and money on recontacting lost customers who are poor prospects for future business. One database strategist we interviewed described the peril this way:

> I have a phone line downstairs in my home that I use for occasional business purposes. Never a long distance call. And about every six months, I get an offer I can't refuse and I switch the thing from one long distance carrier to another. I always get a callback from the carrier I just terminated trying to woo me back. Why would they even want me back? I make no long distance calls. I'm more expensive for them to process. And they call back every time which tells me there is no profiling, no segmentation being done. It's just reactive.[1]

The best segmentation plan for lost customers we've found thus far is a two-step process outlined by Stauss and Friege.[2] First, lost customers are segmented based on second lifetime value. Next, these same customers are segmented a second time based on reason for defection. Let's look at this segmentation process step by step, including a third step of combining the information from Steps 1 and 2.

Step 1. Segment and Grade Lost Customers by Second Lifetime Value

In Chapter Two we examined customer lifetime value (LTV). With lost customers, the lifetime value of the terminated relationship is not as important as the value of the relationship once the customer is regained. Stauss and Friege call this new value the second lifetime value (SLTV). There are at least four reasons why a customer's second life cycle can differ greatly from the same customer's first life cycle: (1) the defected customer is already familiar with the services offered, (2) the service provider has more data about the likes and dislikes of this particular customer than about those of any first-time customer and can offer a more targeted service, (3) the personal recognition of the customer in the course of a successful win-back could lead to a sales performance better than that generated by the typical anonymously recruited first-time customer, and (4) the length of the *prospect phase* and the *new customer phase* may well be shorter in the second life cycle than in the first one. Only a detailed analysis of customer data for each business will reveal whether that business's typical LTV is smaller, the same, or greater than the typical SLTV. The relationship between the two might be different for different customer segments as well.

Just like calculating LTV, calculating SLTV requires the application of facts and reasonable assumptions. Figure 3.2 develops a second lifetime value estimate (again defining lifetime as three years cumulative value) for a regained customer for ABC Product Company. Here's an overview of some of the numbers.

• Year 1 represents the first year of win-back rather than the calendar year.

• ABC estimates that this customer will place an average of five orders in the win-back year, with an average order value of $400, and seven orders in the next year, with an average value of $515. Because the regained customer is, like the retained customer, already familiar with services offered, the SLTV analysis assumes the win-back customer will reengage with ABC at a higher order rate and value than a new customer and then increase the number of orders, paralleling the behavior of retained customers as shown in Figure 2.9.

• Because ABC has more data on the likes and dislikes of this win-back customer than it does on any first-time customer, the SLTV allocates a revenue contribution for cross-selling (15 percent of order revenue) and information value (10 percent of order revenue). Cross-selling revenue, as we pointed out earlier, comes from additional products and services the win-back customer will likely purchase over and above core purchases. Accessory items are one example. Information revenue is earned when insights gleaned from the win-back customer are turned into revenue contribution. For example, suppose ABC learns, through field sales and customer research, that its win-back customer will open a new satellite operation in the next six months and that the new facility will have an immediate need for ABC widgets. That insight represents information value that can be quantified for SLTV. (In some companies cross-selling and information value may be appropriate in calculations of LTV too, but the opportunities

Figure 3.2. Second Lifetime Value Calculation.

	Win-Back Year 1	Win-Back Year 2	Win-Back Year 3
Revenue			
Orders per year	5	7	8
× Average order	$400	$515	$550
= Base revenue	$2,000	$3,605	$4,400
+ Cross-sell	$300 (15%)	$540 (15%)	$660 (15%)
+ Information value	$200 (10%)	$360 (10%)	$440 (10%)
= Total revenue	$2,500	$4,505	$5,500
Costs			
Direct cost	$1,500 (60%)	$2,703 (60%)	$3,300 (60%)
+ Win-back cost	$750 (30%)	0 0	0 0
+ Retention cost	0 0	$450 (10%)	$550 (10%)
= Total costs	$2,250	$3,153	$3,850
Profit			
Gross profit	$250	$1,352	$1,650
Cumulative SLTV	$250	$1,602*	$3,252*

*Before net present value adjustment.

for such leveraging are often greater with a win-back customer, so we calculate only these values here.)

• In Chapter Two we took a conservative stance on additional revenue from referrals because of their unpredictability. We take the same conservative stance on referrals in calculating SLTV as well. The good news is that some win-back customers may be so thrilled with the personal recognition they receive in the course of a successful win-back effort that they become very strong referral sources soon after returning. But other win-back customers may prove to be forever cautious about referring, and still others may behave somewhere in between. The key to effective forecasting of revenue contributions associated with referrals, cross-selling, or information value comes down to tracking real purchase information. The more you know about actual successes in these areas, the better you can be at forecasting these three areas effectively. (To see referral rates included in SLTV, refer to Appendix B, which provides a more detailed example of an SLTV calculation for ABC Product Company.)

• If you choose to incorporate referral revenue, calculate the referral revenue as a percentage of sales revenue. As we recommended for LTV, when estimating referral revenue for SLTV, consider using an escalating percentage beginning with the year of win-back (for example, Year 1, 5 percent; Year 2, 7 percent; Year 3, 10 percent). This escalation is based on the premise that the longer your relationship with the customer, the more likely he is to make a referral.

• Like LTV, SLTV may be estimated for an unlimited number of years. As real purchase information is collected, the second lifetime value estimate should be periodically recalculated and reestimated to reflect this latest learning.

IDENTIFYING YOUR FIRM'S UNIQUE SLTV INDICATORS. Experience is a great SLTV teacher. Every industry and every firm develops rules to guide its SLTV calculations. For example, magazine publishers have discovered that indicators such as lapsed-subscriber time (the more time that has passed since the last subscription, the less the SLTV) and lapsed-subscriber source (SLTV is higher if the lapsed subscriber was recruited through a subscription card for the specific publication as opposed to a secondary subscription source that handles multiple subscriptions, such as American Family Publishers) are important considerations when calculating SLTV. Every firm should use its past retained customer and win-back customer histories to help identify the indicators that drive SLTV calculations.

RECALCULATING WHEN THE SLTV IS IN FLUX. In some industries a lapsed customer's SLTV can resemble a moving target. In the cellular market, for example, the marketplace changes rapidly and may be making new demands. One cellular marketing executive we interviewed described the challenge this way: "Cellular is a declining category in terms of revenue. The interesting thing is, when you lost them a year ago, they may have been $100 a month customers. But now, because cellular pricing is going down, they are $50 a month customers."

If your firm competes in an industry with severe pricing and promotion turbulence, periodic recalculation of SLTV estimates may be required. The longer a lapsed customer stays away and does not repurchase from your firm, the more important it becomes to periodically recalculate that customer's second lifetime value to ensure your assumptions about the customer's value still hold.

CALCULATING SLTV WHEN YOU'RE SHORT ON DATA. What if you have a file of lost customer names but almost no additional data from which to predict SLTV? Here's how one firm faced that challenge and got what it needed. An optical company in the Northeast with three store locations and a database of fifteen thousand to twenty thousand lapsed customers contacted us about winning back lost business. The firm's information about these customers was very limited, so to determine their future value, we recommended that a sample of these lapsed customers be contacted by phone, starting with customers with the most recent purchase dates. Figure 3.3 shows the questions the customer representatives used to gather the needed information.

From this information, the optical company could estimate SLTV and segment lost accounts. Generally speaking, the lapsed customers with the highest SLTV would be those who (1) are still wearing prescription eyewear, (2) use multiple types of prescription eyewear, (3) have multiple family members with eyewear needs, and (4) expect to make a prescription eyewear purchase within the next six months.

Step 2. Segment and Grade Lost Customers by Reasons for Defection

Once you've assigned SLTV estimates to lost customers so you can segment them by value, it's appropriate, as Stauss and Friege's segmentation model tells us, to further segment these same lost customers by reason for defection. Why? Because a customer's reason for defection can offer valuable insight on whether or not she is a good win-back prospect.

FIVE KINDS OF DEFECTORS. Stauss and Friege have identified five distinct defector categories: (1) intentionally pushed away, (2) unintentionally pushed away, (3) pulled away, (4) bought away, and (5) moved away.[3]

Figure 3.3. Optical Firm Customer Questionnaire.

Hello, Mr. Smith. My name is _____ and I'm calling you from ABC Eyewear. According to our records, the last time we served you was _____ [*give date*]. Does that date sound correct? [*If "yes," continue. If "no," correct the date per the customer's input.*] We appreciate your past business and want very much to serve you in the future.

1. Are you still wearing prescription eyewear? [*If "no," terminate call. If "yes," continue.*] We'd like to send you a gift certificate for your next purchase of prescriptive eyewear. To do that, I'd like to update our records by asking just a few questions.

2. What type of eyewear do you use and when did you last replace it?

   _____ Full-time wear   Date last replaced _____

   _____ Prescription reading   Date last replaced _____

   _____ Prescription sunglasses   Date last replaced _____

   _____ Distance only   Date last replaced _____

   _____ Contact lenses   Date last replaced _____

3. Who else in your household wears eyewear? What type of eyewear?

4. Thinking about your next eyewear purchase, what type of eyewear is it most likely to be?

5. When do you expect to make your next eyewear purchase?

6. What was the major reason you stopped shopping with us?

   _____ Product quality

   _____ Product selection

   _____ Service concerns

   _____ The attitude of an employee or employees

   _____ Price considerations

   _____ A relocation

   _____ Change in insurance carrier

   _____ A better arrangement with a competitor

   _____ A mishandled complaint

   _____ Billing problems

   _____ Other

   Mr. Smith, we truly appreciate your past business and want to earn more business from you in the future. As I stated earlier, we'd like to send you a gift certificate for your next purchase of prescriptive eyewear.

7. Is this your correct home address? [*Read the address on record, and correct it if neccessary.*]

8. Do you have an e-mail address for our records? [*If "yes," record the e-mail address.*]

Intentionally Pushed Away Customers. Intentionally pushed away customers are unprofitable to serve, and for that reason the firm does little to encourage their ongoing patronage. Contracts are not renewed or the service level is reduced in a way that encourages customers to defect by themselves. Examples include customers who have proven to be poor credit risks or whose service costs are greater than the profits they create. It's important that companies identify intentionally pushed away customers and exclude them from win-back initiatives.

The unreasonable demands of unhappy customers whose needs do not fit with the company's capabilities can consume excessive resources and wreak havoc on employee morale. Glenn Holley, vice president of Holley Dodge in Middleton, Connecticut, recalls "a customer who essentially never wanted to spend a dime at his dealership. Any time anything was repaired, he thought it was not right, and then he refused to pay a bill that we were entirely correct in charging him for." After a number of incidents, Holley reached a solution: the customer didn't have to pay the bill, but Holley invited him to take his business elsewhere.[4] Similar circumstances have prompted outstanding service organizations such as Nordstrom department stores and Southwest Airlines to regularly "fire" customers they cannot properly serve. Says Southwest Airlines CEO Herb Kelleher, "The customer is sometimes wrong. We write to them and say, 'Fly somebody else. Don't abuse our people.'"[5]

To manage unprofitable customers, some companies are creating sophisticated processes that match service levels to customer value. This technique can push away low-profit customers, or at the minimum, limit the costs of serving such customers. For example, when you call AT&T with a question about your long distance service, you are routed to one of many different call centers. AT&T computers use Caller ID to identify your phone number and call up your monthly bill. If it's high, you get what AT&T calls *hot-towel service*—human operators who remain on the phone with you. Spend less than $3 a month, and you get no such coddling—just more automated voices. What if the cut-rate service drives off lower-paying customers? AT&T has done the math and determined that many low-paying customers are unlikely to grow into bigger customers. The company loses $500 million a year on its fifteen million to twenty million "occasional communicators," who rarely make long distance calls yet cost plenty to acquire, bill, and service. "We've gotten a lot smarter about separating the customers we do want from customers we don't," says AT&T CEO Michael Armstrong.[6]

Unintentionally Pushed Away Customers. Unintentionally pushed away customers are those you want to keep but who leave because the company's performance does not meet their expectation. Here are some of the reasons commonly cited by these customers for no longer buying from a supplier:

- *Unhappiness with product delivery, installation, service, or price.* A single incident is unlikely to lose a customer, but several incidents of poor quality, late delivery, or inaccurate shipment may do it. A price rise may have the same effect, especially if your customer hasn't been given much advance notice.

- *Improper handling of a complaint.* A single incident here can lose a customer. Someone who feels a complaint isn't taken seriously, or is displeased with your resolution of it may search out another supplier.

- *Disapproval of changes.* Whenever you make a change in price, policy, product, or salesforce, you risk offending some customers.

- *Feeling taken for granted.* Established customers, though highly profitable, are often treated in an offhand way by salespeople. This is a major error. Every customer should be resold in every transaction.

Some firms have learned from the customers they unintentionally pushed away. Zane's Cycle, an independent bicycle retailer in Branford, Connecticut, had annual revenues in 1996 of just under $1.5 million—much higher than most bike shops' earnings. Owner Chris Zane expected that revenues would pass $3 million the following year. "From the customers we've lost that we've then been able to get back," says Zane, "we've heard that they just thought we didn't care whether they came in or not. It wasn't that the price was bad, it wasn't that the products were bad—they just felt when they came in that no one really cared that they were here."

These experiences have taught Zane to look for ways to let customers know he appreciates them. One way is to offer free coffee and soft drinks to customers. "A lot of our customers come in on Saturday mornings to have coffee, hang out for 15 or 20 minutes, read the paper, and leave," says Zane. What has helped Zane reduce the number of customers unintentionally pushed away is that he thinks of such customers in terms of relationships, not transactions.[7]

Pulled Away Customers. A competitor may pull customers away from you by offering a better value, an advantage that often goes beyond price. Perhaps service was more personable or more reliable, or product quality was higher, or the product was more innovative. Studies show that often customers will switch even when the new provider is more expensive or less convenient if they perceive that the value proposition is stronger.

A company that has created a value proposition that routinely pulls customers away from competitors is Price Automotive, a group of dealerships in Northern Delaware. Since converting to a one-price sales policy (no more haggling over price between customer and salesperson), Price has shot up to fifth in sales among the 125 Dodge stores in its zone and seventeenth among 134 Toyota stores. Moreover, service dollars have doubled, and the dealership enjoys one of the highest percentages of customer-pay work (versus warranty work) in the United States. Even more remarkable is the fact that these solid performance numbers have been achieved without any media advertising. Says dealership general manager Michael Price, "Our results validate that people hate to negotiate, and that happy customers really do spread the word."

What's the pull? In addition to a frictionless pricing system, every customer who buys a new or used vehicle from Price gets an estimated $1,600 worth of services over five years. This includes several free oil changes and free diagnostic service inspections, emergency roadside assistance that exceeds the manufacturer's plan, and mobile repair services. Says Price, "In an industry where location is king, we capture and keep customers based on no-hassle sales and service. If anything, our location is a bit of a nuisance. We're surrounded by industrial parks and high-density housing. In fact, at our Dover location, on summer weekends beach traffic is so heavy that you can't pull out of our lot for a demonstration ride."[8]

Bought Away Customers. For some customers, price is all that matters, and competitors make low-ball, introductory pricing offers to get them. Defecting customers are considered bought away customers when they are attracted by these introductory pricing offers. These customers feel a low level of company loyalty and are open to switching providers back and forth.

One company that has experienced the fickleness of such customers is Super Embroidery Inc. A three hundred–employee Phoenix firm that does automated embroidering of hats, caps, and jackets, Super Embroidery has hundreds of customers. Sometimes business is lost to new companies that price very aggressively in an effort to get accounts. Says company president Anna Johnson, "Most of those I get back within three months because competitors fail to keep their promises." But others don't return. "There was one customer we lost because of three cents a hat," says Johnson, even though the customer was completely satisfied in every other way. That customer's buyer called Johnson a few months later, complaining that her new supplier was slow and the quality of its work was below Super Embroidery's—but the customer still wanted Johnson to reduce Super Embroidery's price by three cents a hat to get back the order. Johnson declined to reduce the price, and the lost customer did not return.[9]

The lesson of bought away customers is this: cutting your price to snare such a customer is probably pointless—you'll get less money, and you probably won't keep the customer anyway.

Moved Away Customers. Moved away customers drift away from the consumer-oriented service provider because they have relocated or because their needs are different due to age, life cycle changes, or a change in geography. For example, a manufacturer of women's pantyhose loses customers because slacks and pantsuits have replaced skirts and dresses as the working woman's wardrobe of choice. A day-care center loses a child because the parents buy a home in a neighboring town. Or a printing company loses a business client because a regional office is closing and the printing will now be handled by corporate headquarters three states away.

But for many companies, moved away losses that were once unavoidable due to changes in customers' geography can now be greatly reduced through e-commerce. For example, Pat Jameson, a working mom in Indianapolis, does half her shopping on the Web. She uses the Web to get quick access to her favorite high-end retailers, which weren't accessible to her in pre-Internet days. For example, a former Californian, she missed Nordstrom after her 1991 move to the Midwest. Now she does much of her clothes shopping with Nordstrom via the Internet.[10]

GUIDELINES FOR UNCOVERING THE CUSTOMER'S REAL REASONS FOR LEAVING. Successfully identifying and classifying your lapsed customer's reason(s) for defection is crucial to your segmentation plan. Oftentimes, uncovering the real reasons for losing an account is easy; at other times it requires a sort of Columbo-style detective work for which many companies are ill prepared. Gathering full information and conducting customer exit interviews are two important techniques for uncovering a customer's reasons for defection, along with watching your timing and distinguishing emotional from logical reasons for termination.

Get Both Sides of the Story. When investigating a lost customer as a possible reactivation candidate, getting to the real termination issues is critical and not always easy. Says *Austin Business Journal* advertising director Patrick Asbra, "Be aware, particularly if your predecessor is no longer in your company (and perhaps even if he is), that you may not get all the facts. You'll likely get one side of the story (your organization's). This will become apparent when you talk to the customer and find his story is somewhat different." For example, in considering accounts to reactivate, Asbra reviewed an old account file on a construction company client. At first blush it seemed that the account had been lost over the client's inability to pay. But as Asbra dug deeper and then went out and talked to the client, a different story emerged.

"The construction client had soured on us because of problems," explains Asbra. "They were unhappy because their former ABJ account executive was running the wrong ads on the wrong dates, and the ads were running at poor quality. The construction client complained, was assured it would be fixed, but nothing happened. Then bills were sent out for the advertising that had not met specification. Awaiting adjustment to the bill, the client withheld payment, and the accounting department was not informed so they started sending overdue notices to the client. Meantime, the account executive just ignored the problem and didn't inform accounting. The problem just snowballed."

With some real effort, Asbra was able to piece together the real story and determine that the construction company was indeed a good prospect for future business. With these new insights, the construction company was successfully won back as a client.[11]

To smoke out the details surrounding a client defection, use these guidelines.

- Review account history with those in your company with information. Seek out sources with first-hand knowledge but be aware they may not know all the facts.

- Read through old customer files.

- Look for signs of cause in letters, call reports, and the like.

- Look at the pattern of the orders, and compare it to the date of any change in your company or in the customer's situation.

- Meet with a lost customer to compare your "facts" with his or hers.

- When appropriate, ask noncompeting salespeople about their purchase experiences with this customer.

- Keep an open mind.

- Be prepared to hear the unexpected.

Conduct Exit Interviews. Call the departing customer and request an exit interview. You might say, for example, "My upper management wants to know why this happened, and they want details. I want to go back to them and say, 'We need to correct these problems so we don't lose more business.' Can we have a short meeting so you can fill me in on the particulars of your decision?"

Research conducted by Marketing Metrics has found that at least 50 percent of departed customers will participate in an exit interview, and 30 percent will even tell you what you can do to win them back.[12] Key questions to ask on an exit interview include these:

- Why did you stop buying from us?

    The quality of merchandise (unintentionally pushed away)

    The quality of service (unintentionally pushed away)

    The attitude of an employee or employees (unintentionally pushed away)

    A competitor had a better price (bought away)

    A relocation (moved away)

    A better arrangement with a competitor (pulled away)

    A mishandled complaint (unintentionally pushed away)

    An invoice or billing problem (unintentionally pushed away)

    Other

- Did you inform us about your problems before you stopped purchasing?

- If we fixed that would you try us again?

When possible, meet with the client in person. Body language and demeanor can tell you a lot. However, conducting an exit interview by phone is appropriate as well at times. Make sure you do not use this time to sell to the lost customer but rather to gain crucial insights on how to avoid a similar problem in the future. Consider this an opportunity to reestablish in your client's mind the picture you want him to retain: that you are on the ball and willing to go to great lengths to make sure your company is doing its best for its clients.

But simply conducting an exit interview doesn't ensure you'll get real answers. For example, an associate of ours recently quit doing business with a bank. The bank didn't offer some services she wanted. She told us, "I went to a competitor. I wasn't lured or bought away. I was just annoyed!" But when she was called by a bank representative and interviewed about the reason for her exit, the representative listened to the explanation and then checked a box on the computer screen that said "competition." How much will the bank learn from that information? Not much. The bottom line on exit interviews is that they must be designed to offer enough options so that frontline people can report accurately what the client says.

Watch Your Timing. Cellular One director of revenue Fernando Roman has found that many newly departed customers are often reluctant to share the real reason they left. They may be embarrassed to say they're leaving and will compensate by giving easy reasons for defection. Says Roman, "In the cellular phone business, a departing customer will say, for example, they no longer need their cell phone, but their last bill was $300, so they're obviously using it quite a bit. If you call them a month or two later, and specifically ask them why they left, then they will tell you the truth."

Roman sees parallels between this lost customer behavior and the breakup of a romantic relationship. "The lost customer has landed somewhere else. They're happier now and ready to tell you the real truth. They want you to know why they left. It's kind of like boy-girl relationships. When you break up with one person and you're happier with the next one, you can't wait to brag about it. It's just like that."

Besides running the risk of receiving inaccurate termination information, calling too soon after defection can hinder the rebuilding of the relationship in other ways. Says Roman, "If you call the customer up immediately, it's almost annoying to them. Their first response is, 'Why are you bugging me? You should have cared for me before I left.

I'm not going to change back now, so why are you calling me?'" Calling later (in Cellular One's case that means in thirty to sixty days), communicates to the customer that he is not forgotten and that the door is open for return. Calling later also means that you are recontacting the customer after he has had some experience with the new vendor. He now can make a clearer assessment of his former relationship with your company. That also helps you get some honest feedback. Roman observes, "We have taken that feedback and implemented rate plans based on what customers that have left us have said. Moreover, we've had several customers who have come back because they realized that their new vendor was not as good as it claimed."[13]

Identify Reasons as Emotion or Logic. Finally, you may need to make sense of what you learn about termination. Sometimes you may uncover a reason for termination that doesn't fit neatly into any of the five conventional categories we discussed. That is because termination is not always a logical decision. It can be an emotional decision that is outwardly justified with logic, as Roy Chitwood, president of sales training and management consulting firm Max Sacks International discovered when working with an engineering client.

"What I hate about salespeople," this vice president of engineering confided to Chitwood, "is that they drive the wrong way around the parking lot all the time."

"What?" asked Chitwood, stunned.

"You know, we have arrows in our parking lot. They don't follow them," the client replied, quite irritated.

The point, Chitwood says, is that dozens—and perhaps hundreds—of salespeople had struck out or been fired by this man primarily because they went the wrong way in his parking lot. "Now what's this Stanford Ph.D. going to say? That you're losing the account or not getting a new piece of business because you *drove* wrong?" Of course not. So he must justify it some other way—which is exactly what a sale is, explains Chitwood. "An emotional decision, justified logically."[14]

There is good and bad news about emotional defectors. The bad news is that the lapsed customer who defected on an emotional issue may be a drifter of sorts who journeys from one vendor to the next due to boredom or indecision or super ego or any of a number of other psychological reasons. Such lapsed customers are often more trouble than they are worth and make poor win-back prospects. The good news is that a defected customer's reason for leaving, emotional as it was, may be judged by the vendor to be a manageable or fixable issue or a one-time incident that is unlikely to recur. In these circumstances, emotional defectors make viable win-back prospects. Like other win-back candidates, an emotional defector's win-back worthiness should be carefully evaluated according to second lifetime value and reason for defection.

Step 3. Segment and Grade Lost Customers by Combining SLTV and Reasons for Defection into a Master Segmentation Plan

Steps 1 and 2 examined how to calculate the SLTV of a lost customer and how to identify and segment lost customers by reasons for defection. In this third and final step, these two variables are combined to form a master segmentation plan for lost customers. This segmentation plan can help you target your resources at the lost customers with highest win-back potential. Following the Stauss and Friege model, this step is accomplished in two parts. First, divide your lost customers into four SLTV segments: A (the top 10 percent), B (the next best 20 percent), C (the next best 30 percent), and D (the last 40 percent). Second, within each SLTV segment, cluster the unintentionally pushed away customers and pulled away customers and place the remaining customers in an "others" category. In Figure 3.4, you will note that the division between "UP + P" and "others," as indicated by the width of the bars on the graph, is about 50-50 for the A group, about 70-30 for the B group, about 60-40 for the C group, and 50-50 for the D group. These percentages simply reflect the number of unintentionally pushed away customers and pulled away customers in each of the four segments in the Stauss and Friege example. These percentages will vary based on the composition (how many unintentionally pushed away customers, for example) within a firm's SLTV segments.

Generally speaking, unintentionally pushed away and pulled away customers in each of your four groups (A–D) are your best win-back candidates. Why? Because bought away, moved away, and intentionally pushed away customers left for reasons that would probably jeopardize any success in keeping these customers loyal in the future: (1) Bought away customers have shown vulnerability to competitors' pricing bribes. Given the expensive up-front offer that would be needed and the expected short customer life cycle, it seems unlikely that these customers will ever become profitable. (2) Moved away customers' needs have shifted away from your offerings, making their long-term loyalty very questionable, except in some circumstances when long distance buying is viable. (3) Intentionally pushed away customers have proven unprofitable or incapable of being well served, making it unwise to invest resources to win them back. (Intentionally pushed away customers are technically part of a firm's lost customers, so they are included in the "others" category in the Stauss and Friege model outlined in Figure 3.4.) While there are exceptions to these rules, generally your best win-back candidates are unintentionally pushed away and pulled away customers.[15]

As you will recall from discussion earlier in this chapter, the motivation behind segmenting and grading customers is to shed light on the following decision point: "Win back—yes or no?" Returning to Figure 3.4, these segmentation results suggest that the firm's largest win-back resources should be spent on unintentionally pushed away customers and pulled away customers in Group A followed by UP and P customers in Groups B, C, and D. For reasons stated earlier, other customers in Groups A, B, C, and D should be given secondary win-back consideration or eliminated from win-back programs altogether.

**Figure 3.4. Segmenting Lost Customers
by SLTV and Reasons for Defection.**

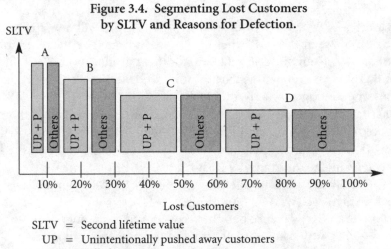

SLTV = Second lifetime value
UP = Unintentionally pushed away customers
P = Pulled away customers

Source: B. Stauss and C. Friege, "Regaining Service Customers," *Journal of Service Research,* May 1999, p. 351.

DECISION POINT: WHEN YOU DON'T WANT A LOST CUSTOMER BACK

Earlier in this chapter we discussed numerous situations in which lost customers should be retired from future win-back initiatives. Intentionally pushed away, bought away, and, in some circumstances, moved away customers are examples of lost customers you often do not want to recover. Take care to leave these customers with as positive a feeling about your company and its services as possible. While these customers themselves do not represent significant future purchase potential, their positive word of mouth can be valuable (and their negative word of mouth can be harmful).

But there are some lost customers who may not be good candidates for winning back right away but who should not be crossed off the books altogether.

For example, across its 230 private membership clubs, ClubCorp loses between thirty-two thousand and thirty-five thousand members a year, most of whom are in the uncontrollable moved away category. Statistics show that 65 percent of the attrition is attributable to financial difficulties, death, divorce, and so on. Although many of these lost customers are not immediately win-back worthy, it's important to keep the door open, because a number of them are likely candidates for future reinstatement. Delivered in person or in writing, here's the key message offered to these departed customers: "We hope that circumstances will soon change such that we can look forward to welcoming you back to the club. We appreciate your past membership and the opportunity to serve you."[16]

Customer reps should be able to make a note in a customer's file of any special circumstances. In some cases, you may want to call the expired customer from time to time to determine if circumstances have changed.

DECISION POINT: WHEN YOU DO WANT A LOST CUSTOMER BACK

With every lapsed customer, you are typically faced with a quick win-back opportunity or a longer-term win-back opportunity. A quick win-back opportunity takes place on the spot, immediately upon discovering the customer has departed. The longer win-back requires a more lengthy recovery process. Let's look at both situations.

Quick Win-Back Efforts

You sometimes have an opportunity to do a quick win-back. Suppose, for example, you are the club manager of a golf club and you have a member, Mr. Freemont, who has submitted his resignation because of unhappiness with the club. With some quick action, you just might win back Mr. Freemont by phoning him to say:

> Mr. Freemont, I am really sorry to hear about your experience, and I want you to know that I am going to take care of this as soon as we hang up the telephone. As a matter of fact, I'm going to credit your club dues for the upcoming month, because I want you to see that the problem has been rectified. I'll hold your resignation in my drawer here in my office during that time. If you still want to resign at the end of next month or if you feel we have not corrected the problem to your liking, we'll process your resignation at that time. I'll just make a note to call you in about six weeks.

More often than not, your company's credibility is in serious question at this juncture in the relationship. To save this customer now requires an authority figure with skillful listening and contrition skills. When talking with the customer:

- Listen carefully to the customer issues and acknowledge the customer's pain.
- Be decisive about solutions. Avoid the "I'll talk to my manager and get back to you" scenario.
- Be generous in your resolution offer.
- Give the customer some options.
- Be equally gracious whether the customer says yes or no.

When your quick win-back strategy works, do five things: (1) be thankful the customer returned; (2) look closely at your operating processes and make any necessary changes to prevent a similar reoccurrence with another customer; (3) determine why your win-back approach was successful and use this approach, when appropriate, in other quick win-back situations; (4) move this successfully recovered customer into retained customer status and resume normal communication; (5) be sure this win-back history is captured and recorded in the customer's file.

Longer-Term Win-Back Efforts

Often when a customer terminates, there is no opportunity to immediately win back the lost business. For example, the magazine advertising executive who lost the hotel account as described at the beginning of the chapter found out that

> Some new people came on board at the [hotel's advertising] agency and this created some shifts in strategy. They felt that they needed to do something on the hotel account that was on an even grander scale and more immediate than what our magazine could deliver, despite the fact we're a weekly. The agency elected to shift from about 15 percent to 25 percent broadcast to about 75 percent. So after they had described to me what they felt their needs were, it was pretty hard to argue with the logic. By the time I was informed, the decision had already been made. The agency was in final production for the broadcast commercial. They were cutting the music. There's not anything that I personally could have done to get them to change this direction. The only thing I can do here is to go to Plan B.

When this happens, you should do some immediate housekeeping on the account and then move to the longer win-back plan (Plan B). First, consider three ways to maximize your position in the short term.

1. *Let the customer off the hook.* We all know better than to display anger; burnt bridges are hard to recross. The more typical reaction is "to fight for the business, to attack your competition, to try to meet prices," reports sales veteran Donald C. North, president of Impulse! a Toronto company that sells novelty and gift items to large retailers. It's human nature to fight hard, but one worth repressing for one key reason: trying too hard to save the account at this stage makes you look as though you are twisting in the wind. That's the wrong impression you want to leave with your former customers—one of you squirming while they're thinking, "Boy, he's taking this hard. How can I get rid of him?"

"The better move at this juncture," says North, "is to relieve the pressure and let your customer off the hook. If you're sure the loss is a fait accompli, be gracious and reassure the client about the decision. Make 'good sportsmanship' statements like: 'Your company hasn't gotten to be so successful by making mistakes, so I'm sure you're making the right call.'"[17]

2. *Position yourself for reentry.* Getting fired from an account is a critical moment that is laden with opportunity. The customer is often feeling guilty, and she's not 100 percent sure she's made the wisest decision. Sizing up the situation and identifying the next best opportunity can help you win more business in the future. To master the art of reentry, use one or more of the following strategies:

- *Go for the second prize.* If your relationship with the client has been good, and you make a reasonable pitch for a portion of the business you're losing, or even a new ancillary piece of the business, you can very often get it. And that leaves you in an ideal position to woo the main attraction again later, because you'll continue to be an established supplier.

- *Ask for a timed reevaluation.* If your attempt to get a portion of the business fails, consider a timed reevaluation strategy. This means getting the customer to agree to meet with you again— perhaps in six months—to discuss how happy she is with her new choice and whether she would consider letting you pitch the business—or a portion of it—again.

- *Ask for permission to stay in touch.* If the timed reevaluation strategy doesn't work, take heart. Your fallback position is still a good one: ask the lost customer for the opportunity to stay in touch. She'll almost certainly say yes, out of guilt if nothing else, and you'll be in the top-of-mind spot when the other vendor runs into problems.

The executive at the news magazine discussed earlier who lost a big chunk of business knew when it was time to move on:

Plan B is to uncover your next best opportunity with this lost customer. Now that I've lost the big piece of business, I need to be probing the customer to say, "What other tactical opportunities do you face, Mr. Client, that I could stay on top of or be attuned to, that might produce an opportunity for us to do some more business this calendar year?" The second part of the reentry strategy is this: as soon as this [new] campaign is up and running, and they've had a chance to begin to monitor it, the question is, how is it doing? Is it meeting expectations? Are there any opportunities to expand further into print next year and change that 75 percent/25 percent broadcast/print relationship? Surely there will be opportunities once this campaign gets up and going. They're going to think about how they can go bigger and better. With that percentage devoted to broadcast, they're going to have to bring it back to 50/50 parity or 60/40 broadcast versus print. Part of Plan B is having patience.

3. *Make the departing customer an ambassador.* Even when a customer no longer has a need for your services, he will come into contact with people who will. Say you're running the Canyon Vista Country Club. If you provided a fond farewell when that customer left, he may be heard responding to his new neighbor's inquiry about local country clubs with, "You ought to go over and take a look at Canyon Vista Country Club. I used to be a member there, but when my arthritis got bad and I quit playing golf I just couldn't justify it anymore. But I sure hated to leave. They really care about their members and go out of their way to do things right."

Once you have "treated" the account in the short term, you can begin the long-term win-back process. To begin a long-term win-back plan, you need to take the following steps:

STEP 1. GRADE AND SEGMENT LOST CUSTOMERS. As discussed, SLTV and reasons for defection are the two criteria for prioritizing lost customers.

STEP 2. RESEARCH THE CUSTOMER'S PRESENT NEEDS. Don't assume that your customer's needs of a year or six months ago still apply. The marketplace changes rapidly and may be making new demands. In fact, this change may give you the opportunity you need to capture the customer's interest. For example, a major international retailer of jewelry, apparel, and collectibles that reached customers through various electronic means such as the television shopping channel used its database to identify those customers who had once had a high value but who had not purchased in over two years. In many cases, they had purchased ten or more times from television offers. These customers represented a very small percentage of the retailer's total customer base, but they had spent thousands of dollars since first converting from viewers to buyers. Many companies would have written these customers off because of the long lapse in time since purchase. But this company was unwilling to do that without learning more about why their purchases had fallen off.

Loyalty research that targeted the reasons for these customers' dramatically reduced buying activity showed that (1) they still considered themselves active customers of the retailer and (2) they had the economic resources to continue purchasing at or near their prior rate, but they had made all the general purchases they wanted, sometimes in a very short span of time, and had bought all the gifts for friends they desired. Now their interest in continued purchasing had become more specialized. The retailer then asked each customer to complete a product purchase interest profile, and customized shopping program schedules were sent based on the individual customer's profile. As a result, more than half of these dormant customers were reactivated.

STEP 3. CREATE A PLAN THAT REINSTATES TRUST. Put yourself in the shoes of your lapsed customer. The customer originally bought from you for a reason. Through your acquisition efforts, expectations were established. And you succeeded in getting the customer to buy at least once and in some cases many times. But then something happened so that your offerings either disappointed or at minimum, didn't make a large enough difference to the customer to keep her returning. In many ways, through this underdelivery, a trust was broken with the customer and now she is at best indifferent and at worst gravely disillusioned with you as a supplier. The result? Your win-back marketing plan must be designed to regain the customer's trust. Every aspect of your reapproach must start to rebuild the perception and trust that a dollar spent on your offerings represents a better value than a dollar spent with your competitor.

Your reapproach must strongly communicate a compelling reason to return. You can plan this reapproach process by addressing five key areas:

- What value message(s) will you convey in your reapproach?
- What medium (or combination of media) will you use to recontact the departed customer? In addition to one-to-one contact, what other influential sources can you use to support your recovery efforts?
- With what frequency will you recontact the departed customer? How many attempts will you make to reactivate her?

- What alternate strategies will you try if customers continue to say no?
- When will you retire the relationship?

Choosing Your Reapproach Message. Relevance and personalization are the name of the game in successfully reapproaching a lost customer and rebuilding trust. Says Joe Udell, CEO of a direct marketing firm:

> A reactivation program has to be driven by a high degree of relevance. I recently paid off my credit card, and I got this generic letter that said, "we want you back." Obviously, the credit-card issuer thought I had jumped ship and transferred my balance. In actuality, I simply had paid off my credit-card balance. Had the credit-card company taken the time to analyze their processing data, they could have differentiated between a balance transfer to a competitor versus my check. But instead, their letter to me in effect said they had no understanding about what was going on with me or my account. I am a platinum member with a large credit line and have been with them loyally for eight or ten years. So I would have thought they would have chosen something other than this generic message to send me.[18]

One of the surest ways to successfully win back lapsed customers is to communicate in a way that lets your customers know you know who they are. Beware of the generic one-size-fits-all communication when addressing lost customers. It can backfire. For example, a friend recently told us about a letter she received from a well-known clothing retailer in her neighborhood. She had shopped there a few times in the past but had not been in for quite a while before receiving the letter. It was a handwritten note on expensive, wedding invitation–quality paper. Here's the note:

Dear Clarice,

   How are you? It's been quite a while since I've seen you in the store. I just wanted you to know how much great new product we have gotten in. Don't hesitate to give me a call if you have any questions. Maybe you would like to set up an appointment. I'll be here for you.

   Thanks!

   Louise

Clarice decided to have a little fun. She wrote Louise back, and here's what she said:

Dear Louise,

Thank you for writing to me. I can't tell you how empty my life has been. I don't shop, I don't eat, I don't sleep. I am so depressed!

For a long time now, I've spoken only to my therapist and my dog, but then your note arrived. What a wonderful day! What a miraculous occurrence! I am so thrilled that you are there for me. Can we have lunch on Tuesday? Would you like to become my new best friend?

Love,

Clarice

Little wonder Clarice didn't take Louise's letter seriously. It lacked evidence that the writer had any knowledge about the departed customer. Ironically, that lack of knowledge and specificity can be what drives defection in the first place. Think about it: many customers leave because they feel unrecognized, underappreciated, and undervalued. Others simply forget about your business and stop buying because they feel no compelling reason to return. That's why, in preparing your reapproach message, it's extremely important to know as much about these lapsed customers and why they stopped buying as possible and then to address these customers with specificity.

With even limited information about the customer's reason for defection, here's what Louise might have written:

Dear Clarice:

Our records show that we haven't served you in over a year. Whenever I learn that a valued customer like you has departed, I get very worried. Losing a good customer is like losing a good friend. Was it something we did? If so, we'd like to make it up to you.

Our new fall line has just arrived. I know you've enjoyed our sportswear in the past, and this season's selections are exceptional. We have a wonderful array of coordinating jackets, skirts, and slacks in many new styles and colors. You don't want to miss it.

I want to offer you the enclosed "We miss you" savings certificate good toward your next purchase. It's our way of showing you how much we value your business.

Won't you call or come in soon? I'll be delighted to assist you.

Sincerely,

Louise Robertson

555-1111

Whether you are reapproaching the lost customer by letter, on the phone, or in person, your message should include five key points. It should

- Acknowledge the customer's past patronage.
- Point out improvements and changes made since the customer's departure.
- Emphasize the ease with which the customer can reengage.
- Be sent, when possible, under the signature of someone the customer is likely to recognize.
- Provide a possible financial incentive.

Choosing Your Reapproach Media. What's the best way to reconnect with the customer—e-mail, fax, regular mail, telephone, on-site visit, or some combination of these? When recontacting the lapsed customer, should you make the contact yourself or assign it to someone? Find the answers by reviewing what you know about the customer's preferred ways of working.

Your goal is to build a synchronized communication plan that delivers high value to the customer, reestablishes trust, and uses in-person contact (phone, office visit, and so on) in the most effective manner. There are quantum cost differences between contact media (the cost of an e-mail is $.01, for example, whereas a field sales call can cost anywhere from $40 to $400). So you want to satisfy the lapsed customer's contact preferences but in a way that balances costs with expected revenues.

In addition to direct communication, here are two other ways to deliver your value message to lapsed customers.

- *Use customers who are still sold on you to heal lost customer wounds.* Bill Cone of Norwest Bank (now Wells Fargo) finds a way to let win-back candidates rub elbows with customer advocates in a light, social setting. He invites six to eight carefully chosen current and former customers to a luncheon hosted by Norwest. Says Cone, "We try to build the right group. We don't deny [at the luncheon] that we had difficulties. We don't look the other way and say it didn't happen. But it's a positive way to get your message out. We're happy when our current customer says to a former customer, 'We had a few problems too, but, boy, they have their act together now. We've taken out this new line of credit and we just signed up with them for a 401(k).' Selecting the group makes all the difference," says Cone. "There's no better advertising."[19]

• *Put your best foot forward. Austin Business Journal* advertising director Patrick Asbra found that belonging to some of the same associations as a valued lost customer can be important. He describes how in one instance, "I got at the heart of the problem with the lost customer and discussed it, but they were still leery of us. Over time, the *Austin Business Journal* was very involved in an association the customer belonged to. . . . This lost customer saw us at these meetings on a regular basis. Our paper was recognized at every event, and the association was saying good things about the paper, etc. The more the lost customer saw of us in this venue the more trust was being rebuilt."[20]

Choosing Your Reapproach Frequency. The reapproach frequency varies greatly by industry. Once a year or no more than twice may be a good rule of thumb in some industries, whereas many more contacts per year may be justified in other industries. Let experience teach you what your ideal communication frequency looks like. But always remember that your communication goal is to reestablish a top-of-mind value awareness with the lapsed customer yet not become a nuisance. It's a delicate balance to strike.

• *How* Inc. *magazine does it.* Let's look closely at three aspects of *Inc.* magazine's renewal subscription program for more insights:

1. *The frequency plan. Inc.* uses a seven-part win-back series that involves six varying reminder mailings spaced out over six months and finally, within thirty days of the subscription expiration date, one well-planned telephone call.

2. *The message. Inc.* tests a lot of approaches for the telephone contact with those who have not responded to the previous six renewal messages. Says *Inc.*'s John Titus, "The approaches are carefully scripted. We test a lot of different messages that range from reiterating the benefits of subscribing to the urgency of acting now. We also appeal to people's sense of convenience by reminding the nonrenewers that if they say yes, we'll restart the subscription at this great savings and bill them later." Titus cautions that it's unwise to offer lower pricing in the later months. "If you do, you're rewarding the nonrenewer for delaying his renewal, and that's the wrong message."

3. *Recycling to the new prospect file.* If the subscriber does not respond to the telephone follow-up, he is considered an "expire." If, six months later, renewal has still not occurred, he is considered a "dead expire." From this point forward, this nonrenewer is reapproached as a new prospect. These dead expires are graded by age (that is, how much time has passed since the last subscription) and source (did the nonrenewer come in as a direct subscriber, or did he come in through a secondary subscription source such as American Family Publishers?). This grading will determine which decile of prospective subscribers the nonrenewer is assigned to. Says Titus, "When we go out and do new subscriber solicitation, we mail to both new subscribers and dead expires. At this point, we treat dead expires as new prospects. They are probably in the first profitable decile of the lists we mail to. Our message is simple: Here's the magazine. . . . Here's the price. . . . Would you like to subscribe?"[21]

• *Patience pays.* Pete Wayman, former president of Prudential Relocation's southern region, also knows the merits of patience with lost customers and the benefits of staying close. You never know when your competitor might stumble. ·

We were one of two suppliers for a client who decided they wanted to consolidate to a single supplier. The contest was close, but we lost the account because our client perceived our competitor as offering a better service for a cheaper price. We worked hard to ensure an easy transition of files and similar materials to the competitor. We told our client that while we certainly hoped that things worked out for them [with their new supplier], we wanted them to know that we were still very interested in getting them back. We explained that we were assigning a key contact person from Sales for continuity. Sales was immediately notified, given the full history of why the client cancelled, and a "keep in touch" plan that stressed easy re-entry and continuity.

The client stayed with the competitor for a year and a half. They then came back to us and said they were not seeing the service orientation, the value-added, or the benefits that they had expected to see. They were impressed with our transition over to the competitor and our consistent follow-up.

The client asked if we'd be willing to talk. We immediately got on a plane, went up there, and told them that we understood that they tried what they thought was a better idea. We still had the same people involved and the same team, so we were able to jump right on it with no loss in continuity. We got them back as a major account. We're now very close to securing them as a total outsourcing account, which will double our business with them.[22]

• *Trying an alternate strategy.* If your research was adequate and your approach is right for the lost customers, you're likely to get an open-minded reception. Remember, this is a business and not a social situation. The customer's major interest is not in keeping a feud going or in dealing with friends but in getting the most value. If you can offer something the customer is not getting now—benefits, services, quality, or any other extras—you'll have a chance. But if you are still hearing no, drastic measures may be required.

For Judy Kearney, for instance, it was just plain hard to lose a good customer to a competitor. As a Holiday Inn director of sales and marketing, she knew customer service had weakened for a time as the hotel went through some internal changes. She had asked a valued customer to "hold on" through the transition, but to no avail. Kearney stayed in touch for any new opening, but the decision makers at the account said they were completely happy with Kearney's competitor. Calling once a month and following up with letters was getting her nowhere.

Then Kearney hit on an idea. Because the decision-making managers weren't the ones actually using the hotels, she wondered if the employees were as happy with the change as the bosses who told those employees what hotels to use. "We were still friendly with some of their employees," explained Kearney. "Without risking managers' ire over an end-run, we asked questions and a different picture emerged: many employees liked the good old days with us."

Armed with this knowledge, the next time Kearney talked to the managers at the account, she planted a seed. Did they ever survey employees to gauge their satisfaction? Did they know if employees liked the suppliers management gave them to work with? She stressed how such surveys could help staff retention and team work.

Management did the survey, and results showed that when it came to hotels, employees liked the old supplier (Kearney's hotel) better. The managers conceded they were surprised by the results, but Kearney didn't win back the business right away. The managers agreed to come out to tour the hotel, but only with an eye on the next time the hotel contract would be up for bid. They made it clear that other hotels would be looked at too.

"That's when I decided to take a huge risk," says Kearney. I said I understood and I'd be delighted to do a lot of their work for them. I set up a tour of our facility, but I helped them line up all the other visits as well on the same day—and volunteered to drive them around to the competitors." Kearney was nervous about this offer. The last thing she wanted was to hand-deliver this customer to a competitor. But her efforts were rewarded. The managers said they couldn't get over what Kearney had done. They signed a new $60,000 contract and got out of the competitor's contract early. Kearney sums up her win-back lesson this way: "The experience taught me that mere persistence isn't enough. You continually need to change your approach to get attention—and exceed customers' expectations."[23]

• *When to call it quits.* There is an old saying about the uselessness of beating a dead horse. In some cases it becomes more costly to pursue win-back than to give up on the lost customer. If you have collected all the pertinent information you can find, have tried all the options you can imagine, and the customer still says no, it is time to move on and spend your time and energy on someone else. Although you may give up on winning back a customer, you should not, however, completely forget the customer. At some point this customer can be reapproached as a new prospect. After all, you have spent a good deal of time and energy in collecting information about this person or firm. That information needs to be kept and used if possible. Adding a lost customer (along with what you've learned about that customer's needs) to your new customer list may pay off years down the line. Perhaps new people will come on board at the firm. Circumstances are always changing. So knowing when to give up is important—but never give up completely!

STEP 4. MEASURING, EVALUATING, AND REFINING YOUR WIN-BACK PROGRAM. Some of your win-back efforts will work and others will not. That's why each win-back program must be measured for success. Without measurement and evaluation, you cannot know which initiatives work and which do not. But what criteria should be used to measure win-back success? To help answer that question, consider the program Retail Resources devised for a retail client.

After carefully tracking customers and the number of months since last purchase, a high-end national women's apparel chain had realized the need for reactivation. A significant group of customers who were at one time very valuable had defected, and the retailer wanted to recapture these customers' patronage. The retailer, catering to a unique and narrow niche market, couldn't afford to lose many customers.

Retail Resources developed a personal letter to be signed by the retailer's president. The letter, which included a $50 gift certificate and no minimum purchase, was sent to customers who hadn't shopped in seven or more months and who carried a lifetime value greater than $400. The letter was mailed to approximately ten thousand customers.

With the guidance of Retail Resources, the retailer calculated these key measures of the three-week event's reactivation success:

- Reactivation offer (gift certificate) redemption rate (4.3 percent)

- Sales generated from reactivation offer ($100,000)

- Average event purchase versus nonevent average (+$50)

- Postpromotion purchasing habits of reactivated customers (75 percent bought again over the next six months)[24]

Sales-related benefits aren't the only enticements for conducting win-back programs. Win-back analysis also generates strategic insights that can be extremely important to your firm's success with its retention and acquisition initiatives. Earlier, we discussed *Inc.* magazine's renewal subscription plan. In addition to realizing sales benefits, circulation director John Titus wanted to better understand what distinguished a renewer from a nonrenewer, and his department conducted a survey to determine the differences.

Subscribers were divided into those who renewed and those who did not. Wanting to compare apples to apples, Titus and his team then narrowed the groups to only those subscribers who had been on board during a given five-year time period and had seen the evolution of the magazine. *Inc.* wanted to better understand how these two groups differed in their overall perception of the magazine and what caused some subscribers to renew and others not to.

"We found out," reports Titus, "that the people who had not renewed felt that the magazine was writing for a company much larger than their own. They felt we provided less practical, how-to, service-oriented articles than there had been when they first signed up or than they thought there would be." In contrast, the renewers tended to be from slightly larger companies and were more able to apply concepts from a wider variety of companies and industries. Says Titus, "These renewers didn't need someone to say, this is about a company that's a little bit larger, but the lessons that could be learned here are A, B, C, and D."

Inc. also found the renewers and nonrenewers dividing between two other lines: the renewers were generally people who like to read a somewhat longer article and draw their own conclusions and get five or six pertinent ideas or points from it. The nonrenewers wanted the information in a more cut-and-dried format. They wanted to be able to skim it in ten minutes and say, "Here's how we can do X, Y, and Z."

How was this information used? *Inc.*'s circulation department shared the information with the editorial department to help the editors in understanding how to please as many subscribers as possible and put out the best possible product. "But the real purpose of the survey," says Titus, "was to help us target the messaging of our new subscribers and renewal notices. This information helps us play up the high points and not emphasize something that perhaps these subscriber groups don't care about. From the research, we also got confirmation that our biggest asset is *Inc.*'s name recognition and the reputation we have built over time. We recently celebrated our twentieth anniversary. People remember that we were there first and that the brand is important and it stands for something. That's probably our biggest asset to leverage."[25]

BELLSOUTH MOBILITY PUTS IT ALL TOGETHER

Throughout this chapter we have seen that developing and executing a win-back marketing plan to recapture lost customers requires specific decision tree choices. Once the decision is made to begin a long-term win-back process, there are four steps:

1. Grade and segment defected customers (according to SLTV and defection reasons).

2. Research the customer's present needs.

3. Create a plan that reinstates trust.

4. Measure, understand, evaluate, and refine.

Let's look at how BellSouth Mobility met these challenges for a successful win-back program.

Ed Evans, director of field operations for BellSouth Mobility, knew he had to communicate to lost customers in a relevant way to successfully tackle his company's daunting churn problem. As a major provider of wireless services in the Southeast, BellSouth had one million subscribers in its twenty-eight cellular systems. Even though the company was growing at an annual rate of 45 percent and adding more than twenty-five hundred customers each day, it was also losing five hundred customers every day. It costs on average $350 to add a customer, and the average active customer contributes around $60 per month in revenue.

In an industry where churn averages 18 percent or more per year, Evans knew that winning back lost customers was a cause worth fighting for, but how to go about it? Part of Evans's strategy was think big, start small as he went about testing a win-back plan in a BellSouth market of 1,065,000 subscribers, one in which BellSouth had a 65 percent market share. Evans's goal was to win back 10 percent of BellSouth's lost subscribers.

Step 1: Grade and segment lapsed customers. BellSouth's first step was to determine which lost customers were most appropriate to reapproach. To help answer that question, BellSouth called and queried a large sample of lapsed subscribers about why they had terminated their relationship with the company. The research found that

- Twelve percent of the lost customers "no longer needed the service."
- Eighteen percent of the lost customers said their "company no longer pays the bill."
- Twenty-four percent had "moved out of the coverage area."
- Thirty-four percent had "switched to the competition."
- Twelve percent had "other reasons" for terminating.

This analysis identified the 34 percent who switched to the competition as being the key win-back target.

Step 2: Research the customer's present needs. To identify what was required to win these customers back, four focus groups were conducted among former customers who were active customers of BellSouth's competitor. The respondents were asked why they had switched and what could prompt them to return. Most of the lost customers felt that BellSouth's system coverage, customer service, and billing system were better than the competitor's. The key reasons for defection were

- BellSouth did something that upset me.

- BellSouth wouldn't issue a credit [$.50] for a dropped call.

- BellSouth gave free phones to new subscribers, but not to me.

- BellSouth wouldn't give me the current [free air] promotion.

Many of these customers were open to the possibility of switching back to BellSouth, but they indicated their current contract obligations would limit their ability to switch back immediately. Moreover, they wanted air time or a phone as an incentive to return.

Step 3: Create a plan that reinstates trust. As part of its win-back plan, BellSouth decided to give a $.50 credit for all dropped calls. It sent thirty-five hundred customers who had switched to a competitor a direct-mail reactivation offer that included a free phone or free airtime and featured the news about the $.50 credit for dropped calls. However, this offer was met with disappointing results: after thirty days, it achieved only a 3 percent initial response and a 1 percent reconnection rate. This program cost a whopping $800 per reconnected customer and was considered a failure. Additional customer research revealed that although respondents rated the offer strong, current contracts with other cellular companies and misplacing or never receiving the direct-mail card prevented lapsed customers from switching back.

Step 4: Measure, understand, evaluate, refine. Recognizing its mistake, BellSouth repeated the offer to one thousand former customers who had left eleven months before, reasoning that these customers would soon be free to switch back. BellSouth followed up the letter with a phone call. The results were much improved. The second letter produced an 8 percent response rate and a 3 percent connect rate. When the company followed up with a phone call, it was rewarded with a 10 percent connect rate.

The costs per customer dropped to $325. Since 1997 BellSouth has mailed to about one thousand lost customers every month, using the same selection criteria as before. At last report, it was expanding the win-back program to its other twenty-seven markets.[26]

BellSouth's reactivation program provides four win-back lessons:

- *Develop and work your plan around the real customer defection issues.* Don't guess about these issues. Go out and uncover these client issues and requirements.

- *Communicate relevancy.* Communicate to your lost customers that you know why they left and what you are prepared to do about it.

- *Think big, start small.* Rather than rolling out an untested program on a large scale, test it on a smaller scale and learn from your efforts.

- *Timing is everything.* You must understand your customer's restrictions in returning as customer. Time your win-back program to coincide with the customer's ability to switch.

SUMMARY

- You can learn to recognize when a customer is defecting.

- When a customer is lost, you have a choice—try to win the customer back or do not try.

- One essential step in making this choice is calculating the second lifetime value (SLTV) of lost customers.

- Another essential step in making this choice is identifying lost customers' reasons for defection.

- Some lost customers are best forgotten.

- Some lost customers can be won back quickly; others take more time.

- The key to success is understanding lost customers and having a well-conceived win-back plan.

CHAPTER FOUR

How to Save a Customer on the Brink of Defection

~~~

Ruthie McDowell is a lifesaver of sorts. As one of forty "save" reps at Cellular One's call center in San Francisco, McDowell takes around fifty calls a day—and every caller has a cell phone problem. Some callers are reporting lost or stolen phones, but most of the callers routed to McDowell are on a burning mission to cancel their service. In many cases, they're angry. They're frustrated. They're belligerent. And it shows.

"Your company stinks. I'm taking my business elsewhere. Cancel me and do it now!" These were the first words a recent customer yelled into the phone at McDowell. The customer was a commissioned salesperson, and her livelihood was tied to keeping close to customers via phone all day long. In this customer's mind, Cellular One was letting her down.

But Ruthie McDowell doesn't flinch. In a strange sort of way she finds comfort in the customer's venting. Extensive training in the art of saving angry customers has taught McDowell that letting customers vent is the first step to a successful save. McDowell takes save calls from some of Cellular One's highest revenue customers. And with a save rate of over 50 percent, she gets results. In this case the customer agrees to a phone replacement (multiple dropped calls are often due to phone failure, not network failure) and a thirty-day trial. McDowell makes a note to follow up in the third week, but the customer beats her to it. This once-angry customer calls back happy as a lark. She loves the replacement phone—it's smaller, lighter, and has more options than before, and best of all, no more dropped calls. She thanks McDowell profusely for her time and her attention and is glad to remain a Cellular One customer. McDowell is even happier. This three-year-old customer has a stellar payment history and consistently high call volume.

How does McDowell celebrate these happy endings? "After the final call concludes," says McDowell, "I sometimes stand up at my cubicle and joyfully yell out to my colleagues around me, 'Save!'"[1]

If your business is like most, about one-third of your customers are in some phase of defecting. But most firms are ill equipped to recognize and manage this turbulence. To better understand why customers leave we conducted the nationwide survey discussed in Chapter One to compare sales managers' and marketing managers' perceptions with the perceptions and needs of the purchasing agents who buy their products and services. Our win-back research found that more than 60 percent of sales managers and marketing managers surveyed had no system or process for identifying customers who are at high risk of defection. This same study also found that over 75 percent of purchasing agents surveyed reported giving suppliers advance warning about possible termination of the account. Yet these agents also reported that only about half of their suppliers responded assertively to this warning. This chapter will explore what to do when you learn your customer is on the brink of defection.

TREATING AT-RISK CUSTOMERS WITH CPR

Opportunities to save defecting customers manifest themselves in two basic ways: (1) the customer calls and says "I want to cancel my service," or (2) the customer says nothing, but other indicators tell you the business is about to walk out the door. Take heart! Even at this late date you can still save that customer using three key steps: comprehend, propose, respond (CPR). Just as cardiopulmonary resuscitation is used to treat medical emergencies, this CPR is used to treat loyalty emergencies—customers on the brink of defection. We look at these three steps and then at examples of using CPR on the individual and large-scale levels.

Step 1. Comprehend

Quickly identify the at-risk customer, determine the customer's lifetime value, and then get to the heart of the customer's problems.

IDENTIFY AT-RISK CUSTOMERS. It's important to have processes that tell you when customers are at risk. These processes fall into two general categories.

Ask for Customer Notification. Having a process that requires the customer to notify you about canceling service can be a big advantage in saving customers on the brink of defection. This is a lesson that many Internet service providers are starting to learn. A manager from a leading Internet service provider (ISP) explained it this way: "In some ISP companies, a customer is allowed to cancel on-line by just sending an e-mail that says, 'I don't want to stay with you anymore.' Under this plan, the ISP loses the opportunity to understand why people are leaving and then take proactive save steps. At our ISP, our customer contract requires that the customer actually calls to cancel the service. That way we have some chance of saving the business, or at least, we can find out why the customer is leaving us."

Rely on Other Processes. When customers are not required to notify you of their intentions of leaving, they often just silently walk away. To combat this reality, this chapter outlines seven key sources of information, including purchase data and complaints captured by frontline staff, that can guide processes for identifying at-risk customers, Effective save programs are only as good as the firm's ability to identify at-risk customers.

HAVE A QUICK AND EFFECTIVE METHOD FOR DETERMINING AT-RISK CUSTOMER VALUE. All save protocols begin with a quick assessment of the customer's future value to the firm. Simply speaking, the greater the customer value, the more aggressive the save should be. Depending on the industry, this assessment, as we have been discussing in the earlier chapters, can include a number of variables, including the following:

- Revenue from customer
    Average usage or purchase frequency
    Average annual spending levels
- Cost to serve customer
    Frequency with which customer calls in with problems that require operator time
    Frequency with which customer calls in with billing questions
    Frequency with which customer asks for credits
    Quality of customer's payment history
- Customer's likelihood to churn or not to churn
    Customer is on a price-sensitive plan
    Customer has signed an annual contract
    Customer signed up as a result of a promotion

Most firms provide these variables in a computer data file that their save representatives can access. Reps are trained on how to evaluate these variables and then to use their discretion in conducting a save.

In a perfect world, you would have instant access to all the information you needed about the customer's lifetime value. But that's not usually the case in the real world. For example, one ISP manager we interviewed commented, "We're not as sophisticated as the financial or banking industry in terms of member profitability. We're moving in that direction, but we're not there yet. When the customer calls, we input their name on the screen and up pops how long they have been a customer and whether or not they have had billing problems. Overall, we have a simple rule of thumb: the longer the customer has been with us, the more we want to work to save the business."

Yet even some smaller businesses have found more sophisticated approaches to determining the value of at-risk customers. Consider ScrubaDub Car Wash, a chain of highly successful, family-owned car washes in metro Boston and Warwick, Rhode Island, which offers full-service and self-service car washing as well as auto detailing. As is typical of service businesses, ScrubaDub's customer base is dominated by infrequent users. Robert Paisner, the president, and his father, Marshall Paisner, the founder of the chain, look at their customers according to segments—five groups ranging from very low to very high patronage—and calculate their value based on acquisition, development, and retention costs; gross and net annual contribution; and average duration of customer business. From these data, they are able to determine the net relationship value to ScrubaDub of each customer.

This analysis helps ScrubaDub divide its customer base more generally into two key groups: the Great Infrequents and the More Valuables. The Great Infrequents are customers who wash their cars only a few times each year—perhaps on holidays, when the car is extremely dirty, or when the customer has a special event to attend. Moving these customers to purchase more often is extremely difficult, so ScrubaDub invests very little to save these customers when they are at risk. The More Valuables drive utility vehicles, are more often female, and have newer (under three-year-old) vehicles. ScrubaDub estimates that these customers represent only about 13 percent of its customer base but account for virtually all of its profitability. ScrubaDub's database can identify whether any of these customers are at risk due to car washing damage, quality issues, or other factors, such as location change. With this information, ScrubaDub can then begin save initiatives.[2]

If your company is midsize or large, the variables for determining lifetime value will likely be more complex. For example, cost-to-serve factors are wide ranging and may include multitiered sales costs, different customer support levels, regional and national media costs, promotional expenses, Web site development and upkeep, and competitive response. Sophisticated software products are rapidly emerging to assist large companies with sizable and diverse customer bases to determine both the identity and the value of at-risk customers. NCR, for instance, has developed a process for using customer purchase behaviors to create *profit pools* that enable comparison of customer value. Moreover, the cost of customer save programs can be factored into these analyses to better evaluate the lifetime value of at-risk customers.

But remember that the whole point of determining lifetime value is to make a decision about whether to use save initiatives with the customer. There are some customers on the brink of leaving that you will want to lose. Don't be afraid to retire a customer relationship. If the lifetime value isn't there, it's a wise decision. Some customers are marginal at best in terms of revenue generation and use of services and are not worth the effort to save.

GET TO THE HEART OF THE CUSTOMER'S PROBLEMS. Listen carefully to understand customer needs. Successfully saving a customer means identifying what is important to that on-the-brink-of-defection customer. Effectively saving a customer often means isolating and addressing three key customer needs: *trigger need, driving need,* and *original need.* Each of these needs requires somewhat different approaches.

Identify the Trigger Need. When you begin talking with any unhappy customer, you'll want to listen for the trigger need and consider how to best address it. Think of the trigger need as the straw that broke the camel's back. It is typically the latest in a series of unmet needs experienced by the customer. By itself, the trigger need may not be enough to cause the customer to defect. But as the latest in a litany of problems or service failures experienced by the customer, the trigger need can cause the customer to finally say, "That's it! I'm leaving."

Your first save goal is to identify the trigger need and treat it immediately. At the same time you should be looking deeper to uncover other larger, more significant unmet needs. Here are two effective probes for identifying and treating the trigger need:

- Why are you considering leaving us?
- I'm sorry you're having problems. Please give me the details so I can help.

In addressing the trigger need, two factors are critical to success. First, frontline employees need to be empowered to take care of problems quickly and efficiently. Your chances for successfully saving a customer with a trigger need will be severely reduced if the defecting customer encounters an additional complication in getting this immediate problem resolved. We explore this fact in more detail later in this chapter.

Second, because customers often enter the defection process in an angry mood, considerable staff skill is needed to defuse the anger. Upset or severely disillusioned customers require special attention. It often helps to visualize the person as having a *psychological sunburn.* If you attempt to save the customer without treating the burn, you may get a violent reaction. Help the customer recover from the acute stage of this sunburn by doing these two things:

- Let the customer blow off steam. Don't interrupt. Don't argue. Just listen for a while. Such statements as "I'm sorry you've had problems; please tell me the circumstances so I can help you," will encourage the customer to explain and in doing so cool off a bit.
- Let the customer know you understand her problem. It's critical that your perception of the issue matches the customer's. Listen carefully; paraphrase the problem so the customer can hear that you understand it.

It is sometimes possible to respond immediately with added value. For example, when faced with a highly irate customer with a fussy toddler in tow, a service rep for furniture giant IKEA quickly retrieved a colored ball from the store's playroom and gave it to the child as a gift. The child loved the ball, and the customer appreciated the gesture—enough so that this irate customer was no longer so irate and the service transaction could be completed.

Identify the Driving Need. In comparison to the trigger need, the driving need is a bigger, more complex unmet need or set of needs that has been festering for some time. Because most customers do not like confrontation, they remain silent and internalize their unhappiness. Yet the longer this driving need goes untreated by the vendor, the more of a driving force it becomes for the customer. When, finally, the trigger need and the driving need intersect, the customer becomes fully motivated to defect.

To effectively save a customer at this level, you must move beyond the trigger need and identify and treat the driving need as well. Here are three key driving need probes:

- Have you had problems before?
- If you leave us, where do you plan to go?
- What attracts you to [*competitor's name*], and why does it attract you?

Your goal is to understand this driving need and determine how to reposition your product or service in the mind of the customer to best deliver the value the customer is missing.

Identify the Original Need. Customers tend to have short memories about positive experiences, and it's important to remind a customer on the brink of defection about the key reason(s) he became your customer in the first place. If you can identify those original needs that have been effectively met, chances are that those same needs are still legitimate in the customer's eyes, and reminding the customer of them can be very helpful in saving the customer on the brink of defection. Here are two useful probes for identifying and reminding customers of these original needs:

 • What were you looking for when you first became our customer?
 • Which of our service features do you use most? Why?

Step 2. Propose

Once the comprehend steps are complete, you're ready for the propose phase of the CPR protocol. You are ready to make a conciliatory offer that matches the customer's pain. We suggest you begin this propose step by asking the customer how he or she would like the situation to be resolved. The key question to ask is this: We very much value your business. What can we do to make this up to you and keep you as a customer? Asking the customer is important because often the customer can be saved with far less than the company is willing to offer. When planning your proposal, consider the following principles.

MAKE THE PENANCE EQUAL TO THE PROBLEM. In the mind of the customer, your proposal must show that you recognize the problem and its seriousness and that what you offer to make amends is commensurate with the problem and its severity.

CREATE A HIERARCHY OF OFFERS. It's helpful to construct a series of offers that are layered according to cost, with the noncost offer first. Train your win-back representatives to look for opportunities to apply the noncost, or *value,* level first, before escalating to the more expensive levels. Remember the old lesson that you don't need a sledge-hammer to kill an ant, and use the same principle here.

For example, assume you are a customer service rep for ABC Internet Service Provider. A customer calls to request her service be cancelled. You use probing questions to uncover and understand her unmet need, and based on this learning, you look for ways to customize your save offer so it matches that level of need. Your first goal is to save her with noncost or low-cost offers. However, you have higher-cost offers available to use if you need them, as outlined in the following sections.

Level 1: Value Solution. There are two basic approaches to creating a noncost, or value, solution:

• *Find hidden value.* Is it possible to show the customer that there is value he is not receiving from the service? This option costs nothing but adds value in the eye of the customer. For example, is a misunderstanding or incomplete information causing the user to get marginal value from an ISP service? You might discover the user does not understand how to use e-mail or that the user is an active stock trader who is unaware that free stock quotes are available on the ISP site. Once you assist the customer in using these services to get more value from the site, he is willing to remain as a customer.

• *Add more value.* Is there information you can provide to help the customer get more value from the products or service? As part of our research for this book, we were invited to listen in on save calls between customers requesting to cancel their credit cards and credit-card save reps. On several occasions, the save rep told the customer about a "benefits book" the company was mailing to customers that outlined key features of the credit-card services. In some cases the customer and the save rep made a date to talk again once the benefits book arrived. It is of course very important that the save rep initiate this follow-up call at the time committed to. Otherwise, trust will have been violated in the mind of the customer and the save will fail.

Level 2: Low-Cost Solution. If adding value is not sufficient to save the unhappy customer, consider low-cost offers that may soothe her. For example, suppose the customer is upset about an item on her monthly ISP statement. You offer to credit the hourly charge rate that the customer disputes. This incurs minimum costs to the company and validates the customer's belief that she was correct in the first place.

Level 3: Higher-Cost Solution. Sometimes problems are major enough to require a more substantial investment to save a customer. For example, the customer is upset about the constant busy signals received when trying to access the ISP network. You apologize about the heavy call volume and offer the customer one free month of service for her inconvenience. If necessary, you are authorized to offer up to two months' free service. In addition, the company should have a process for hearing about such problems from the reps so it can take steps to deal with the cause of the problems.

Step 3. Respond

There are several ways that customers can respond to a proposal. Their reactions will determine your response as the save representative. Let's look at handling agreement, tentative agreement, and disagreement.

GO ALONG WITH AGREEMENT. If the customer happily accepts the offer, then execute the plan cheerfully and swiftly. But if you sense the customer is not happy with the proposal, it is important to keep the dialogue flowing. Monitor the customer's tone of voice and speech pattern. Long pauses, monotone responses, or a general absence of enthusiasm are signs that the save is not yet complete. Continue to probe the customer to solicit more information. Ask what she would consider fair. Most customers will be fair, and if you can meet her requirements, do so.

ENCOURAGE EVEN TENTATIVE AGREEMENT. Sometimes the best approach to saving a customer on the brink of defection is to introduce a new offer and request that the customer try the new service on a trial basis. This was Ruthie McDowell's technique in the save effort described at the beginning of this chapter. She suggested the customer try the replacement phone for thirty days as an alternative to immediate cancellation. This offer worked and the customer was saved.

A business-to-business client of ours recently described to us a good example of a buy-more-time strategy that he used with a high-value account on the verge of defection:

One of our vice presidents sat down with the clients, understood what their issues were, and asked for six months to get the problems corrected. The clients said that we had earned that because of our past track record. They told us they'd give us six months to turn it around. So, we're three months into that process now. We have added a manager to that account and we've put in some "stay" bonuses to ensure that we don't lose people on that account. In essence, we've upped the fire power. We haven't gotten our most recent survey back yet, but we are in regular discussions with them and we're on track.

COPE WITH DISAGREEMENT. When you and the customer cannot agree on a solution to the problem, you have to reconsider the situation. In the case where the customer's demand exceeds the customer's value to your firm, it is still important to leave the customer on the best terms possible. Restate your best offer and reinforce your keen desire to keep him as a customer and your appreciation for his past business. Above all, you want to limit the amount of ill-will the customer feels toward your firm so that future word of mouth is at least neutral if not positive. Even when the customer leaves, not all is lost. Move him into new prospect status, so he can be recontacted along with other lost customers at an appropriate time in the future. In the interim, the company should keep careful records about the reasons customers are defecting in order to support internal process improvement and to improve save messages and offers in the future.

Saving customers is hard work. Yes, the payoffs are tremendous, but the effort required on the part of reps can be extensive. One thing is certain: to be successful, the save reps must feel a deep confidence that they are armed with the skills, the knowledge, and the support from their company to do the job. As Fernando Roman, revenue director of Cellular One, counsels, "Your save reps must firmly believe they are the best in their industry and our job as managers is to give them the tools they need to be the best. This means training, this means knowledge of the latest competitive offers, this means well-conceived promotions that the customer finds valuable. With these things, the save rep can be extraordinarily successful."[3]

We look more closely at how to lead a team of win-back and save reps in the next chapter.

How a Stockbroker Provided CPR on an Individual Scale

At a recent seminar where we spoke about win-back, we were approached by Bob, a successful stockbroker for a national brokerage company. His business has seen tremendous change in the last several years due to the increasing popularity of do-it-yourself on-line investing. Charles Schwab, E*Trade, AmeriTrade, and others have been steadily chipping away at the monies Bob has traditionally invested for his clients. More than a few times this stockbroker has needed to save customers on the brink of defection. For example, Bob shared with us this recent experience, which illustrates some of the steps we have outlined here.

A long-time client with a moderate risk portfolio called Bob, distressed that his blue chip stocks were losing money while technology stocks (of which he had very few) were booming. He had been patient enough, he told Bob, but it was clear from his returns that his portfolio was in need of reallocation. The client made it clear he was considering moving his money away from Bob and his brokerage company and into more growth-oriented mutual funds. The stockbroker went into save mode: first, he addressed the trigger need. He agreed with the client that the portfolio was underallocated in technology stocks and that there was a place in it for some carefully selected technology stocks. Probing deeper, Bob identified the client's driving needs. The client resented the fact that he had to call Bob about changes; he thought Bob should be calling him. Also, he was unhappy about relying on monthly statements to track the account. He wanted greater access to his portfolio's performance. To address these needs, Bob suggested he and the client meet every quarter (rather than only for the customary annual review) to discuss the portfolio's returns and possible changes and adjustments. In addition, he reminded his client about the brokerage's password-protected Web site on which portfolio returns could be accessed and monitored daily.

Finally, Bob wanted to reconnect his client with the key reasons the client was doing business with Bob in the first place. Bob asked the client to think back about his original objectives when he first invested with Bob and his brokerage company. The client said he had wanted a reputable, knowledgeable source that could help him achieve his financial goals with moderate risk. And the client now agreed that the only change in these objectives was his desire to add some additional risk to his portfolio. He thought that reputation and knowledge were still important and that Bob and his brokerage company provided these crucial elements.

The crisis was over. By addressing the three needs, Bob saved his client and added more value for the client in the process.

How IKEA Provides CPR on a Huge Scale

Imagine this: a store the size of five football fields containing a huge range of household products, many of which require customer assembly. Does it sound like a formula for disaster?

Not if you're IKEA, the Netherlands-based retail giant that offers a wide range of Scandinavian-style household goods at relatively inexpensive prices.

What's IKEA's secret? Making customer save processes (that is, CPR) a centerpiece in all store operations. And here's how it works. Customers shop IKEA on the promise of affordable prices. Couches can sell for $500 to $600, entertainment centers for $199. Kitchen table chairs can be found at $24.95 each. IKEA is able to offer a wide array of products at relatively low prices in part because it requires customers to assemble much of the furniture themselves. Many of IKEA's products are sold in flat packages that can be shipped and stacked easily. To save on labor costs, stores have a large self-serve warehouse area where customers load up their own prepackaged furniture, pay for it, and then wheel it out to their cars with little or no assistance from the store's staff. It's this self-serve environment that is both the company's strength and its weakness. It can put many customers (particularly new buyers) at immediate risk for defection.

Although customers love the savings they get from the store, a misread product label or bin sign or hard-to-decipher spec sheet can cause major problems once the customer returns home. That's why IKEA takes great pains to ensure that the shopping experience is as flawless as possible. The firm uses mystery shoppers to continually test all aspects of the self-selection shopping experience from point-of-sale signage to wait times for such things as the first approach by the floor service staff or the process of checking out. These initiatives help the retailer prevent problems from manifesting in the first place.

But what about customers who do have problems? IKEA stations a high number of staff (company officials call them *coworkers*) at each store—forty to sixty in the larger stores and fifteen to forty in the smaller stores. These coworkers are extensively cross-trained in sales and stock operations so they can address almost any shopper issue that arises. Moreover, given IKEA's self-serve concept and the demands it places on shoppers, these coworkers are carefully trained to identify, seek out, and care for customers who appear to be struggling or just plain frustrated. Whether the customer mistakenly bought a two-drawer chest rather than the three-drawer model or needs a wall system that is temporarily out of stock, coworkers are empowered to bring the problem to a quick resolution. And they're armed with plenty of ammunition to take the sting out of customer inconvenience—free meals (compliments of IKEA's on-site Swedish-style eatery), free delivery, cash coupons, or even dollars off the purchase. The combination of the fine-tuned self-selection shopping process and the quick customer problem resolution is a big hit with customers. Last year 196 million people visited IKEA's 156 stores worldwide—including 14 in the United States—and spent $8 billion.[4]

TRUST AND ITS INFLUENCE ON SAVING A DEFECTING CUSTOMER

When a customer is on the brink of defection, typically something has occurred that has shaken the customer's trust. Rebuilding that trust is essential to any successful save. Let's examine four trust-breaking events in the context of a customer for a small-disk satellite television service provider and the impact of these events on the company's efforts to save the customer. Then we'll look at three means of rapidly rebuilding trust.

• *Trust-breaking event 1.* A small-dish satellite television customer called the service provider with a big problem. Since his service had been activated, he had not been able to receive signals from any of the major networks and he had poor reception of the other stations. He was seriously considering canceling his service. The provider told him the problems were probably due to an incorrect zip code on his installation record. They assured him the zip code problem would be corrected and his reception would improve; but after two weeks, there was still no change in reception.

• *Trust-breaking event 2.* Increasingly frustrated, the customer again contacted the satellite provider. This time he was advised to write each of the network affiliates in his service area to obtain permission to view programming from a distant affiliate of the same network. Although he thought this was a lot of effort on his part, he did so. The responses from the network affiliates were sent to his home, and he in turn sent them on to the service provider. They were returned because the service provider showed his installation address to be a nonexistent post office box number. (But he noticed the service provider had the billing address correct!)

• *Trust-breaking event 3.* The customer then called a third time to explain that the material had been returned because of the incorrect post office box number. He was a big tennis fan and wanted to view the Wimbledon tennis tournament, which was coming up soon on the NBC affiliate. The service provider's representative advised him to have the affiliate, temporarily, change his address to the nonexistent post office box, and fax the notice of changed address to the provider. He did so and was told that everything would be fixed in time for him to see the tournament. It wasn't done, and he was unable to view the event.

• *Trust-breaking event 4.* Amazingly, after all these consecutive service disappointments, this thrice-disappointed customer took one last initiative. He wrote to the company president, recounting his service problems and complaints. In the letter he explained he was on the verge of canceling service unless his problems were quickly addressed. How do you think the president responded? A personal call or letter? How about at least a call or letter from a knowledgeable staff member on behalf of the president acknowledging the problems and outlining a plan for addressing them? Unfortunately, the company chose none of these options. Instead, it simply sent a letter from a customer relations staff member apologizing for any inconvenience and offering a free month of upgraded satellite service and some free movie coupons. To make matters worse, the inconvenience described in the letter was not what the customer had outlined in his letter to the president.

Predictably, within days of receiving the letter, the customer canceled the service. His trust was severely damaged, and he needed more than a general "we're sorry" letter containing some jazzy coupons and a free service offer to repair it. In order to stay with the service provider, this customer needed (and deserved) a hefty dose of personal attention and assurance that his problems were understood and that they could and would be solved. After four consecutive trust breakers, nothing less would do.

What can you do to immediately start rebuilding trust with a customer on the brink of defection? The answer lies in looking more closely at the outcomes a customer wants when making a complaint. A fascinating study conducted by Stephen Tax and Stephen Brown found that when customers voice complaints, they expect fairness.[5] We believe companies need to take this finding very seriously when they are trying to save defecting customers: the more fairness the defecting customer experiences during the save process, the more that customer's trust is being rebuilt.

Tax and Brown's study found that a customer's perception of fairness is driven by three aspects of a company's recovery process: (1) outcome—defined as the results customers receive from complaints; (2) procedure—the policies, rules, and timeliness of the complaint process; and (3) treatment—the interpersonal relationship perceived during the complaint process. Let's examine each of these areas of fairness to determine how they can help you start rebuilding trust the moment a complaint is voiced.

Offer a Fair Outcome

Refunds, credits, repairs, replacements, and corrections of charges are typical forms of compensation anticipated by customers. An apology is also perceived by customers as a compensation for being inconvenienced or treated rudely. In the Tax and Brown study, most customers reported that their complaints were not resolved fairly. They felt the outcomes did not adequately recognize or compensate them for the costs they incurred in getting their complaints resolved. Not surprisingly, the most negative reactions were in response to complaints that were never resolved. The satellite TV customer experienced both inadequate compensation and a failure to resolve his complaints.

The minority of customers who reported positive resolution to their complaints typically pointed to compensation that included reimbursement for the inconvenience associated with the failure as well as basic exchanges or repairs. Customers also reacted more positively when the company offered them compensation options rather than a single prescribed outcome. For example, a hotel might offer the choice of a refund or a free upgrade to a better room rather than just one or the other.

Offer a Fair Procedure

Tax and Brown's study found that fair processes begin with the firm's assuming responsibility for the failure and for the quick handling of the complaint, preferably by the first person contacted by the customer. Customers who judged problem resolution procedures to be unfair had typically been frustrated by a prolonged, inconvenient process that required them to repeat their complaint to several different representatives. The satellite TV customer was told to contact the network affiliates himself, for example.

Offer Fair Treatment

Finally, the Tax and Brown study found that fair interpersonal behavior with customers involves demonstrating politeness, concern, and honesty; providing an explanation for the failure; and making a genuine effort to resolve the problem. This same study reported that oral communication is often better suited for conveying compassion and empathy to irate customers than written communication. Again, the satellite TV customer was treated poorly when he received a general "we're sorry" letter that did not address the specific problems or outline a plan of action.

Most customers who complain simply want a problem solved. They do not want to waste their time or the company's time with long, drawn-out discussions. The more quickly a fair and equitable solution can be found, the more likely the company is to save the customer and earn a valuable customer for life.

THE PHASES OF CUSTOMER LOSS

When the defecting customer's call comes in or the orders stop, it may seem to the company as though the customer is saying good-bye and terminating the relationship abruptly. However, the reality is that a customer typically goes through three distinct phases when ending a relationship. Let's look at these progressive phases of customer defection and how to recognize them. Note that recognizing all three customer loss phases is critical because the sooner you can intervene to save the defecting customer and prevent the later phases the better.

Phase 1. Value Breakdown—
Bump in the Road or Fork?

Every day, customer value breakdowns occur. A delivery arrives late, a product is incorrectly sized, a salesperson misquotes a specification, and so on and so on. For the customer, such value breakdowns can be either insignificant bumps in the road with no long-term consequences or forks in the road that may lead to defection. Value breakdown begins and ends with customer perception. For example, frequent business traveler David Pilgrim hit a bump and a fork all in one week.

As an account executive, David Pilgrim spends an average of two to three nights each week on the road. On a recent trip, he returned to his hotel room to find a letter under his door from the hotel manager expressing a sincere apology for the fact that there was no hot water that evening. The letter offered a free drink and hors d'oeuvres in the bar and a cake to be delivered by room service. Says Pilgrim, "When I say cake, I'm talking about a $25 double chocolate silk cake that was bigger than any human being could eat in one day. When I ordered the cake, I also asked for a glass of milk. I got it too, at no extra expense. The next morning I asked if I could use my free drink and hors d'oeuvres coupon and redeem it against breakfast. No problem, they said. Free breakfast." For Pilgrim, this value breakdown was at most simply a bump in the road.

Contrast that bump with his experience the very next night:

I'm going to be late arriving at my next hotel, so I call in about six o'clock in the evening and they assure me my room will be held. I finally check in about eleven thirty and they give me a key and I head for the door. When I open the door, there are someone's belongings in the room. So I call security, and they come and they bring me another key. This time I open the door to be greeted by a man in his underwear. The guy goes through the roof! I apologize and go back downstairs and talk to the manager on duty. Scott, the manager, tells me the hotel is having computer problems. He gives me another key and I find that room is also occupied! That makes three keys, three occupied rooms.

It's now 12:30 A.M., and David Pilgrim is beat. What's more, he must leave for the airport at 5:45 A.M. to catch an early flight. He goes back to the front-desk manager and asks that the manager check the next available room. When he finally gets in the room, he discovers that the air-conditioning unit for the entire complex is right above his room, creating a constant flow of noise. Reports Pilgrim, "I called the hotel manager again and told him this wasn't going to work. He told me he gave me the last room. I tell him that I'm a frequent business traveler and stay at his chain's properties around the country. I tell him about my experience the night before with his competitor. And I say that I wonder if customer loyalty matters to him and his hotel. I will leave it up to him to rise to the occasion and make good on all this inconvenience." Pilgrim got nothing—no discount, no coupon for a complimentary night, no letter of apology. Did he see this as a bump or fork? Definitely a fork![6]

From the provider's point of view, value breakdowns should be seen as opportunities to stabilize the customer and avoid having to save that same customer later. If the error is quickly identified and remedied, the customer relationship can often be stabilized and brought back under control by first-line staff.

Consider Wachovia Bank's Relationship Recovery program. When a customer, either by visiting a branch or telephoning the call center, registers a complaint or indicates interest in closing an account, front-line staff are empowered to address the problem immediately. This may mean moving the at-risk customer to another kind of account or waiving fees and the like. In addition, high-value customers often receive a follow-up call, letter of apology, or gift from the area manager. Wachovia has built a bankwide process to stabilize a customer as soon as possible after identifying a value breakdown, and the payoffs have been substantial. On average, Wachovia saves 50 percent of customers who express an interest in closing accounts. Even better, Wachovia's Relationship Recovery program saves around 70 percent of high-value customers.[7]

One of the leading overnight package delivery services has a recovery program that engages virtually every operating area. When a problem, especially one threatening the continuing customer relationship, is brought to the company's attention, whoever first receives the problem or complaint owns the handling of it. Any functional group of the company can be called in by the problem owner to participate in resolving the problem and ensuring that at the least the customer's needs have been met. By immediately and aggressively addressing problems as they are voiced, the company keeps bumps in the road from becoming forks in the road.

The payoffs can be huge for companies that address and remedy value breakdowns. Left untreated however, value breakdowns put customers increasingly at risk. Perhaps an industrial chemical distributor said it best when he commented, "Customers recognize that we're not perfect. Lots of things can go wrong. The one thing customers will not tolerate is a supplier who does not recognize the error." Let's look more closely at how unaddressed value breakdowns can lead to a high probability of customer loss.

Phase 2. The Season of Discontent

After a value breakdown experience or a series of them, the customer will generally begin to exhibit specific behaviors and actions that indicate a weakening in the relationship. Warning signs may include lower or flattening sales, lower than expected performance ratings, a slowdown in proposal approvals, less accessibility to upper management, and a shortening of plans for future work. At this stage, customers have not yet left; but by their actions they are demonstrating their intentions to do so. Left unaddressed, this discontent can lead to termination. But when it is effectively addressed, this defecting customer can still be saved. Here's how one corporate account manager described his season of discontent experience and the steps his company took to save the customer:

> We signed a Fortune 100 company as a client. We did a fabulous job, so they kept us for ongoing business. Then, we had some staff turnover. The account executive changed, and the new account executive didn't line up as well. So, surveys [of our performance] that were coming in at a 10 dropped to neutral, let's say 5 or 6. We did the standard recovery steps—I went up there, we sat down, we talked about it and agreed on some changes.
>
> What was disturbing was that three months later, we got a letter from them—even though [we were in ongoing discussions with them] during this time—saying that "despite all your efforts, things still aren't improving." So we had gone from the verbal warning to the written warning. It looked just like our progressive staff discipline system. You know, "Dear Dave: We talked about this three months ago, and I know you've been doing a lot of things; but it still isn't any better. So this is your formal notice that we really expect you to do something about

it." I thought to myself, "Oh my gosh, this is the written warning in my personnel file."

We went up there again and said, "We've *really* got an action plan now!" It was drilled down to a weekly plan and update. We just got their survey back, and they've now graded us much higher, and they said things are great. It's not perfect yet, but we know what we have to do to get there. The nice thing about this improvement is that they recently helped us with references to secure another major division within their corporate family.

Phase 3. Termination—But Not the End

In the termination phase the customer either officially puts you on notice that your services are no longer needed or you hear nothing and the customer just goes away. In either case you want to apply effective save tactics and avoid this fate. And as we have said before, even if your business is terminated, take heart. You can move the account into win-back status and use the process outlined in Chapter Three.

IDENTIFYING AT-RISK CUSTOMERS— SEVEN IMPORTANT SOURCES

An understanding of the three phases of customer loss and of the fact that the sooner intervention with a customer begins the easier and less expensive it usually is to fix the problem makes it clear that the best plan is to have a system for identifying at-risk customers as soon as possible. Yet as our nationwide win-back study showed, a majority of sales managers and marketing managers have no system or process for identifying customers who are at high risk of defection.

The best first-alert system for any company is one that receives input from a variety of sources. Think of these sources as important nerve centers throughout your organization that constantly feed you information about customer defection risks. We have identified seven information sources for identifying at-risk customers, and we summarize them here. Some of these first-alert sources are reactive. They report to you after the fact about a value breakdown and the customer discontent that has resulted from it. Other sources are more proactive. They help you anticipate the trouble spots and problems looming on the horizon that may adversely affect customer loyalty.

Let Your Purchase Data Tell You

Purchase data are one source of information about defecting customers. The customer churn analysis presented in Chapter Two, which tracks customer revenue decile assignments from one period to the next, is a critical tool for evaluating customers' propensity to defect. In the Chapter Two example (Figure 2.10), nearly half the customers in the top two revenue deciles in one year had migrated down into lower deciles for the next year. Such data are a sure sign that high-value customers are already spending elsewhere and that additional defection risk among this group is very high.

In addition to the customer churn analysis, other data analyses outlined in Chapter Two can provide insights about defection risk. For example, the more time that has lapsed since a customer's last purchase (recency of purchase analysis), the higher the risk of defection. Likewise, the fewer the number of products a customer is buying from you (product penetration analysis), the higher the risk of defection.

Fortunately, there's more and more software available to help you evaluate purchase data and discern purchase trends. Analyzed correctly, purchase data can help you identify at-risk customers.

Let Listening Posts Among Frontline Staff Tell You

Relatively few customers, whether at risk or not, actually complain, especially in consumer products and services. So a number of companies use frontline listening posts to help spot at-risk customers and take action on their behalf. Let's look at two of these companies.

Frontline employees who are in frequent touch with customers represent a huge opportunity for identifying at-risk customers and more. No organization knows this better than USAA, the San Antonio–based financial services giant that serves an all-military clientele of over two million customers and policyholders and manages over $20 billion in assets. From its earliest beginnings, USAA realized that its telephone sales and service reps were in a unique position to gather important customer information. This realization led to the creation of ECHO, a state-of-the-art on-line information collection system used by USAA's six thousand sales and service reps to gather data related to feedback, complaints, and competitive threats as well as market trends and new product opportunities. When an issue that might put a customer at risk is discovered, a service rep assigns it to an internal *action rep* for quick resolution and customer recovery. When a service failure is noted, service reps also report the failure to the appropriate USAA unit, which in turn uses the data to change faulty processes. These frontline listening posts provide USAA with a significant competitive advantage, which enables the company to achieve a 98 percent customer renewal rate.[8]

Moreover, if you think listening posts belong only within your company's four walls, think again. Listening posts can be anywhere your staff is found. For example, a small five-branch bank, Enterprise Bank and Trust in Lowell, Massachusetts, establishes listening posts throughout the community by encouraging employees to take part in neighborhood and town meetings and activities. A community bank is only as strong as its reputation, and Enterprise Bank uses listening posts throughout the community to help ensure that its reputation remains stellar.

Let Your Customer Research Tell You

Customer research can keep track of your performance with your customers overall as well as with specific customer groups and individual customers.

MONITORING OVERALL SCORES. Well-conceived customer surveys can give you valuable insights into the defection risk of high-value customers. For example, in 1998, Royal Bank of Scotland received some troubling feedback. It conducted a customer survey showing that a shocking 69 percent of its customers agreed with the statement: "I don't have a relationship with Royal Bank; all I do is pay money." This insight, coupled with equally troubling facts regarding customer value and trust issues, provided Royal Bank with confirmation that they had a large number of at-risk customers.

Management acted quickly. A one-to-one customer relationship program was designed for the bank's most valuable customers. The program consisted of multiple telephone contacts with both new and long-standing customers. The message conveyed to customers was kept simple and direct. It said, "Here are ways to get more value from the services you already use with our bank," and, "We're here to help. What other financial requirements can we assist you with?" During the calls, customers were encouraged to ask any and all questions they had about Royal Bank services. Additionally, customers were asked if they would agree to regular follow-up calls by a bank representative. More than 80 percent of customers agreed to the calls.

Once the program was underway, Royal Bank surveyed customers on their feelings about the one-to-one contact program. Research showed the customers were extremely impressed with the level of service and care they were now receiving. Customers noted that they were pleased with the bank's willingness to proactively solicit questions and that they felt reassured by the bank's ability to provide a personal touch.

Among the follow-up study's other findings were the following:

- Eighty-six percent of Royal Bank customers now felt valued by the bank (23 percentage point increase).

- Twenty-one percent of customers agreed with the statement, "I feel low on Royal Bank's priority list" (25 percentage point decrease).

- Forty-four percent of customers agreed with the statement, "I don't have a relationship with Royal Bank; all I do is pay money" (25 percentage point decrease).

- Ninety-six percent of customers said they would know how to contact Royal Bank to buy another product or service (43 percentage point increase).

- Ninety-eight percent of customers agreed with the statement, "It would be easy to contact someone at Royal Bank if I had an inquiry or problem" (19 percentage point increase).[9]

Evaluating customer surveys can be key in keeping customers satisfied in any business, perhaps especially in health care. Open enrollment is a perilous time for any health care management organization (HMO). That's the period each year during which a member can elect to stay or leave for another health care provider. Being well regarded by members before open enrollment is critical to any HMO's ability to maintain a stable member base. It's a lesson PacifiCare Health Systems learned in the mid-1980s when it conducted extensive research among its members. A key finding was that if primary care physicians did not demonstrate a cooperative, helpful, and respectful attitude toward members and their families, these members developed a high risk of defection. With this information, PacifiCare then identified medical practices with the highest percentage of such members, and trained the providers and their staffs in member relations improvement strategies. Disenrollments dropped substantially for PacifiCare as a result of this intervention.[10]

MONITORING INDIVIDUAL SCORES. One service company we interviewed has a very comprehensive plan for monitoring an individual's account to track risk of defection. Here's how it works:

First, each customer is surveyed twice a year. If the results from the performance and value delivery questions show declines in key areas, that customer is considered to be at risk. The company's action plan then goes immediately into effect. It calls for a company officer to conduct an in-person review with the customer to get more depth on the root causes of the problem. Once a problem is identified, a performance improvement program is codeveloped by the customer and the company. In effect, a partnership plan is created, complete with benchmarks, completion dates, and proofs of performance. Second, to support this plan, the company maintains an active database on the customer, which includes the research, call reports, action plan updates, and anecdotal information by contact staff.

One company officer described the process this way: "My contact and his boss gave us a 6 on a 10-point scale [on the client survey], and they wrote in a couple of things that they thought we should be doing differently. I got the survey and immediately scheduled an appointment with them, flew up to Washington, D.C., sat down, and basically listened to them." The officer wanted to understand the client's perspective and understand what it would take to make that 6 turn into a 10. After detailed talks the officer went to work on a plan that would make that happen. He sent the plan to the client along with a letter that said, "This is what I heard. This is the action plan I'm putting in place. Did I hear correctly, and does this action plan seem appropriate and aggressive enough for you?" The client confirmed that the plan was acceptable. Once there was an agreement on what needed to be done, checkpoints were established to make sure progress was being made. At each step along the way, revisions could be made to be sure that the plan was working to satisfy the client's needs. For example, said the officer, "We discovered that a big problem was that our staff and their staff did not approach problems in the same way. We created a training forum so that both sides could come together and work out the problems together. On the next survey they gave us a 10. The bottom line was that the client was amazed at the level of our response to a few shortfalls. What they saw from our response was just how valuable a customer they really were to us."

Let Accounts Receivable Tell You

Ask Bruce Woolpert, co-CEO of Granite Rock, a one-hundred-year-old family business that quarries granite, about his company's number one method for saving at-risk customers, and he'll tell you about the short pay method. *Short pay* is a term used in the construction industry to describe paying less than you were invoiced for. You short your invoice by subtracting what you feel you don't owe and pay for what you feel you do owe.

For example, if a customer gets an invoice from Granite Rock for a load of gravel that was delivered late and caused a delay on the construction site where the gravel was needed, the customer might opt to short the invoice, subtracting a portion of the payment for this inconvenience. Explains Woolpert, "What we've told our customers on the back of our invoices is if there is something, product or service, that we provided to you and you're not happy with it, subtract it from the total, pay us what we earned, and don't pay us what we haven't earned."

By now, you may be tempted to discount Woolpert's save strategy, but do so at your peril. Why? For one thing, Bruce Woolpert finished first in his class at Stanford Business School and for eight years ran a software division of a little company called Hewlett-Packard before taking the reins of Granite Rock with his brother in 1987. Since then, the company has won the Malcolm Baldrige National Quality Award and in December of 1999 was named number eleven on *Fortune* magazine's One Hundred Best Companies to Work for in America. Granite Rock has a dozen locations between San Francisco and Monterey, and its customers pay, on average, 6 percent more than they would with the competition. Not a bad margin in an industry where the low bid typically reigns supreme!

Woolpert's save strategy is simple but sound. "The reason we did this is we wanted to come up with a very easy method for customers to complain. We know from countless research studies, that 90 percent of customers don't complain. They just go away." So Woolpert devised a way to leverage the emotion of an unhappy customer. "There are two times when customers are the most emotional about our product or service. One of those times is when we don't perform. The second time is when they receive the invoice," explains Woolpert. "The client sits there thinking, 'I don't really owe them this money, but if I don't pay them, they will turn it over to their credit department and it will turn into a big hassle, so I might as well go ahead and pay them.' But I can guarantee you that as those unhappy clients start to write out the words 'Granite Rock' on the check, . . . about the time they get to the word Rock, they've decided this is the last check they'll ever send us. You can ask credit departments all over the United States, How are customers? And they will say customers are just fine, and that customers are happy. But a lot of those checks are their last but they just don't know it." Granite Rock, says Woolpert, learns quickly from a short pay episode and quickly improves internal processes to prevent problems from reoccurring.[11]

Bob McAdams, managing partner of Carneiro, Chummey & Co., a San Antonio accounting firm, is acting on similar beliefs when he encloses a short questionnaire with each invoice. It saves stamps, but there's another reason for doing it. "When a customer pays the bill, it's the ultimate evaluation," says McAdams. "It's one more snapshot of how we're doing."[12]

Let Your Customer Network Tell You

Much has been written about getting customers to sell for you, but how about getting customers to listen for you? A customer listening on your behalf can help you save a valuable piece of business. Here's how one relocation manager rescued a piece of business, thanks to the good listening skills of a loyal client.

One of our clients was attending a corporate human resources conference. During a break he was sitting in a conference room reading his *USA Today,* and he could overhear two other attendees at a nearby table, whom he did not know, talking about relocation. As it turned out they were talking negatively about one of our company's services (and actually called the program by name). On returning from the conference, my client called me. He told me what he overheard and said that although it wouldn't be appropriate for him to tell me who it was, . . . "If you have a client in the (he named the industry) in (he named the city), that you provide (he named our product) for, you may want to check to see how you're doing, because they weren't talking like they are very happy." I thanked him for giving me the heads up. I checked up on the client, discovered a serious problem, and got the issue resolved.

Let a Sophisticated Churn Model Tell You

Thanks to continuing advances in data mining software, more and more companies are applying computer churn models more complex than the basic analysis we described in Chapter Two in order to identify those customers at risk of leaving. Sophisticated churn models evaluate the interplay of multiple purchase and behavior variables to uncover defection patterns that might otherwise go undetected.

For example, churn modeling helped the Liverpool Victoria Friendly Society in England (friendly societies are financial services companies that were originally set up to provide burial insurance) discover that the majority of those dropping coverage came from only a quarter of the firm's customer base, principally those who had never made a claim, were under thirty-three years old, and had fewer than three Liverpool Victoria financial products. Consider the advantages Liverpool Victoria now enjoyed from this information in both developing customer retention programs and targeting at-risk customers.

Because their customers are so prone to rapid churn, European telecom companies have made considerable progress in using churn models to uncover at-risk customers. For example, SLP InfoWare, a churn modeling consultancy based in France, has developed a comprehensive and highly predictive model for identifying at-risk telecom customers. One of the first things the model considers is incomplete calls. These are calls that the customer terminates because the telephone number is incorrect. In France, for example, customers begin paying after they have been connected for just two seconds. Therefore, a customer who finds charges on a monthly bill for even a few incomplete calls can become a defection risk. Other factors considered by the SLP churn model are length of service to the customer in months or years, the customer's monthly billing data, and the customer's history of customer service requests. With European telecom turnover rates averaging 40 percent annually and an estimated three-quarters of the customers who leave one telecom company going with another company within a few months, churn modeling is proving to be an essential tool for targeting at-risk customers.

Other industries are incorporating churn models as well. At this writing, U.S.–based companies such as Charles Schwab, Wells Fargo,

Hilton, and DirecTV are using E.piphany's E.4 Enterprise Relationship Management System to study customer activity by geographical location, revenue, demographic profile, and other segmentation variables. Using this software system, Schwab, for example, is able to mine and analyze specific information from its account data warehouse for its five million customers. Schwab can personalize approaches to customers at risk, enhancing the relationship and optimizing lifetime value.

Let Account Milestones and Activities Tell You

Some firms, particularly banks, have discovered that certain event milestones closely parallel a high incidence of defection. For that reason they monitor and manage those events very closely. One such company is credit-card issuer MBNA, which loses under 1 percent of its cardholders a year. MBNA's event detection and management works like this.

Customers coming up for renewal are called as their renewal date approaches. If a customer indicates renewal uncertainly or an intention to leave, this information is noted in the customer's file. Soon after, an MBNA telemarketer, trained specifically in customer save protocols, calls the at-risk customer to get specific feedback on the reasons for possible defection and to resolve those issues so that the customer does not leave. Using this proactive approach, MBNA is able to save about half of those intending to defect. Customer research has shown that the at-risk customers often appreciate this additional level of touch and interest, because they feel most other companies either ignore at-risk customers or send out a standardized self-completion questionnaire after the fact.[13]

Another bank we interviewed found a high correlation between certain account activity and client defection risk. For example, a decline in the activity level on a checking account, a decline in account balances, a stoppage or decline in automatic transfers, and a decline in debit card usage were all events that could foreshadow a customer's defection. For that reason, the bank now closely watches for such activity on high-value accounts and takes steps to stabilize or save the account when necessary.

The key is this: pay close attention to defection and the activities that precede defection. These events can become your markers for identifying at-risk customers.

SAVING WEB CUSTOMERS

The Web is here to stay and workable strategies for saving Web customers are becoming critical to every company's processes for saving at-risk customers. By the year 2002, an estimated 43 percent of U.S. households are projected to be actively connected to the Internet, representing an increase of more than 50 percent in household connectivity since 1997.[14] Get prepared for the fact that more and more of your customers will be buying products and accessing information from you on line. Without a doubt, you'll want to attract high-value on-line buyers. But more important, you'll want to keep them. Be ready for a tough fight. Here's why:

• *Higher expectations.* Ask the average person off the street what the Web represents, and you'll likely get responses like "instant access," "easy-to-find information," and "no more waiting in a line to pay." Sure enough, research has found that many customers come to the Web expecting a higher level of customer service than they ordinarily expect in a bricks and mortar environment. Why? Because, they reason, it's on the Web and that means it must be instant. And even thirty *seconds* of wait time spent staring at a computer screen seems like an eternity compared to the expectation of instant service. Given this need for instant gratification, it is little wonder that quick and easy usage drives site loyalty. A recent Jupiter Communications research study finds four key factors are responsible for getting users to return to sites. They are user friendliness and ease of navigation (54 percent), positive usage experience (36 percent), rapid response time (36 percent), and updated, relevant content (27 percent). In contrast, incentive programs, which reward on-line activity with points and prizes, account for only 12 percent of the reasons for customers' purchases and site loyalty.[15]

• *Easy exit.* Moreover, every e-customer's exit strategy is just a keystroke away. Don't like the site? Don't like the product selection? Site too hard to navigate? Just click and you can leave at any time. Your customers don't have to walk out of the store, find their car, and fight the traffic to shop somewhere else. Instead, they simply type in another Web site address and they're gone. Little wonder that Web purchase studies find that, on average, fewer than 10 percent of site visitors make a purchase and less than 2 percent become repeat purchasers.[16]

• *Unpredictable experiences.* Recent studies suggest e-commerce customers are anything but impressed with their on-line experiences to date. A study by Data Monitor found that three-quarters of all attempted on-line purchases were abandoned by customers during 1999. The culprits? Either customers are disconnected at the virtual checkout counter, resulting in a "dropped shopping cart," which forces the customer to fill the cart again, or slow servers cause users to lose patience.[17] Likewise, Resource Marketing, an e-marketing firm that recently spent ten weeks surfing fifteen hundred consumer e-commerce sites to evaluate the state of on-line customer service, concluded the customer experience on-line was "unpredictable at best." This firm looked at fourteen key factors including account administration, security, and returns. The six greatest shortcomings it found were these:

No e-mail response within forty-eight hours	56%
Poor phone assistance	36
No response to e-mail at all	26
Glitches in order processing	25
Late package delivery	14
Package never arrived	6

As Kelly Mooney, Resource Marketing's managing director of intelligence, explains, "It's no wonder that customer conversion rates [percentages of Web surfers who become buyers] hover near 1.5 percent and abandoned on-line shopping carts have soared to as high as 88 percent."[18]

Our strategy for saving Web customers is very simple. Assume every Web customer you have is constantly at risk for defection and act accordingly. Without a doubt, no customer will tolerate for long the Web site shortcomings listed here so get those basic purchase and customer service issues fixed and fast. But don't stop there. To save an at-risk customer, you must get personal. Ironically, the ability to get personal is the greatest advantage an e-commerce marketer has, yet the tools are often unused.

Consider this. Broadbase Software, an e-commerce application producer, recently examined business Web site marketing techniques in its ongoing study *Evaluating the "Sticky Factor" of E-Commerce Sites.* The study monitored communications from fifty leading e-commerce sites as they contacted customers during the thirty- to ninety-day period after purchases were made. In general, Broadbase reports, e-merchants did not use the communicative and personalizing features of the Internet to anywhere near their fullest benefit. For example, sites took an average of 25.6 days to follow up with their first promotional offer. In addition, well under half the offers made efforts at cross-marketing and very few were personalized. More specifically, the Broadbase study found that even the sites that used follow-up marketing within ninety days after purchase left the personalization opportunities largely untapped. For example, the survey results found that only 38 percent of the sites made cross-marketing offers, 11 percent made offers related to customer needs, 16 percent made offers personalized to individuals, and 5 percent made offers related to the original purchase.

Finally, 63 percent of the follow-up promotions and offers were simply sales announcements or monthly specials. It's a fact: a customer at risk of defection is largely unmoved by a generic message. It's the we-know-what-you-like-and-we're-going-to-give-it-to-you message that resonates and gets results.[19]

You can apply the CPR protocol outlined earlier in the chapter to saving e-customers. The on-line communication style makes e-commerce saves a little different from brick and mortar saves. However, the basic protocol is the same. Apply the comprehend, propose, and respond steps, along with some old-fashioned common sense, and fewer of your at-risk e-customers will defect.

Step 1: Comprehend. Have a process for identifying at-risk e-customers (monitor site usage, buying patterns, and purchase data). Have a quick method for determining the lifetime value of the at-risk e-customer (the higher the value, the bigger the save effort). Using any and all customer intelligence available, find out what's motivating the e-customer to defect. In doing so, identify the e-customer's three needs—trigger need, driving need, and original need—and incorporate these needs into your save offer. Finally, consider contacting the customer directly and asking this question: We very much value your business. What can we do to make this up to you and keep you as a customer?

Step 2: Propose. Use the three-tiered hierarchy of offers—comprising value solutions, low-cost solutions, and higher-cost solutions. Try to match the customer with the offer that is least costly but will get results. Customize the offer to relate to the e-customer's specific needs, noted preferences, and so forth. This is the time for the we-value-your-business and the we-know-what-you-like-and-we're-going-to-give-it-to-you communications.

Step 3: Respond. Carefully monitor the customer's response to the offer. No response? Try again. Still no response? Consider upping the ante by going to a higher tier in your hierarchy of offers. If you haven't already done so, this may be the time to telephone the e-customer and talk to him in person. As we mentioned before, research has shown that empathy and concern is best communicated through the human voice. Also, it's OK to call an e-customer!

If you just cannot save this customer, try to exit on a positive note, as you do with other customers. Restate your best offer and reinforce your keen desire to keep the customer and your appreciation for past business. You particularly want to do damage control with e-customers and keep the experience from generating negative word of mouth about your business. As we discussed in Chapter One, the Internet is a giant megaphone, and customers can spread the word in a matter of clicks. So thank the customer for her past business, and tell her you'll welcome her again anytime. Move her into new prospect status so you can recontact her in the future. But take care not to irritate her by calling too soon. Keep careful records of why the customer defected to help you customize your reapproach to this customer as well as improve internal processes.

SUMMARY

- Customers who are on the brink of defection can be won back.
- Putting together a save plan is essential to win back those thinking of discontinuing business.
- CPR is a rescue effort that can save a customer relationship.
- Comprehension is the building block on which all save efforts are founded: you need to learn who the at-risk customers are, learn their value to the company, and understand their problems.
- Proposing a solution and working with the customer often leads to a rescued relationship.
- The response of the customer will determine how successful rescue efforts have been.

- CPR works on both the large and small scale, on both individual customers and huge corporate accounts.

- Trust is an essential element in successful business relationships.

- Lost trust leads to lost customers.

- Rebuilding trust leads to regained or saved customers.

- Customers on the World Wide Web require constant attention and the same sort of intervention to avoid defection as customers in brick and mortar businesses do.

CHAPTER FIVE

Mobilizing and Managing a Win-Back Team

B ehind every successful win-back program is a successful win-back team. Depending on the company and its needs, win-back teams may be mobilized either on a temporary basis or as a permanent function within the organization. In this chapter we address both scenarios, presenting the insights of some seasoned pros who know firsthand what it takes to successfully mobilize and manage win-back teams.

RECRUITING AND MANAGING A TEMPORARY WIN-BACK TEAM

What should you do when a merger or acquisition or some other extraordinary event spooks your customers and they jump ship? The best plan, of course, is a proactive one that anticipates customer defection and works hard to lessen the risk by actively communicating with customers before, during, and after the event. Sometimes, however, despite your best efforts, you're still left with a long list of lost customers. What then?

That's exactly the problem Norwest Bank (now Wells Fargo) executive Bonnie Martinez needed to solve soon after her relocation to San Antonio to assume the position of president of retail banking for twelve area "stores." As part of its customer focus, Norwest calls its banks "stores" rather than branches.

When Norwest Bank came into Texas and bought up several regional banks, a large number of valuable customers departed. Research showed that these customers feared that they would be just another number in this large bank's customer list. So they moved their accounts to other banks where, they believed, they would receive better treatment.

In thinking about a plan for recovering these valuable customers, Martinez considered a number of conventional options such as offering certificates of deposit (CDs) at higher rates than normally available or running bank ads in the local media. But this twenty-six-year veteran banker was unconvinced these methods would recover lost customers, for one key reason: they lacked the personal touch. Intuitively, Martinez sensed that a successful win-back project required a one-on-one reconnection with the customer. Because, after all, the fear of impersonal service and becoming just a number was the major reason for customer defection in the first place. So Martinez began "what if?" brainstorming with fellow managers to mold an action plan:

- What if we personally contacted lost accounts and invited them back to Norwest?

- What if we carefully crafted our verbal and written communication with lost customers to convey a service rather than sales message?

- What if we recruited a team of hand-picked staff members who would temporarily leave their regular assignments in the bank to focus for several months on winning back lost customers?

- What if we created a team-driven environment in which staff closely supported each other's win-back efforts?

These questions led Martinez to develop Norwest's first customer win-back initiative in Texas. It comprised three key elements: people, place and time, and process. Here's how Martinez put her win-back plan into action.

People

Martinez needed four people to serve on her win-back team. Good communication skills and a resilience to rejection were her two key recruiting requirements.

"I took a look at available management and found the people who don't mind hearing no," is how Martinez described her recruitment effort. "I pulled the most aggressive, the person that could care less if there was a rejection. I wanted individuals who were not going to get disappointed and would move forward." She also chose a mix of men and women, and because the calls were to be made to customers in South Central Texas, she made sure at least one team member was fluent in both English and Spanish.

Recognizing that successful win-back required both reestablishing a friendly customer dialogue and ultimately persuading the lapsed customer to return, Martinez wanted her team staffed with, as she put it, "door openers and deal closers." In most cases, members of her team were good at both of these activities. In one case, she knowingly recruited a team member "whose real talent was reopening doors. He wasn't a closer but he was superb at reopening the door. His task was to make the phone call and rekindle the customer's interest and, once that was accomplished, turn the call over to another staff member who would complete the job. Because he was so effective at reapproaching the lost customer, he was assigned many of our high-value lost customers."

What recruitment message did Martinez give her team members? "I told them this was a new and crazy idea (never done before at Norwest), and they needed to think of it as an experiment. I told them we would need to stick together like glue to make it work."

Place and Time

Martinez converted her spacious, high-ceiling office into a win-back Grand Central Station. She had four phone jacks and phones installed (one for each team member), along with a long table and computer terminals. She wanted the team members to be in close proximity to each other to encourage maximum teamwork.

The win-back team devoted a full day each week for three months to contacting lost customers.

Process

How do you make the most of people, place, and time? Plan a process that encourages teamwork and productivity. Here are the key elements in the process that Martinez and her win-back team followed:

• *Daily assignments.* Each morning, the team reviewed the calls for the day and made calling assignments according to who was most familiar with the account. The cardinal rule was that whoever knew the person best made the call. A big flip chart listed the customers to be called. To the right of the name was a space for writing the result of the call. If a lost CD customer agreed to return, for example, the amount of the CD returning to the bank was recorded alongside the customer's name. This flip-chart system served as a highly visible daily tracking system.

• *Call priority.* The win-back team ranked the lost customers by value potential. The bank already had a valuation system in place that assigned customer value based on the number of current relationships—checking, savings, credit card, direct deposit, and so on—that existed between the customer and the bank. The win-back team used this same system for prioritizing win-back calls. Generally speaking, the more customer relationships that had existed during the last year of the account history, the more valuable that customer was to the bank. The accounts with the most relationships were called first.

• *Tools to do the job.* The staff were armed with information about all the bank's product and services. Every brochure and every rate were easily retrievable and at the caller's fingertips.

• *Opening phrases.* The opening sentence can make or break a win-back call. The staff role-played their introductions. Here is one successful opening: "Ms. Smith, this is Judy Moore at Norwest Bank here in San Antonio. Our records show you recently closed your account with us, and we're extremely sorry to be losing your business. I'd like to know more about your decision to leave. May I have a few short minutes of your time?" Once the customer agreed to be interviewed, the rep asked questions like these:

• What's prompting you to leave us?

• Where are you going?

• What attracts you to [*the name of the competitor*]?

• *Follow-ups.* Whether the account was successfully regained or not, the win-back caller handwrote a quick note to the lapsed customer, thanking the customer for his or her time. The staff could write their own messages or choose from a variety of prepared texts. Each note included key phrases however. For example, a note might say: "Ms. Smith, Thank you for taking time out of your morning. I know you are busy and we really appreciate your time. We appreciate your past business and hope we can serve you again soon. Enclosed is my business card. I'd be pleased to assist you at any time." To further sweeten the follow-up, calling cards with $10 worth of free long distance time were included in the envelopes.

• *Real-time recognition.* Whenever a lost customer officially said yes to the invitation to return to Norwest, the win-back team member making the call immediately announced the success and recorded the achievement beside the customer's name on the flip chart. With each reporting, other team members offered hearty, real-time congratulations on the win.

• *Periodic skill builders.* Led by Martinez, the win-back team often huddled for a quick debriefing in the morning and afternoon. The team members reviewed results thus far for the day, talked about successes and challenges, and in doing so, learned from each other. The team members then applied what they had learned to their subsequent calls.

• *Just-in-time coaching.* As the win-back team leader, Martinez managed by walking around and practicing just-in-time coaching. If she detected a team member struggling to describe the bank's CD program, for example, she would debrief with that person at the conclusion of the call. Also, she set a hands-on example by personally participating at times in the process—making calls, writing notes, and so on. This way she demonstrated to the team that both manager and staff were addressing the win-back challenge together.[1]

Outcomes and New Initiatives

Although the actual win-back numbers are considered proprietary and not for disclosure, Martinez confirmed that the program helped the bank regain deposits and win back valuable customers. Says Bill Cone, president of Norwest/New Braunfels, which benefited from the team's win-back efforts, "I think they did a tremendous job of proactively going after lost business. Even if you don't get it back immediately, you still rebuild a bridge and set up the opportunity for future communication."[2]

Moreover, within the Norwest twelve-bank region, the win-back program has spawned important win-back initiatives.

HYBRID WIN-BACK PROGRAMS. The same managers who were part of Martinez's original win-back team have started hybrid win-back programs in their respective branches. And the idea of multibranch teamwork is proving valuable. Recognizing the power of bringing a critical mass of staff together for a common cause, three banks (each represented by a manager and several personal bankers) join together at one branch location for a "Call Night." The purpose is to call both accounts recently classified as closed and accounts that have been classified as growable. Each bank subteam works with its own customer list. Emphasis is placed on enhancing the relationship rather than simply selling more banking products. These sessions last two hours. After each hour, there is a debriefing. Many of the same techniques from Martinez's original win-back program are used in the hybrid programs, including real-time recognition and just-in-time coaching. The personal bankers making the calls give the program rave reviews. Reports Martinez, "Three weeks after their first Call Night, a group of personal bankers asked if they could do Call Nights again. They're the ones who want to continue the program. It's not the manager saying that you have to do this. It's the personal bankers wanting to do this." And the word is spreading throughout the twelve-bank region. Other banks, learning how successful Call Nights have become, are starting similar initiatives. Says Martinez, "It's like the domino effect. They see the success and want to be part of it."[3]

MANAGEMENT OF REAL-TIME DEFECTION. Martinez's original win-back initiative also has pointed the way to on-the-spot win-back opportunities. Both a teller policy and a personal banker policy have now been established at Norwest to guide staff on how to best manage a customer who wants to close an account. For example, if the customer wants to move a $75,000 CD, Norwest trains the staff member to ask if there is anything the bank can do to retain the account. If a better rate is the reason, the staff member is trained on what steps to take to offer a competitive rate. Staff is trained on how to reinforce the bank's overarching message that says "your business matters to us and we don't want to lose you." Even if the account gets closed, the customer receives a follow-up phone call from the branch manager or a banker at that branch, thanking the customer for the business.[4]

RECRUITING AND MANAGING A PERMANENT WIN-BACK TEAM

More and more companies are creating permanent win-back staff positions in which skilled reps routinely work to recover lost customers or save customers on the brink of defection. In industries like telecommunications, win-back staff are important contributors to corporate performance and bottom-line profitability. But win-back is a challenging task and keeping a team of win-back frontliners focused and productive requires skillful management. That's why we sought out two veteran win-back managers, Catherine Sheeran from MCI and Fernando Roman from Cellular One, to learn about the best practices in recruiting, managing, and retaining permanent win-back staff.

Fernando Roman knows a thing or two about managing win-back staff. As director of revenue at Cellular One, he manages sixty win-back call center reps and seven supervisors. This twenty-year telecommunications veteran is a people person, and it shows. His win-back department is consistently among the top-rated departments at Cellular One in both employee satisfaction and overall staff retention. But don't think he's soft on performance. In the highly competitive cellular phone market, this win-back team consistently makes its numbers and then some.

Five years ago, Roman was recruited to Cellular One to manage the win-back area. The department was in chaos. Employee morale was low, turnover was high, and production numbers weren't being met. Staff members from other departments were reluctant to transfer in because of win-back's reputation of being a tough place to work. Today the department is very different. Most of the win-back positions are filled by internal candidates from other Cellular One departments. Moreover, win-back staff are in demand by other departments at Cellular One. They have well-developed analytical skills and proficiency in thinking on their feet, and these are skills much in demand throughout Cellular One.

As director of sales program management at MCI, Catherine Sheeran, along with her team, is responsible for arming the call center reps with the right offers and information to successfully attract, retain, save, and win back long distance customers. That's a tall order when you consider that MCI telemarketing centers call approximately eighty million households every year. The old adage "It's not just what you say, it's how you say it" is a reality that Sheeran and her cracker-jack messaging team of sixteen managers live with daily. Their approach can change in a flash. When a competitor introduces a par-ticularly aggressive offer, Sheeran and her managers go into high gear to evaluate the new competitive offer and, when warranted, develop counteroffers and counterpositions. And that's just the reactive side of the job. Proactive messaging is also constantly under development. For example, the win-back messaging team creates and tests win-back offers that reflect MCI's newest information about what attracts cus-tomers and what contributes to loss.

MCI win-back success rates are typically three to four times higher than new customer acquisition success rates. For example, if MCI were enjoying a 5 percent rate in converting prospects to new long distance customers, it could expect a 15 percent to 20 percent success rate in reactivating lost customers. Why this extraordinary difference? Because there are many drivers for switching from one carrier to another and it's so easy for customers to act on them. A husband switches, but when his wife learns about it, she wants to switch back. A customer switches because of an enticing competitive offer, but the savings don't stack up, and he wants to switch back. Or maybe the cus-tomer was "slammed" (switched without her knowledge), and she wants to switch back. In any event, win-back management is a well-tuned process at MCI and an important contributor to the corpora-tion's bottom line.

What are the critical issues to consider when managing a perma-nent win-back team? Here's what our experts told us.

Recruiting

"People appreciate something more when it's earned" is the underly-ing principle around Cellular One's recruitment program for win-back reps. Cellular One works closely with placement services to screen and select new recruits. Once on board, the new recruits are put on a forty-five-day trial period to see if the match with the job is there. Says Roman, "We're very honest about our policy. We make it clear to recruits that they earn the right through performance to become a full-time employee. That way we send the message that it's an honor to work for Cellular One."

Roman reports that the old adage "Birds of feather flock together" is true and that's why Cellular One offers a cash incentive plan for referrals made by win-back staff. The incentive varies according to the title and responsibilities of the position to be filled. Explains Roman, "People hang around with other people that are very much like them. If you have an employee with very high standards, and you get a referral, more likely than not, that referral is also of the same caliber." Moreover, these referrals come with reasonable expectations about the job. "They have heard from their friend what the job entails. So they are prepared. They also have a sense of loyalty and responsibility to their referral that you don't find with a recruit that comes off the street."[5]

At MCI, win-back reps are recruited from among seasoned reps in other parts of the company's call center. Reports Sheeran, "Win-back reps need an understanding of all of our call plans to work in this area. It requires a depth of knowledge about product that new reps just don't have."[6]

Training

Win-back training is a continual process, a journey of sorts that requires a continual layering of skills. For the new recruits at Cellular One, training begins with basic skill building in a classroom setting where they learn how to overcome objections, manage conflict, and so forth. But Cellular One wants to develop a well-rounded call center rep. That's why new recruits also get experience in taking general customer care calls in addition to their win-back training. Says Roman, "You can't just put someone on the phone with one specific skill set and say, "Sell this widget." You never know when a customer will ask a question about roaming or dropped calls or something completely different. The new recruit needs exposure to these things. So we try to give them enough appreciation for a wide range of topics so they can talk intelligently and know where to look for the answers."

Once the classroom training is complete, the new recruits are put on the phone taking live win-back calls for a couple of weeks. They struggle because they're new. But this struggle helps them identify where their weaknesses are. With this self-awareness now in hand, the new recruits are then paired with experienced reps and, through observation, start filling in the blanks on undeveloped win-back skills.

In addition, at least once a month Cellular One holds a continuation training class for all reps. This training protocol sends a clear message throughout the call center. "We never stop learning. We can always get better."

At MCI, win-back reps already have in-depth experience in the acquisition and prospecting side of the call center. Therefore, win-back training is specific to win-back issues. Training involves a half-day of classroom instruction with a heavy focus on regulatory compliance. From there, the rep starts to practice win-back techniques on the phones, often working one-on-one with an experienced win-back rep to polish the necessary skills.

Managing by the Numbers

Data collection is key to success. It's how a win-back team learns what's working and not working. Reports Roman, "We have an open-book policy on stats. 'Here's how many calls you made, this is how many renewals you obtained.' Everyone sees everyone else's numbers. This fosters friendly, informal competition between reps. They'll challenge each other with taunts: 'I'll bet you a mocha cappuccino at Starbucks that I can beat you on renewals today!'"

Because of the high incidence of success in getting lost customers back to MCI, it's very important that win-back reps keep their call volume high. This means that the rep must strike a careful balance between the need to successfully close the current call and the need to move on to the next call. MCI tracks the win-back success rates, by carrier, from one call cycle to the next. For example, it tracks the number of average win-backs per hour reps produce from customers who recently switched to Ameritech. In the next call cycle, this tracking helps establish a new sales target for Ameritech calls. Bonuses and incentives are based on beating this sales target. As at Cellular One, rep performance numbers are public knowledge. They are posted on a whiteboard each day.

Matching Reps with Win-Back Offers

MCI tests many offers to determine the ones that work best. One technique is a tiered promotion in which the rep starts with a value opening offer and then escalates higher if that's necessary to win back the lost customer. For example, Tier 1: "Would you come back to MCI?" Tier 2: "Would you come back for one thousand frequent traveler miles?" Tier 3: "Would you come back for one thousand miles and $15 worth of long distance calling?" Tier 4: "If you decide now, I can give you three thousand miles and $30 dollars." Another technique is to offer a low-tier offer on the initial call and, if it is declined, putting that lost customer into a five- to ten-day callback cycle. On the callback an escalated offer is made. Success with a particular model often depends on the representative. MCI has found that some reps are more comfortable than others with using an escalation offer. So both of these approaches can work, depending on the comfort level of the individual rep.

Keeping Standards High

When making call after call, people get tired and it's hard to sound enthusiastic on every win-back call. Like all people, reps have bad days. But as a win-back manager, Roman warns, you must make it clear that, while on the phone, reps are not allowed a bad day. "I tell the reps, 'If you need to yell at somebody, come into my office and yell at me. But when you're on the phone, I expect excellence.'" Roman stresses that it's critical that the win-back manager never lowers the departmental standards. "Sure, bad days happen to everyone, but not when talking to customers."

At Cellular One, each win-back rep is given specific quotas for the total number of calls and number of successful win-backs. When these goals are not met, a Cellular One supervisor works with the rep to isolate the problem areas. "We ask them how we can best help them improve," says Roman. "Is it coaching? How can we help?" Supervisors meet monthly one-on-one with reps to discuss performance. Cellular One practices progressive discipline. For example, a rep may be placed on final dismissal notice after failing to meet renewal quotas for three months in a row.

How do you distribute your superstars? Says MCI's Sheeran, "We have found having a mix of talent and performance levels in a group is better than having one superstar group. Spreading your talent around lifts the performance of all the calling, rather than segregating it to just one or two isolated pockets." At MCI, the call center work is conducted in two-week cycles. Between cycles, a high performer may be relocated to another group to boost that group's overall productivity. In MCI call centers, shifting of reps from one group to another is routine, and reps enjoy the prestige of being relocated to a caller group to help boost production.

Fighting Burnout

Burnout is the number one enemy of any win-back manager. What is the best defense? Provide job variety. For Cellular One, this means reps can take time off the phone to assist their supervisor in analyzing data that the team has collected. This way, win-back staff can see firsthand how the information they collected is used.

Like Cellular One, MCI uses job variety as a way to fight burnout. Rotating reps from a prospecting call bay to a win-back bay and vice-versa is common practice. When a rep wants a change and says, "I'm tired of calling prospects. Send me over to a win-back bay," MCI listens and responds.

Call Monitoring

"The purpose of call monitoring is to catch a win-back rep doing something right," declares Roman. "And we reward people for that." Recognizing that for most reps, call monitoring is a dreaded procedure fraught with big-brother-is-watching implications, Roman has turned the tool into a win-win situation for staff and Cellular One. Call monitoring enables staff to showcase their win-back skills and be rewarded for it. Call monitoring can also help identify additional training needed and let managers hear what customers are saying. Roman thinks "it's the most valuable tool we have. No computer in the world will give you as much insight as call monitoring will." But he is also quick to point out that monitoring is not coaching. Moreover, call monitoring takes managers away from the call center floor and affects their ability to be directly available to reps. It takes both call monitoring and coaching, says Roman, to manage a win-back team well.

MCI practices random call monitoring with all call center reps including win-back reps. Government telemarketing regulations are very strict, and violations carry heavy penalties. Therefore, call infractions are taken very seriously at MCI, and reps see the disciplinary action against those reps who don't play by the rules. Experience has taught MCI that the very fact the rep knows monitoring may be taking place keeps standards high.

Using Rewards

Cellular One has a companywide bonus plan tied to performance goals. When the goals are met, all Cellular One employees share in the bonus. Roman and his managers stress the role win-back calls play in making these goals. Beyond the bonus program, monetary rewards are given sparingly. Says Roman, "There was one month when we had a very big target, and I said, 'If we meet this renewal rate everyone gets an American Express check for $100.' And we met it, and everyone got one. But we don't do this very often. You don't want to precondition staff that every time you do this you're going to get $100."

"While money seems to be the most popular reward," says Sheeran, "we try to mix interesting things with the money." For example, awarding running shorts with an MCI Internet logo along with cash has worked well. Other MCI rewards for win-back staff include pizza for the win-back call bay and parking spaces close to the building assigned to high-performing staff members.

Nonmonetary rewards are an important way to keep win-back reps motivated at Cellular One as well. Team outings once a quarter are a mainstay at Cellular One, and "the reps decide where they want to go," says Roman. "We've gone to car races, bowling, whatever. It relaxes people, and it's a lot of fun."

Retaining Staff

With Cellular One's call center located in close proximity to Silicon Valley, Roman is acutely aware of the problems in retaining good win-back staff. The many reps he and his team work so hard to develop are prized bounty for many high-growth high-tech companies seeking talented salespeople. What's the best defense? Continually walking in the staff member's shoes. How does he do it? He is constantly out on the call center floor: "I'm always out with my representatives. We're always talking. I know what they did on the weekend. I can tell by their faces when they are having a bad day. When necessary, I'll invite them into my office to talk. The biggest thing you can do is show respect for them as people and not just as someone hired to make call after call."

"Retention of win-back staff is important to monitor," advises Sheeran. "If we keep a rep ninety days then we have a high probability they'll stay with us provided their compensation meets their expectations."

Managing the Managers

The four departments Roman manages are held accountable, collectively, for each other's results. Explains Roman, "Let's say we have a departmentwide goal of answering 80 percent of all incoming calls within twenty seconds. One department handling incoming calls is at 95 percent, and another is at 50 percent. This imbalance suggests that maybe one department is much more efficient or has employees sitting unproductive between calls. On the other side, I may be working people to death because there is call after call. My question to both managers is why aren't you helping each other to balance this?" Cellular One's quarterly manager evaluation holds managers accountable for process improvement. "I tell my managers that if something is broken, don't wait for someone else to fix it," says Roman. "If you think something is stupid, let's change it."

In his managerial ranks, Roman purposely mixes age groups. "We have very young supervisors and more mature supervisors. I think that people in the same age group tend to think alike, so I purposely combine people to get that different thought process going."

Developing and Monitoring Win-Back Offers

At Cellular One, the win-back team and marketing team work closely together to ensure promotional offers are as effective as possible. Reports Roman, "Yesterday I monitored five calls, and in four of the calls the same competitor was mentioned. I ran that information up to Marketing. We're always collecting information about what promotional offers are working and not working and what we're hearing about competitive offers. The promotional team takes that learning and factors it into planning new promotions. It's important that we work closely with Marketing to get the best results. The market changes so quickly and our data collection and learning make us all better planners."

Roman also knows that this close link between the win-back front line and the marketing department is not a given in every company.

"In other companies this teamwork doesn't always exist. In some cases, you have people in an ivory tower miles away from the customer race making decisions who haven't listened in on a real live call in over twenty years."

Feedback from the front lines also feeds MCI's promotion development. When a rep says, "I'm having a terrible day, and everyone is saying no because AT&T is giving them an hour of free calling," it serves as a call to action for Sheeran and the marketing team. They'll examine MCI's offer side by side with the competitor's offer and brainstorm on overcoming customer objections and on ways to increase the offer's appeal. These approaches then get tested by the reps and refinement continues as necessary.

Managing Through Tough Times

Win-back work is always demanding, but competitive pressures can make some periods harder than others. For example, when a competitor announces a very lucrative offer, win-back results can suffer. Knowing how to manage through these tough times is critical, and pulling the troops together as a team is one way to do it. Says Roman, "When we're going through bad streaks and customers are refusing our win-back proposals, we have lots of team huddles to discuss what the lost customers are saying and, when necessary, change our approach. That way we can learn from each other, and the win-back reps feel the support."

Cellular One and MCI win-back programs are solidly built on the principle that to maximize success, win-back reps must firmly believe they are the best in their industry. Management's job is to provide reps the tools they need to be the best. Training, knowledge of the latest competitive offers, well-conceived promotions that the customer finds valuable, incentive plans that reward stellar performance—all these factors play an important role in managing successful win-back programs.

SUMMARY

- Companies that are successful in winning back defecting customers realize that win-back is a unique task that requires unique skills.
- Winning back customers means making a commitment to gathering information, training staff, and dedicating time and

resources to develop a top-flight team of win-back representatives. Whether the win-back effort is temporary or permanent, it requires sound planning, training, and management.

- Special circumstances may require a major but temporary win-back effort.

- Certain industry patterns require permanent and constant win-back efforts.

- Any win-back effort can be only as successful as its people.

- Training, constant coaching, and team support are essential elements in developing successful win-back reps.

- Management awareness of reps' job stress and management participation in seeing that reps are well supported lead to successful win-back efforts.

- Win-back and marketing efforts can support each other, and they should be discussed by all involved in the process.

- Win-back reps who are well trained and successful can be among the most valued employees of any company.

PART TWO

Making Your Company Defection Proof

Because customer value requirements are constantly shifting, defection-proofing your customer base is a continuing challenge. The second half of this book offers you five tools for meeting this challenge. In Chapter Six, we examine how managing the customer life cycle can help keep your customers loyal. In Chapter Seven, we describe the key elements in designing a customer information system and collecting the right information. Chapter Eight presents strategies for targeting the right prospects, those most likely to become repeat customers. Chapter Nine discusses why companies are using customer-focused teams and how you can put these teams to work for you. Finally, in Chapter Ten we offer the best practices for building a fiercely loyal staff.

CHAPTER SIX

When You Think Your Customer Is Safe from Defection

Although it is a tough lesson to learn, it is important to realize that even your safest customers are constantly at risk of defection—and make your plans accordingly. As you read this chapter, you're probably thinking that you have at least a handful of customers or clients who are immune from the pull of the competition. Yet you're wrong. Sometimes your strongest advocates don't even realize themselves how vulnerable they are to leaving you. Here's one example of how easily it can happen.

"I have to be honest with you. I've been doing business with these people for a very long time and I like them." These are the words Norm Brodsky, CEO of CitiStorage, an archive-retrieval company in Brooklyn, New York, routinely hears from prospects as he starts his process for winning their business. In order to defection proof your company, you need to understand how a shrewd competitor like Norm Brodsky consistently wins away "happy" customers and keeps them. Here's one quick look:

Brodsky got the chance to pitch his firm's capabilities to a large accounting firm in New York City. Through a friend's connections, he met the partner who handles purchasing for the firm. "I knew going in that this firm would be a tough sell," he reports. "The partner had a close relationship with his current storage company, and he didn't try to hide it. He also told me that he planned to show them any proposal we made. My guess was that they wouldn't have to match our bid to keep the business; they'd just have to come close. In effect, he was using us to negotiate a better deal with them. That's all he really wanted."

At the initial meeting with the client, Brodsky asked to spend some time in the firm's record room. "Records management is my business, not yours," he told the client. "I can give you some suggestions on how to improve your system and generate some substantial savings in the process." The partner readily agreed, and Brodsky sequestered himself in the record room in search of internal and external savings opportunities. In the two hours he spent, Brodsky found plenty. He recontacted the partner and scheduled a follow-up meeting. Attended by three staffers from Brodsky's company and seven from the accounting firm, the meeting began at 5 P.M. one afternoon and ran for a surprising five hours! In that time Brodsky accomplished three goals. "First, I was educating the partner and his people about our business. I was teaching them how to save money by being smart consumers of archive-retrieval services. The more I told them, the more questions they asked. It was as if they'd never really understood what they were paying for. Second, I was letting them see what they weren't getting from their current supplier—without saying a negative word. I never bad-mouth my competitors to customers. Third, and most important, I was building trust. How? By giving away our ideas and expertise without any guarantees."

It took eight more months and many hours of discussion about the terms of a possible deal. All the while, the firm was also negotiating with its current vendor, Brodsky's competitor. In the end, however, Brodsky's firm won the contract, and the stunned competitor went from having a happy customer to having a lost customer.

How can you protect yourself against smart competitors like Brodsky? "You have to prove that you deserve a customer's loyalty more than your competitors do," he advises.[1] And that's what this chapter is all about.

WARNING: COMMODITY STATUS IS LOOMING!

Without a doubt, the very best way to avoid having to win back a customer is to ensure the customer doesn't leave to begin with. But the job of keeping customers loyal is harder than ever before. Why? Because today's customers clearly hold the power. There's overcapacity all over the world, and customers in turn have more choices. "Shift," as computer nerds like to say, "happens." And the shift to a marketplace with unlimited buyer choice can quickly transform your product or service into a commodity. With commodities, price is the only point of difference. That's precisely what's happening for many industries, and here's why.

We pointed out earlier that by the year 2002, some 43 percent of U.S. households are expected to be actively connected to the Web.[2] For business-to-business activities, the numbers are even higher. Talk to many brick and mortar CEOs, and they'll tell you a key corporate goal is to transition more of their off-line customers to on-line usage. Why? Because an on-line transaction costs dramatically less than a brick and mortar transaction, there is often less risk for service error, and the firm can more effectively capture and leverage customer information from an on-line transaction, to name just a few advantages. Certainly, the transactional advantages of e-commerce are appealing. But these transactional advantages also bring along a big commodity threat. By its very nature, e-commerce is training your customers to be less loyal. Here are four big reasons why:

• *Easy entry.* The Internet reduces barriers to entry for new competitors. Your customers now have easy access to suppliers worldwide, whereas before your competitors were more restricted. On-line banks, for example, now have virtual locations close to any customer without having to invest in a physical branch network.

• *Easy exit.* With Web shopping your customers are only two clicks away from your competitors at any time. Even the time once required for identifying alternative suppliers and visiting their Web sites has been dramatically compressed. Such sites as mysimon.com search dozens of Web sites for the item of interest and compare pricing as never before.

• *Competitive pricing.* Your competitors can become more cost competitive by sourcing their suppliers on-line and then passing those savings right along to your customers to win them away.

• *Buyer-driven pricing.* On-line consumer buying clubs and centralized purchasing are shifting additional power to the buyer. For example, at Web sites like volumebuy.com, consumers seeking common products or services pool their buying power and win supplier discounts for their members. At priceline.com, consumers now name their own prices for goods and services such as cars and airline tickets. A business-to-business site, worldoffruit.com, allows produce suppliers access to new markets and new customers, provided those suppliers are prepared to sell at less than list price.

When you think about the Internet, it's not the threat posed by other on-line companies in themselves that should alarm you. As we suggested in Chapter Four and will look at more closely later, many Web-based products and services are showing areas of softness in responsiveness and service. What should keep you awake at night, however, is the fear of being considered a commodity by your customers and prospects. As we've seen, the technological revolution is giving your buyers unprecedented access to real-time information about pricing and specs for products and services from all your competitors anywhere in the world. E-commerce is your worst nightmare if all you have is commodity status. Perhaps one-to-one marketing expert Don Peppers most aptly described the dire consequence of being perceived as a commodity in the minds of customers when he warned, "You'd better be prepared to match the lowest price of your stupidest competitor."[3]

With all these changes coming fast and furious, many companies are finding themselves ill equipped to defend their customer base against competitive assault and their products and services against commodification. Our research suggests the problems are widespread.

As you'll recall, we conducted a national customer value study comparing perceptions between purchasing agents on the one hand and sales managers and marketing managers on the other in business-to-business markets. When we asked the purchasing agents in our survey whether their suppliers of goods and services were commodity oriented or customer oriented, only 43 percent (or less than half) said their suppliers were customer oriented, providing optimum benefit and value. When we asked the customer versus commodity question of the sales and marketing folks who call on purchasing agents, the contrast was stark. A whopping 73 percent of the sales managers and 71 percent of the marketing managers believed their customers perceived them as customer oriented. What a disconnect! Some of the attributes on which purchasing agents graded suppliers much lower than the suppliers' sales managers and marketing managers did included these:

- Accurate billing
- Speed of follow-up to requests and inquiries
- Accessibility of supplier contact and service staff
- Rapport and relationship with supplier
- Flexibility and adaptability of supplier

Clearly, there are big disparities between what purchasing agents want and what marketing managers and sales managers are providing. Take note: these gaps create the classic conditions under which real value disappears and a customer reduces a supplier to commodity status! When this happens, all it takes is for a competitor to come along with an attractive offer, and the customer defects with little or no hesitation.

In order to keep that defection from happening, you have to keep on your toes. In the remainder of this chapter we explore two important strategies for keeping your customers safe from defection. First, we'll examine key ways to monitor the pulse of ever-changing customer needs. Secondly, we'll look at some of the latest developments for leveraging the customer life cycle.

TAKING THE PULSE OF CUSTOMER NEEDS

Our research has shown that a big factor in retaining customers and avoiding being perceived as just a commodity is the willingness to treat each customer or customer group as an individual and seek out information about what that individual customer wants and needs. Although the specifics may differ from industry to industry, the attitude and approach is generally the same. Let's look at some examples and a model for value delivery.

How Starbucks Tapped into Unmet Needs

What's behind big disconnects between companies and their customers? And why aren't firms better equipped to ward off the commodity threat and prevent customer defection? One fundamental problem is that many companies remain trapped in the past. Perhaps Karl Albrecht said it best in his book *The Northbound Train* when he wrote, "The longer you've been in business, the less likely you know what's going on in the minds of your customers."[4] Need convincing? Just ask the makers of Nescafé or Maxwell House coffees about the challenges of spotting coffee drinkers' emerging needs and how "the way it's always been" can get in the way of "how it could be."

What coffee manufacturer wouldn't lust for a loyal legion of coffee drinkers who visit their company-owned store eighteen times a month on average and spend on average $3.50 a visit? Those are exactly the stats that Starbucks now enjoys because it has revolutionized the way Americans buy coffee. With close to three thousand stores and still expanding, the company is producing sales and profits that have each grown more than 50 percent annually through much of the 1990s.

But things weren't always that way. In 1983, Starbucks was a tiny, little-known Seattle coffer retailer. While on vacation in Italy, however, Howard Schultz, now Starbucks chairman, was inspired by the romance and the sense of community he experienced in Italian coffeehouses and bars: "Starbucks sold great coffee beans, but we didn't serve coffee by the cup. We treated coffee as produce, something to be bagged and sent home with the groceries. We stayed one step away from the heart and soul of what coffee has meant throughout the centuries."

So Starbucks began to focus on building a coffee bar culture by opening coffeehouses modeled after the Italian ones. Equally important, however, was the company's strict control over the coffee itself, from the selection and procurement of the beans to their roasting and blending, all the way to the ultimate consumption. How does Starbucks deliver value and in doing so earn premium prices for its coffee? For starters, by appealing to the customer's five senses: the enticing aroma of the beans, the rich taste of the coffee, the product displays and attractive artwork adorning the walls, the contemporary music playing in the background, and even the cozy, clean feel of the tables and chairs. And don't forget those personable staffers with upbeat attitudes and friendly smiles.

Unlike the old consumer packaged goods model that used price reductions as loss leaders to attract triers and buyers, Starbucks approached the challenge in reverse. It looked deeply at what was missing in the coffee drinkers' value equation and then created ways to provide that value. Starbucks proved the axiom that price is important only in the absence of value and by creating supreme value, Starbucks consistently earns premium pricing.[5]

Value Is a Lot More Than Money

One industry that has historically provided low price at the expense of overall value, and has suffered for it, is the service station industry. Industry research shows that as many as 85 percent of service station customers are not loyal. Mobil Oil wanted to know why. The company conducted its own market research among over two thousand motorists and found that only 20 percent buy strictly on price. Although wanting competitive pricing, most buyers also desired things like more human contact, fast service, clean restrooms, ease of getting in and out of the facility, and attendants who recognize them. So Mobil went to work to improve its stations with better lighting and cleaner facilities and attendant friendliness and responsiveness. The company's initiatives were rewarded with revenues increasing by 15 to 20 percent at many of their stations.

"Our customer survey basically told us customers are looking for a fast, friendly convenient place to buy gasoline. We're trying to provide that," says Steve Lundgren, area manager for Mobil Oil. And this means continuing to look for fresh, new ways to add customer value. For example, the customer's desire for fast service has led Mobil to introduce Speedpass, a system that enables customers to stop at the service station, pump and pay for their gas, and be on their way in record time. Similar to state-of-the-art electronic payment systems used to reduce waiting time at highway tollbooths, Speedpass technology uses an electronic transponder attached to the motorist's key chain or affixed to the rear window of the car. When the customer pulls up to the gasoline bay, the electronic system located in the pump "talks" with the key chain or window tag, provides instant access to the grade of gasoline the customer selected when she enrolled in the program, and bills her credit card automatically. Customers have quickly embraced the new technology. More than one million customers were using Speedpass just nine months after its introduction. Today, approximately two million customers use their Speedpass devices at gas pumps at more than thirty-five hundred locations.

What effect has Speedpass had on customer loyalty to the company? According to Mobil, a Speedpass customer makes an average of one fill-up per month more than a non-Speedpass customer does.[6] One independent research study reports Speedpass customers are "twice as loyal to the brand as any other type of customer."[7]

Value and the Kano Model

Understanding the customer's perception of value is a continual learning process for all of us. Customer's needs may lead them to put different values on things that might seem similar in some ways but that to customers have critical differences. Consider the lesson learned by Morris the auto mechanic. He was removing the cylinder heads from the motor of a car when he spotted the famous heart surgeon Michael DeBakey, who was waiting for the service manager to take a look at his Mercedes. Morris shouted across the garage, "Hey DeBakey! Is dat you? Come on ova' here a minute." The surgeon walked over to where Morris the mechanic was working on the car. Morris straightened up, wiped his hands on a rag, and asked argumentatively, "So Mr. Fancy Doctor, look at dis here work. I also open hearts, take valves out, grind 'em, put in new parts, and when I finish dis baby will purr like a kitten. So how come you get da big bucks, when you an' me is doing basically da same work?" DeBakey leaned over and whispered to Morris, "Try doing it with the engine running."

Delivering value on your customers' terms is critical to your success in the marketplace. The penalties for underdelivering and overdelivering value can be severe. Provide too little service or the wrong kind of service, and your customers will defect; provide too much service, even of the right kind, and your company will go bankrupt after pricing itself right out of the market.

Some of today's most groundbreaking work on effectively delivering value comes from Noriaki Kano. Kano is a professor at the Science University of Tokyo and an international consultant and lecturer on quality management, marketing, and statistics. He is well recognized for his analysis of what he calls *attractive quality* versus *must-be quality,* also known as the Kano model.

Kano has challenged the conventional customer satisfaction beliefs that the better a company delivers on each product or service attribute, the more satisfied its customers will be. He finds instead that not all service and product performance is equal in the eyes of the customer. Some performance creates higher levels of loyalty than others. Kano's model defines three performance levels:[8]

• *Basic.* This is expected or must-have performance. For an overnight shipping firm like Federal Express, for example, accurate billing and prompt telephone assistance are basic services. Failure to deliver these basic performance factors will result in customer dissatisfaction. Doing them well, however, will not increase customer loyalty because customers perceive them as minimum requirements for performance.

• *Expected.* This is the level of performance that the leading suppliers in an industry provide. For FedEx, delivery by 10 A.M. on the next business day is an example of expected service. Providing expected products or services results in neither increased nor decreased customer loyalty because most primary competitors offer these things. As a market leader, a company must do these things to simply stay even with the competition.

• *Unanticipated.* This is the exciting, surprising, and attractive level of performance. Unanticipated value increases customer loyalty. It is what makes companies different from their competitors. As a company begins to deliver at this performance level, customer loyalty accelerates. FedEx was the first to offer on-line customer tracking via computer, for example. Customers could track where their package was during transit and the time at which the receiver accepted it. At the time of its introduction, this was considered a major, unanticipated service perk. Since first introducing its tracking system, FedEx has added other tools to improve tracking effectiveness, such as providing drivers with handheld computers and transmitting devices. The more unanticipated value a company provides the deeper the loyalty. Says FedEx chairman Frederick Smith, "I don't think that we understood our real goal when we first started Federal Express. We thought that we were in the transportation of goods. In fact, we were selling peace of mind."[9]

How a Food Store Operates at the Unanticipated Level

When you think about not-to-be-missed travel destinations for central Texas visitors, several sites in Austin immediately come to mind: the state capitol and rotunda, the University of Texas campus, the Lyndon Baines Johnson Library, maybe the governor's mansion. But who would expect a grocery store to be on the list? But by understanding grocery shoppers' definition of value and operating at the unanticipated level of performance, Central Market has earned a place on that list.

When UT student Stephanie Larson wanted to entertain her parents who were visiting from South Dakota, she took them to Central Market. After spending more than two hours in the store, Paul and Nickey Larson described it as the highlight of their weeklong trip. "I've never seen anything like this anywhere," Paul Larson said of this store that offers rare foods and extraordinary selection—including eight varieties of bananas, three hundred brands of beer, and a fresh olive bar.

Strolling the well-merchandised aisles, shoppers like the Larsons are fascinated by unique produce and hundreds of sauces and products that simply can't be found anywhere else. What they don't see are many of the standard items most grocery stores carry. Coffee is a case in point. Although there's no Maxwell House coffee on the shelves, there is a coffee section with enough variety to challenge even the nation's most upscale coffeehouses. And breads? Don't look for the Wonder brand, but be prepared to choose between challah and tortillas, bagels and babkas.

In fact, when sales reps for giants like Coca-Cola, General Foods, and Nabisco called on senior food buyers for the parent company of this flagship store prior to its opening, they were in for a shock. The sixty-three-thousand-square-foot store planned to carry only limited quantities of their products. Instead, the store would be stocking more exclusive, hard-to-find products and lots of specialty items.

Central Market is designed around the Kano model's three levels of value, and that design is paying off in fiercely loyal customers. At the basic level, the store offers the standard products, services, and operational functions such as express checkout and debit-card machines—the things customers take for granted when they do their food shopping. The expected level is evident in ordinary take-home foods like cooked chicken and salads from a salad bar. The excitement, the unanticipated value, is generated in the vast selection of unusual foods and in products and services like gourmet take-home fast foods, a pasta bar, a flower shop, and an in-store cafe with numerous stations featuring everything from Cajun to cowboy cuisine.

On the weekends Central Market offers live music on the patio. There's even a full curriculum of gourmet cooking classes—patrons can learn to make the perfect pesto or send their children for baking lessons. Unlike most grocery stores, where customers are hurrying to get in and out as quickly as possible, Central Market has effectively slowed people down and enabled them to make the shopping experience more like an outing, someplace you would want to take visitors from another city.[10]

According to Central Market vice president John Campbell, operating in the unanticipated is an integral part of the store's core strategy for earning customer loyalty. "Our commitment is to give the Austin shopper what they're looking for and some things they've never asked for," says Campbell. "Nobody ever asked for Central Market."[11]

WAYS TO SEARCH OUT VALUE

Clearly, it is essential to learn what your customers truly value. Attending to customer feedback, conducting surveys, listening to complaints, and asking the right questions about customer loyalty are all ways of discovering customer wants and needs (see Figure 6.1; also see Appendix A for a more detailed explanation of the PACE process).

Attending to Customer Feedback

The customer's value definition is always changing and no one knows that better than Adrian Slywotzky, vice president of Mercer Management Consulting and the author of a trio of books examining the quest for value in a rapidly shifting business landscape. For Slywotzky the question any business should ask is not the proverbial "What business are we in?" Instead, insists Slywotzky, the real question is, "'What is the next-generation business model that we should be running?' That is, the one that best responds to customer priorities and is so resource-efficient that it becomes highly profitable."[12]

No one asks that question better than John Chambers, CEO of Cisco Systems, a maker of hardware and software for global data networks. Cisco dominates its markets and has a market capitalization that is second only to Microsoft's. Leading the company since 1995, Chambers spends 40 percent of his time with customers. He focuses particularly on customers who are unhappy and in some state of attrition to understand why Cisco isn't measuring up and in what direction the customer is headed. He gives his private office number to customers and urges them to call if they have problems. Every evening, he reviews the day's results for fifteen to twenty critical accounts among Cisco's one hundred thousand global customers, accounts that have been flagged as "at risk" or requiring "top guy" attention. Says Slywotzky, "The best business design innovators are always outside

Figure 6.1. PACE: A Proven Process for Searching Out Customer Value.

Do you want real insight on ways to build and sustain customer loyalty? Our Customer Loyalty Compass can help you get the answers you need. It's a research process involving four key steps: prepare, assemble, comprehend, and employ (PACE). A more detailed summary is given in Appendix A.

Step 1: *Prepare* for the research process

Before anything can be done to encourage customer loyalty, a business must first know what makes a customer loyal and what factors exist in the company that discourage loyalty. Start by interviewing management and staff as well as reviewing existing information, including prior research, sales reports, complaint data, and so on. Determine (1) what the company knows about its customers and competitors and (2) what insights are missing.

Step 2: *Assemble* customer needs and wants

Use qualitative research methods to uncover customer-defined needs, expectations, problems, and complaints. With this information, you can design your quantitative customer questionnaire.

Step 3: *Comprehend* customer priorities

Use your questionnaire to survey randomly selected customers and identify customer loyalty drivers. Analyze the survey data, employing user-friendly graphics and models that prioritize your firm's performance areas according to improvement needs and opportunities.

Step 4: *Employ* your findings

You will now have a clear understanding of what is driving customer value and loyalty. Based on your research findings, develop action plans, programs, and processes for improving customer loyalty.

---

listening to and arguing with their customers. They get more of the data directly, to understand what the next two or three patterns of strategic change in their industry are going to be. And then it takes a courageous manager to say, 'The thing that has carried us so far is no longer going to be enough.'"[13]

Remember Granite Rock and its co-CEO Bruce Woolpert from Chapter Four? Woolpert started a customer value "listening tour" for Granite Rock back in 1986. His motivation? Sustainability. Other people had managed to bring Granite Rock to its eighty-sixth year, and the question on Woolpert's mind was what he and his team were going to do to ensure that it continued for another eighty-six years. Years of experience in the electronics industry had taught Woolpert just how competitive the business landscape really is and that to thrive, his firm needed answers to hard questions, not the soft ones. But learning how to solicit that information turned into a lesson all its own. Explains Woolpert, "We went out and we asked customers, some of whom had been customers for seventy-five years, please tell us what we're not doing well. Now I have to tell you that customers were very reluctant to say something. The customer starts talking about the weather, kids, etc., trying to change the subject." But Woolpert learned two ways to cope: (1) stay seated and (2) stay on the subject. "It becomes uncomfortable for you," says Woolpert, "you want to get up. But it's when the uncomfortable level reaches a peak that the customer says, 'There is one thing I'd like to tell you.' That's the moment of honesty," explains Woolpert, "because the customer is basically saying, 'I'm going to tell you the truth about the first thing your company could do better and if you take that successfully, then I'll tell you number two, three, and four.' So you learn to sit quietly, keep your mouth closed and listen very carefully."

What Woolpert learned by sitting quietly and listening was that his customers perceived his company as doing a very good job of providing the basic and expected services but as being pretty weak on the unexpected: "If you asked us to supply a product during normal operating hours, which in the construction industry are from seven in the morning until three-thirty in the afternoon, we were great at that. But if you asked us for something special, like something after hours, or a special product, you would typically get the runaround."

Customers weren't told outright that special services weren't available; instead they were told such excuses as "I'll check" or "I can't find a supplier" or "I'll call back." But then there was never a follow-up. Woolpert gives this example: "I remember a customer called and asked us to deliver concrete to them adjacent to San Francisco Bay, at low tide, Sunday morning at 2 A.M. And this customer told me that we had relayed to them all of the difficulties we would have in meeting those needs. 'Do you know how difficult it will be to find a plant operator who wants to work Sunday? How will we possibly find mixer drivers who want to work Sunday? etc.' And so eventually the customer says, 'The heck with it, you make me tired just listening to you.'"

The problem with not meeting special needs is complex. Not only is the customer disappointed and perhaps a little disgusted that you weren't able to meet his specific need, he also becomes ripe for the picking by your competitor. Granite Rock's thinking on special orders began to shift: "In our industry, it could be very dangerous to only meet the standard needs and wants of our customers. For example, that guy who wanted concrete on Sunday morning that we gave excuses to, would probably go to Joe's Concrete for his order. To the customer, that special business is crucial and he may start thinking, 'Well, if Joe will do that for me, why not give Joe all my business?'"

As a result of the conversations with customers, Woolpert and his team decided it was time to make a change. Granite Rock instituted a new standard service policy. It is called "Yes we will." It means that anytime a customer asks for a special service, as long as it's not illegal or immoral, Granite Rock will do it. In addition, to make the new service policy work, every person in Granite Rock has had to become "a custom service delivery representative. And that means that everyone in our company needs to know our products thoroughly to be able to deliver on these special needs and requests." One result of the new policy was that "immediately when we started implementing 'Yes we will' and told our customers about it, our telephone started to ring." Another result is that there is much better communication now between Granite Rock and its customers. Because it is constantly in contact with customers about special needs, the company knows how customers are changing, what their needs are and how these needs are evolving, and how they perceive Granite Rock is meeting those needs. As a result, the company is ready to move quickly when any problem begins to arise.[14]

Paying attention to special needs is key to finding out what trends are at work in any industry. The first time a customer asks for a low-calorie salad dressing at a restaurant should be a signal to that restaurant that diet matters to people. And yet every single day, people walk into businesses, ask for special needs and wants, and no one writes them down. These requests are the best source of market research information that any company could have.

Using Customer Surveys

Formal customer surveys can help identify and prioritize those elements of value delivery that most leverage loyalty and also identify the elements that cause customer attrition.

In addition to carrying out face-to-face evaluation sessions with clients, Granite Rock also uses customer surveys to find out what's important. Again, the findings have changed the way the company does business. Explains Woolpert, "We thought in the concrete business what was really important to the contractor was the quality of the concrete. We were very proud of the fact that the concrete inside our Granite Rock mixer truck was the best in the world. It is. But when we surveyed our customers, they said the most important thing is that the concrete arrive on time. It suddenly became clear to us that, for years, the dispatching role and the kinds of things that UPS does well, were not priorities for us."

As a result, delivery time became Granite Rock's number one priority, and it started measuring arrival times much more closely. When the company started paying attention, people began watching the clock. They allow themselves only fifteen minutes on either side of the promised time. Says Woolpert, "That means we're on time if we're fifteen minutes early or fifteen minutes late. And we went from 65 percent on-time delivery to 95 percent on time. Meanwhile, our competitors haven't changed."

But the survey taught Woolpert even more about how the customer defines value. "We thought we had done a great job after we had done our mining process and run the rock through the plant, and created these beautiful, uniform stockpiles of rock." But customer research taught Woolpert and his company that getting customer trucks loaded and back on the road was more important to this segment of customers. "And so we developed a new system called Granite Express with our benchmarking partner Wells Fargo Bank. Our new system automatically loads trucks like an ATM machine." The truck driver simply swipes an authorization card that closely resembles a credit card, pulls the truck in, and a machine loads the truck automatically. This loading service is available to drivers twenty-four hours a day, seven days a week. Woolpert reports that "it used to take twenty-four minutes from the time you left the public road to get loaded, get your sales tag, and be out on the public road again. We've got that down to seven minutes now. And in California, a trucking minute is worth about $1.20, so that seventeen minute savings is now something that cities and counties and contractors and individuals who come into our quarries can benefit from."

Granite Rock's payoff for better alignment with customer value has been significant. Market share has doubled. And, explains Woolpert, "We did it not by cutting prices, not by stealing our competitors' salespeople, or any of those kinds of things. We did it by changing ourselves."[15]

Hearing Customer Complaints

Our earlier books have examined in depth the fact that the more customers complain, have their problems resolved, and feel positive about the resolution experience, the stronger their likelihood to repurchase and recommend. Yet most customers don't complain. For example, Hepworth & Company, a Canadian marketing research and consulting firm, found that in industries like financial services, food and beverages, and pharmaceuticals, between 55 percent and 90 percent of customers never complain.[16] But don't think it's because of a shortage of complaints. Consumer advocacy groups have determined that over 50 percent of the buying public have one or more complaints about the products and services they purchase. In business-to-business situations, the stats are just as bad. So why won't customers complain to their suppliers? Here are seven key reasons:

- They don't know where or how to complain to the supplier.
- They are too busy and can't, or won't, take the time.
- They consider complaining an annoyance they would rather avoid.
- They don't believe the company will do anything about it anyway.
- They don't see any direct value or benefit to them from complaining.
- They fear some postcomplaint hostility or retaliation on the part of the company.
- They can get what they want from a competitor, so it's simpler and easier to switch.

As a result of this hesitancy on the part of customers to make their dissatisfaction known, it is necessary for businesses to constantly seek out information about customers' experiences. The successful business will be aggressive every day in uncovering complaints and making the most of what it learns. Here's how:

- *Make it easy for customers to complain.* Regular customer meetings, toll-free numbers, e-mail, write-in spaces on payment vouchers, and opportunities for dialogue with a representative at point of purchase are some ways to encourage customers to share.

• *Train customer contact staff to use assumptive questioning for uncovering complaints.* For example, the front-desk staff at the Renaissance Hotel in Orlando asks departing guests at checkout this question: "What's one thing we could have done better to improve your stay?" Assume customers will not complain, and look for ways to help them speak up.

• *Get resolution quickly.* Hepworth & Company found that most complaints required three contacts for resolution. What's worse, only about one-third of the customers in that cross-industry research reported positive resolution of their issues, with high-tech companies being the biggest culprits.[17]

• *Positively acknowledge every complaint.* By mail, telephone, or e-mail, let the customer know his feedback was appreciated. Avoid form letters. Instead, send communications that demonstrate a real person is behind the acknowledgment. At Ben & Jerry's, for instance, every letter and contact receives a written thank-you.

• *Enforce a closed-loop complaint management system.* Ensure complaints are routinely gathered and analyzed for insights. Then loop that learning back into systems and processes for continual improvement. One definition of insanity is doing the same things again and again while expecting a different response. The closed-loop complaint system helps remove the possibility of that kind of behavior in your business.

• *Conduct customer loyalty research to truly understand customer value.* Ongoing one-on-one dialogue with customers about what you're not doing well will give you an edge. But couple that input with some broad-scale quantitative customer surveys, and you will have a real value road map to follow.

Recognizing the Difference Between Satisfaction and Loyalty

As you seek out customer values, it's important to ask questions that help you distinguish between customer satisfaction and customer loyalty, as ClubCorp learned a few years ago.

There's no hotter sport in the new millennium than golf, and the world leader in delivering golf, private club, and resort experiences is Dallas-based ClubCorp. Founded in 1957, this $1.4 billion corporation owns and manages more than 230 properties on five continents.

Some of the firm's crown jewel courses include Pinehurst, the world's largest golf resort and site of the 1999 U.S. Open, and Mission Hills Country Club, home of the Nabisco Dinah Shore Classic. But golf is just half of the story. Dining services are a big part of the firm's livelihood. It annually prepares fourteen million meals in seven hundred dining rooms, including the Metropolitan Club in the Sears Tower in Chicago, the City Club in San Francisco, and the Capital Club in Beijing.

Watching closely over membership loyalty and retention is Kathy O'Neal, ClubCorp senior vice president of marketing. O'Neal and her team monitor member termination very closely for clues about new ways to keep members and prevent defection. The year 1998 provided some important insights. Terminations showed that 25 percent of the members who had resigned had been members for a year or less. Digging further, O'Neal and her team discovered that those members who resigned for reasons other than bad debt (bankruptcy), death, and relocation (moving to a city where ClubCorp does not have a club) left for two key reasons: discontent with club services and nonuse.

Anxious for more insights on how to improve services to eliminate both discontent and nonuse, O'Neal looked at the data from previous member satisfaction surveys, a tool ClubCorp had been using for years. Reports O'Neal, "The survey asks what do you think about the locker rooms, what do you think about the quality of the service, what do you think about the quality of the food, what do you think about the club manager? We asked about all of the tangibles. What we discovered was 95 percent of those members who left and had taken that survey gave us very high marks on the satisfaction level." What O'Neal quickly concluded was that the survey wasn't asking the right questions. "We weren't asking about intangibles like clubby atmosphere, the ability to meet other people of similar interests, the ability to network for business and social purposes. These are often the primary reasons why members are joining. What it told us was we needed to throw our member satisfaction survey out of the window and develop a member loyalty survey. Satisfaction was not enough to keep members. They are satisfied and still going out the door. We need to drive them to the loyalty stage."[18]

There's lots to know about conducting well-designed loyalty research. To do it right, we urge you to seek help from research experts who have strong track records in conducting loyalty research. Here are some guidelines to help keep you on task:

• *Choose the ideal quantitative survey method for your circumstances from among telephone surveys, mail surveys, Web-based surveys, and so on.* Choose the method that (1) maximizes response rate probability, (2) enables you to best capture rich feedback on open-ended questions (which require more than a yes or no answer), and (3) avoids respondent self-selection bias, allowing you to survey a truly random and representative sample of the respondents you want.

• *Ask customers how they would rate your performance rather than how satisfied they are.* We find performance is a more rigorous, disciplined, and reliable overall measure. Respondents typically give higher scores on satisfaction-based questions and lower scores on performance. To avoid inflated scores, use performance-based questions.

• *Measure your customer's likelihood to repurchase and likelihood to recommend.* What is the probability that your customer will buy more, less, or about the same from you in the future? Would your customer pass your name along to another person?

• *Use an 11-point scale (0–10) for written surveys and a 5-point scale (1–5) for telephone surveys.* Respondents can more easily deal with an 11-point scale in a written survey; a 5-point scale is easier to comprehend over the phone. For example, on the phone you might ask, On a 5-point scale, how would you rate our firm's performance overall, where 5 is excellent and 1 is poor? To get necessary detail, ask, Why do you say that? on scores of 8 or below on an 11-point rating scale and 4 or below on a 5-point scale.

• *Use customer-defined attributes.* Employ qualitative focus groups or in-depth interviews to identify the right attributes to ask questions about. Don't rely on self-defined standard industry attributes. Your marketplace is undergoing rapid change and customer needs are evolving. Include performance attributes pertaining to things with tangible results, things like time, cost, accuracy, and completeness, but also address intangibles like communication, relationship, reputation, and reliability. Measure importance to the customer and performance ratings on all attributes.

• *Focus on top scores.* For example, in calculating your firm's performance rating, calculate the percentage of respondents who gave your firm a 5 on a 5-point scale. This is a more stringent measure than counting respondents who gave you both 5's and 4's, for example. Above all, avoid using mean or average scores. For example, an average score of 4 on a 5-point scale looks pretty good, right? But it's possible that if you looked behind that 4, you would find that 40 percent of the respondents gave a 5, 20 percent gave a 4, and another 40 percent gave only a 3. You should be very concerned about the loyalty of those 3's; yet with an average score of 4, you might never look at the scores at each level.

• *Ask about complaints.* Learn what the complaints are, whether they are being voiced, and how well you are doing at resolving them.

• *Before beginning your research process, ensure that your research methodology will produce actionable findings.* Ask your research team these questions: How will the findings be presented? How will I know what actions to take based on the findings? For example, customers' ratings of the importance of each attribute and of your performance on each attribute can be mapped on a matrix to indicate relative value, as illustrated in Figure 6.2.

The upper-left quadrant in the figure contains attributes with low performance scores and high modeled importance scores. Modeled

Figure 6.2. Customer Motivation Matrix.

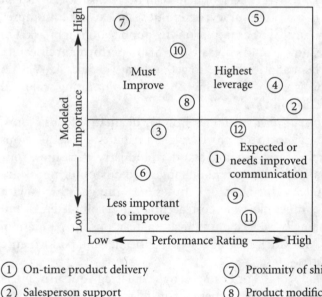

(1) On-time product delivery

(2) Salesperson support

(3) Customer service

(4) Products true to specifications

(5) Price

(6) Product quality

(7) Proximity of shipping points

(8) Product modification flexibility

(9) Product development leadership

(10) Product performance

(11) Billing services

(12) Delivery flexibility

importance means the degree of relationship between attribute performance levels and future purchase intent (for each attribute and relative to each other). Modeled importance results typically offer more insights than standard importance ratings because the former are based on a mathematical importance formula called simple regression or correlation analysis. This means that rather than simply relying on a respondent's reported importance ranking, this mathematical model can help determine the attribute's real importance in relation to the respondent's intent to repurchase. Within this upper-left quadrant, there is a high correlation with negative intended action (that is, customers are unlikely to remain loyal given these performance ratings), so the company must target attributes in this quadrant for improvement.

The upper-right quadrant contains attributes with high performance scores and high modeled importance scores. There is a high correlation with positive intended action (that is, customers are likely to remain loyal given these ratings), so these are attributes that offer probable positive leverage for the company and that it should continue to emphasize.

The lower-right quadrant contains attributes with high performance scores and low modeled importance scores. These attributes, although performed well, have relatively little leveraging potential. They may represent areas about which the company needs to communicate better, or they may simply be expected attributes that must be performed well but need not necessarily be improved.

The lower-left quadrant contains attributes with low performance scores and low modeled importance scores. There is a low correlation with positive intended action, so these are the attributes that provide little value to the customer or the company. If possible, the company should downscale or even eliminate activities in these areas and instead divert resources to the attributes needing the most attention or offering the most opportunity.

LEVERAGING THE CUSTOMER LIFE CYCLE

Customer loyalty doesn't happen overnight. It's built and earned one customer experience at a time. In keeping your customers safe from defection, it's important to recognize that customers typically evolve through loyalty stages in the customer life cycle. For off-line customers, six stages can be defined:[19]

1. *Suspect:* anyone who might possibly buy your product or service
2. *Prospect:* someone who has both a need for your product or service and the ability to buy
3. *First-time customer:* someone who has bought from you one time
4. *Repeat customer:* someone who has bought from you two or more times
5. *Client:* someone who buys everything you have to sell that she can possibly use
6. *Advocate:* someone who buys everything you have to sell that she can possibly use and encourages others to buy from you

On-line customers can evolve through seven stages in their customer life cycle: (1) surfer, (2) first-time site visitor, (3) repeat visitor, (4) first-time buyer, (5) repeat buyer, (6) client, and (7) advocate. Stage 3 may be skipped. However, an on-line customer may move from surfer to first-time site visitor to first-time buyer in one site visit. In any event, the most effective relationship management programs are those that are organized around specific customer loyalty milestones such as these stages and that continually "grow" a customer from one level of loyalty to the next.

Effectively managing the customer life cycle is a critical part of any firm's retention program. Our previous books on customer loyalty have examined basic ways to leverage this life cycle. In the remaining pages of this chapter we highlight some of the newest developments in turning first-time customers into repeat customers, clients, and advocates.

How Not to Turn First-Time Buyers into Repeat Customers

What happens early counts. Now more than ever, customers have a strong sense of the monetary value they represent for a vendor. And they expect big things in return. Some customers take baby steps to becoming high-value customers, but Sara and Jim Bonner went from prospects to high-value clients in just one meeting. Sara's and Jim's banks had been bought up by big regionals, so the couple decided to move all their accounts to a large bank with branches in Manhattan (where they work) and Connecticut (where they live). Their bank of choice waived fees for a year as part of a program to attract new customers like Sara and her spouse. Over the course of a few months, the Bonners, both self-employed, moved all their accounts to their new bank. "We had a business account, a tax savings account, two personal checking accounts, one joint account, and three credit cards. We consolidated a lot of business there. So we thought it was great."

Several months later the Bonners were heading to London on vacation. About a week before departing, Sara Bonner received a client check for $17,000. She deposited it in her personal account thinking that would give her plenty of money for ATM withdrawals during the trip. When she returned, she would distribute the remaining cash into other accounts.

Soon after arriving in London Sara stopped at an ATM machine for some cash. She was declined. When she called the bank, a personal banking rep looked up her account and told her a ten-day hold had been placed on the check. "The woman said, it was a three-day hold for being an out-of-state check and then a further five-day hold because the check was over $5,000. Now mind you, when I add three and five, I only get eight and they put a ten-day hold on it. But I wasn't in any position to argue."

Sara found herself "angry and frustrated. I've done marketing consulting for banks, and I know that I was the perfect new customer. I had done everything any banker would want a new customer to do. They want you to consolidate all of your accounts with them. They want you to put both your business and personal with them. They want you to have your credit cards with them. I did all that stuff and I got absolutely nothing for it."

Upon returning home, Sara got in touch with the bank again. "I called my account manager, and she was not the least bit apologetic. She said the bank had to protect itself against bounced checks. And that because of strict policy about commingling personal and business accounts, it made no difference that I had ample funds in other accounts." Sara added, "Funny, they sure didn't talk that way when they were trying to get us to consolidate everything together as a new customer."

What's next for the Bonners? Sara is diligently doing research to identify another bank. This time she'll look hard for a bank with a program for people who are self-employed or have small businesses and where she can be sure this kind of thing won't happen again. She declares, "For the time being I am still [the bank's customer]. But talk about no loyalty; they have already lost me."[20]

How to Turn First-Time Buyers into Repeat Customers—The Right Way

One of the most powerful strategies for turning first-time buyers into repeat customers is *wondrous entanglement*. It means learning more and more about the new buyer's needs and then matching your products and services against those needs. The goal of wondrous entanglement is to earn the customer's dependence on your firm in as many ways as possible. In effect, you are building a strong partnership with the customer over time, and in doing so you are getting your products and services wonderfully entangled in the customer's day-to-day operations.

Practicing wondrous entanglement means executing a three-part process:

1. Identify all of your products and services that might possibly benefit your new buyer.

2. Over time, motivate your new customer to use as many of your products and services as possible.

3. Prove to your customer that your products and services provide tremendous value in ways that can't be found anywhere else.

The Bonners' new bank was well on its way to practicing the first two steps of the wondrous entanglement strategy. Then it failed miserably in the third step (proving that the Bonners' account consolidation would truly make their lives easier), and it lost these new and valuable customers because of that failure.

Here are three examples of companies that have mastered the process of turning first-time customers into repeat customers.

CLUBCORP DOES IT BETTER. One firm that understands the concept of wondrous entanglement and has built successful internal processes around it is ClubCorp, introduced earlier in this chapter. Experience has taught ClubCorp that the first year of membership is critical for anchoring long-term loyalty. Members' usage habits are often formed in the first twelve months, and ClubCorp knows that the more activities and club services the member becomes involved in, the more likely that member is to remain. Because of this understanding, Club-Corp uses various tools to encourage participation and activity in its golf and city clubs. One of its newest initiatives is member mentoring programs. All members are brought in by a sponsor, and during the initial enrollment process, the club's membership director learns more about the interests and needs of the new member. With this information, the membership director now matches the new member with an existing member who can act as a mentor. The mentor may have similarities to the new member in family, work, or some other area. At least once a quarter, the mentor, as a guest of the club, invites the new member to lunch or to attend a special club event and at that time makes as many introductions to other members as possible. The mentor is also asked to call the member once a month to see how things are going. All of this is designed to integrate the new member more quickly into the club.

Senior Vice President Kathy O'Neal told us about a recent member-mentoring match: "There was this neat lady who was joining one of our clubs. Her husband had passed away recently, and she wanted a safe environment in which to meet more people and have a social life. The membership person knew a wonderful member who had lost her husband a year ago. So she got them together at lunch, and the two ladies became fast friends. That's what we're looking for. We're looking to drive long-lasting relationships that will make a major difference in peoples' lives and, in turn, drive loyalty for us."

ClubCorp communicates carefully with new members as well. Important tools include a club newsletter and new member access to ClubCorp's virtual club Web site, featuring a virtual pro shop, a photo gallery, member forums, golf trivia, a schedule of member outings, and even a wine cellar. Says O'Neal, "It's always about providing value-added for members, both new and established."

But don't think all this focus on new members means established members get ignored. When an established member's activity level drops, ClubCorp also takes action. For example, a club manager might have the accounting office pull the names of members who have not used the club in the past 120 days. The manager then goes through a five-point program for contacting those inactive members and reigniting interest. ClubCorp knows that nonuse is frequently a key reason why a member terminates. So this five-point program is designed to remind members about the pleasures of using club services. Managers may offer complimentary dinner vouchers, tickets to a special club event, and the like. Usage is carefully tracked, and if the member remains unresponsive, other options within the five-point program are considered.[21]

Such customer personalization and usage tracking are even easier for Web customers. Yet, as we discussed in Chapter Four, a 1998 Jupiter/NFO research study suggests that many Web sites are slow to personalize their communication with customers.

GET FEARLESS WITH YOUR OFFERINGS. It's a fact: you can't expect to practice wondrous entanglement with your customers without providing products and services they really want. Yet many companies continue to try to earn customer loyalty with tired, outdated products and service offerings that don't meet the real needs of today's customer. Not Commerce Bank, headquartered in Cherry Hill, New Jersey. Beginning in 1997, when other banks in the area, occupied with mergers, were eliminating branches and cutting back on service (and still raising fees), Commerce Bank did just the opposite. Its customer research confirmed that large pools of attractive customers wanted one-stop shopping for financial services. So Commerce Bank aggressively expanded its locations, opening nine new branches in 1997, close to twenty in 1998, and twenty-five more in 1999. Positioning itself as "America's Most Convenient Bank," this company has focused squarely on providing superior service that aligns with customer needs rather than traditional banking policy. Take hours of operation, for example. Brushing aside the banker's hours mind-set of most of its competitors, Commerce is open 7:30 A.M. to 8 P.M. weekdays, 7:30 A.M. to 6 P.M. on Saturdays, and 11 A.M. to 4 P.M. on Sundays. And how about the day after Thanksgiving, typically the busiest shopping day of the year? All Commerce branches open at 6 A.M. so that business clients and consumers alike, preparing for the "Black Friday" shopper rush, have the banking support they need. Locations are heavily concentrated in the bedroom communities of major urban areas so that customers can easily visit a branch, a key want according to Commerce research.

But earning wondrous entanglement with customers is an ongoing process. That's why Commerce Bank is continually identifying new ways to maximize involvement with its customers. For example, for customers who use the bank's personal investing services, Commerce offers such privileges as no-fee, interest-bearing checking accounts, discounted commissions on personal investing service transactions, and no-annual-fee credit cards. Although many banks are slowly transitioning to on-line banking, Commerce is in the full-speed-ahead mode, with e-mail customer service and on-line banking that includes loans. Says Commerce executive vice president Dennis DiFlorio, "We are drastically different from most other banks. The merger mania that is going on—cutbacks in service and movement away from the community branch banking role—gives us tremendous opportunity. Other banks compete on rate. We compete on service and convenience."

Commerce Bank's strategies are clearly striking a chord with customers. Since starting its new initiatives, the bank has consistently enjoyed two-digit growth as illustrated by its 14 percent increase in deposits and 23 percent increase in revenues for 1999 over 1998. Net income increased by 34 percent for the same period.[22] At this writing, deposits, revenue, and income are all up about 25 percent for the first half of 2000 over the first half of 1999.[23]

As ClubCorp and Commerce Bank both demonstrate, practicing wondrous entanglement means having the right *products* and *services* at the right *time* for your specific customers. It's how you truly become indispensable.

WIN REPEAT CUSTOMERS THROUGH OLD-FASHIONED SERVICE. How does a dot-com with lots of not-com experience turn first-time customers into repeats? Look no further than Cameraworld.com. During its twenty-two years as a profitable retail and mail-order business, Camera World Company honed its expertise in fulfillment, customer service, and supplier relationships. And it's that deep, back-end not-com experience coupled with the opportunities of the Internet that is catapulting the company to new heights. For example, during the 1999 holiday season many of the company's three hundred thousand customers returned in droves and spent on average $600 each. In December, the site handled an average of twenty-five thousand unique users a day, and Web sales rose by 245 percent over the previous year's figure for the month. (Concurrently, the mail-order business shot up 67 percent and sales at the company's downtown Portland, Oregon, store were up 22 percent.) On average, 90 percent of Web and mail-order shipments left the warehouse within twenty-four hours. Return rates for Web sales paralleled mail-order and in-store return rates, hovering at around 4 percent.[24] Contrast this performance to that of ToysRUs.com. That e-tailer was buried by the demand of on-line holiday traffic and was unable to fulfill orders on time. The company's delivery infrastructure was designed to send truckloads of products to stores rather than to ship single orders to millions of consumers.[25]

Jupiter Communications analyst Cormac Foster finds that "an awful lot of web sites don't realize that customer service should be a priority. They focus on customer acquisition but don't spend time on the unsexy stuff, like customer-support infrastructure. Infrastructure doesn't get you headlines, but if you don't have a staff of people to take care of business behind the firewall, you won't get much."[26]

An average day means fifteen thousand unique visitors and four hundred transactions for Cameraworld.com. And there is lots of support for customers when they need it. The customer service department is staffed with professional photographers who respond to customers by e-mail or phone. A twenty-four-hour turnaround on e-mail is the action standard. Customers even receive an e-mail notice showing them where their question is in the queue. An Internet telephone feature lets customers whose computers are equipped with a sound card and a microphone connect over the Internet to talk with the sales and support staff. Couple this support with an on-line auction area, on-line chats with celebrated photographers, a selection *wizard* that helps customers choose the right camera by assessing their expertise and frequency of use, and it's little wonder that Cameraworld.com customers are transitioning from customers into advocates.[27]

Turning Repeat Customers into Clients and Advocates

When considering ways to turn repeat customers into clients and advocates, a *frequent buyer program* deserves careful consideration. Indeed, frequent buyer programs (also referred to as *loyalty programs* and *reward programs*) have become a critical retention tool for firms searching for unique ways to add value and in turn build customer loyalty. Recent estimates show that over sixty million Americans belong to frequent flyer programs. But beyond airlines, buyers can now earn points when they grocery shop or use the dry cleaners, telephone, or even their HMO.

Perhaps the greatest misjudgment many companies make in offering frequent buyer programs is failing to understand that their return on the program includes more than the point-based sales revenue generated. It also includes the buyer information gathered through the program about purchase habits and preferences, information that when used correctly, allows a firm to sell more to its most valuable customers. Remember ScrubaDub Car Wash from Chapter Four, the firm that divides its customers into the Great Infrequents who wash their cars only a few times a year and the More Valuables who wash their cars with a much higher frequency?

Several years ago, as a way to attract and keep more high-value customers, the firm set up a frequent buyer program called the Car Care Club. For a fee of $5.95, good for the life of the car, customers joined the club and got four key benefits: twenty-four-hour rain and snow insurance (a free wash if it rains or snows within a day), a three-day clean car guarantee (a free wash if the car gets dirty for any reason within three days after purchase of one of the deluxe services), a frequent wash bonus program (for every ten paid washes, get one wash free), and a $5 waxing rebate.

To date, the Car Care Club has brought in more than thirty-five thousand members who wash more frequently and spend more money. When a customer signs up, ScrubaDub puts a bar code on the member's vehicle and then scans that code at the beginning of each visit. This provides information about the customer's buying habits for the company's database and also gives ScrubaDub a tool to add value with each visit. Once the bar code is scanned, the attendant can address the customer by name and offer suggestions for special services like vinyl top cleaning or waxing.

About two or three times a week, ScrubaDub shocks one of its club members by washing his or her car for free. It happens whenever one of the club members comes in for a wash, and the database shows that the car is within the clean-car-guarantee period. The attendant tells the customer, "You were just here three days ago." Says company president and CEO Robert Paisner, "We hand them their ten dollars back and they're blown away."[28]

Expect to see more loyalty programs introduced in every market space. Technology is making these programs easier and less expensive to do, and customers have come to expect them. High-value customers will be looking for innovative programs that provide them with the highest return for their participation. When designing your own frequent buyer program, consider these tips:

• *Avoid one-size-fits-all reward plans.* Customers are increasingly drawn to programs that recognize their particular interests and lifestyle preferences. As a five-time winner of the J. D. Power Award for Customer Satisfaction (among high-usage long distance customers),

Sprint knows such recognition comes only by going the extra mile. That's why Sprint spent almost a year conducting extensive research to truly understand what program rewards its customers would find most valuable. Customers said they wanted customized rewards relevant to their particular interests. So Sprint relaunched its member reward program on these terms. Now, a Sprint Rewards member who is a travel lover can redeem earned points for a Mediterranean cruise and a family with small children can choose a series of children's videotapes.

• *Use the hook principle.* Studies find the hook principle (which states that the more products and services a customer buys from one source, the less likely that customer is to leave) is central to any sound loyalty strategy. Designing your loyalty program so that members can sample and experience as many of your offerings as possible lessens the risk that another competitor will woo your customers away.

Boots The Chemist is Great Britain's leading health and beauty retailer, with thirteen hundred stores. The point structure of Boots's frequent buyer program is designed to encourage members to enjoy products that they might not otherwise readily buy for themselves— like a special fragrance or a luxurious skin care line. Boots calls this "guilt-free indulgence," and it helps hook customers and make them more loyal. Sprint designed its reward program so that members can earn rewards more quickly by using a wide range of Sprint communication products and services. Again, introducing members to multiple product solutions helps ensure long-term loyalty.

• *Create a program that rewards your best customers.* Make sure your loyalty program rewards your best customers and deepens their purchase commitment. Chart House Restaurant's Aloha Club, launched in 1993 in all sixty-three of the company's fine dining facilities in twenty-one states, does just that. Renewal, ordinarily commanding a $20 annual fee, is free if the customer spends at least $250 per year with the chain. After three visits, members get a $25 dining certificate. The club offers a newsletter that contains restaurant information, a Web site, and a members-only 800 number. One especially interesting feature of the Aloha Club is a free trip for two around the world for any member dining at all sixty-three Chart House Restaurants. With over three hundred thousand members in the program, Chart House has given out over $2 million in dining certificates—and thirty customers have completed the restaurant circuit to win the round-the-world trip for two.

In the quest to reward best customers, Musicland's Replay, a reward program that targets high-profit customers who shop in Sam Goody or Musicland mall stores, has achieved some impressive statistics. Launched in 1993, Replay has 750,000 members, with 50 percent identified as active. Members outspend nonmembers 2:1. The program works like this: there is a $9.95 fee to enroll, but members get an immediate sign-up bonus of 15 percent off regularly priced merchandise purchased that day. Members get 1 point for every dollar spent, and when they reach 150 points, they get an automatic $15 store certificate. There is a bimonthly magazine with industry news, music and movie reviews, and new releases. In addition, the program offers a cobranded credit card that earns a 5 percent rebate on store purchases.

• *Make your staff program evangelists.* No loyalty program can truly thrive without the understanding, enthusiasm, and support of staff. Who better to firmly establish the benefits of loyalty program participation than the frontline staff who constantly are in touch with customers? When planning your program, think about selling your customers and your staff. Boots The Chemist signed on all sixty thousand sales associates as members of its Advantage Card program six months prior to the official launch. This way, associates could earn treats themselves and appreciate firsthand the benefits they would soon be offering customers.

On-Line Tools for Turning Customers into Advocates

Amazon.com CEO Jeff Bezos says, "To have someone be an evangelist, you have to create something 10 times better than what they're used to. You can't just make something marginally better. That will make them happy, but it won't make them an evangelist."[29]

No company can create advocates without a true understanding of customer preferences. Not surprisingly, many of the innovative and groundbreaking techniques for listening to customers are coming from the Web world. Let's look at some of these tools and their impact on capturing and keeping loyal advocates.

• *Self-selection clicks.* Rather than simply listing products and services on its site, PRM Consulting, a network management company, opted to categorize its site by industry. Site visitors choose from five different market segments—insurance, pharmaceuticals, manufacturing, hospitals/healthcare, and banking/financial institutions. Choosing a segment, customers work their way through levels of choices to reach specifics. Why the drill down? Because the choices allow PRM to better learn whom it is best reaching (and not reaching) on-line. Moreover, this information capture drives additional customer customization.

• *Answer-dependent pathing.* It's a fact: the right series of questions can help you add more value for your customers. People will almost always fill out a questionnaire that helps them select the right product or service. Consider Adam Golf's Flex Finder survey that helps site users select equipment by asking questions such as: How old are you? What is your official handicap? and, Do you have any physical limitations? Two things are accomplished by asking these questions. First, as customers type in their options, the site is gathering rich data that the company can use to better serve (and sell) this customer in the future. Second, when customers mold their own requirements, they typically feel better about their purchases.

• *One-to-one chat support.* Want an alternative to customers calling an 800 number and waiting in a queue? Consider this new on-line support feature. A site visitor clicks on a chat link, a chat room opens, and a company rep—often depicted in full color beside the chat window—extends a greeting in text. Visitors then have the opportunity to type in their questions or comments, to which the rep replies on the spot.

• *Private Web pages.* An effective way to understand and leverage both current and emerging customer needs is to practice *consultative selling.* In contrast to the more transactional selling style in which reps simply make a sale of what the customer selects, this style requires lots of probing and lots of listening, and that takes time. Want to free up your sales reps' time so they can do more consultation? Private Web pages may be the solution. Inside sales reps at Dell Computer, for example, create and maintain Premier Pages for corporate customers. Dell has now established more than twenty thousand of these password-protected private Web pages. Premier Pages offer people at companies like Ford and Procter & Gamble a wide range of services, including the ability to order predetermined or preapproved configurations negotiated in advance with Dell. One Dell client allows all of its fifty thousand employees to view and select Dell products on-line through the client's Premier Pages. At recent count, a reported 40 percent of Dell's multinational customers use Premier Pages, freeing Dell sales reps from routine selling to play a more consultative and less transactional role with their customers.

• *E-mail discussion group.* One profound way to really know what your customers are thinking is to get them talking to each other. Consider asking customers to subscribe to an e-mail discussion group about your company or industry. Internet strategy ace Jim Sterne describes the experience this way:

> The progression of on-site discussion groups is fairly predictable. First, your customers introduce themselves. Then they begin bragging about their expertise with your product and how they have used it to great advantage. Then they fall to bickering about the best ways to use it. Then they begin asking for and receiving help from one another. And then something surreal happens. They turn on you. You, the maker of the products they love. You, the person who brought them all together. You, their host. They will link arms and demand that you do something about problems they all face when using your products, and they won't be satisfied until you promise to act. Mission accomplished: Do you know of a better way to entice your best customers to help you redesign your offerings? To get them to tell you how to get them to spend more money? There's nothing like a light flaming to teach you what you need to know to stay competitive.[30]

SUMMARY

• Every customer is vulnerable to competitive pull when better value is offered elsewhere.

• The key to making your business defection-proof is delivering maximum value to your customers.

• Continual monitoring of your customers' definition of value and delivery of that value at every stage of the life cycle earns customer loyalty.

• Offering not only good value but also unanticipated value will surprise and please customers.

• Getting customers to complain and then acting on those complaints will make your business more competitive and your customers more loyal.

- Satisfaction and loyalty are not the same. Loyalty is the goal.
- Old-fashioned good service is still important to customers.
- Loyalty clubs, frequent buyer programs, and other special offerings can turn repeat customers into advocates and your business into a success.

CHAPTER SEVEN

Building a Customer Information System That Drives Loyalty

W alk into the product development room at ChemStation, a $25 million company based in Dayton, Ohio, and you'll see a space with a split personality. Scattered about on the room's black Formica countertops are Bunsen burners and beakers brimming with multicolored liquids, giving the room the look of a chemistry lab in a high school. But in the center of the room are lots of grease-covered engine parts that remind you more of a mechanic's bay in a filling station. Perched on a stool, surrounded by engine parts, is chemist Kathy Hansen, who is patiently applying drops of pale green fluid to one of the machine parts. Her goal? To determine if the carefully formulated detergent she's applying will remove the grease from the metal in the way the customer needs it to.

Hansen's job and the job of two other chemists is to formulate cleaning products, one by one, for the eighteen-year-old industrial detergent company. ChemStation's clients are varied, ranging from the U.S. Air Force to car wash firms. And the formulas Hansen and her colleagues create must be equally diverse—thus the wild array of props, because some customers ship their cleaning dilemmas directly to the lab to assist the chemists in their pursuits.

The chemists don't work in isolation. They must coordinate closely with ChemStation's salespeople, who spend most of their time in the field at customer sites collecting information about various operations' cleaning needs. For example, they investigate the kinds of dirt customers are battling and what particular cleaning properties— smooth, foamy, gritty, or just plain flat—their customers most want in a cleaning agent.

A central database called the Tank Management System (TMS) integrates all the information from the field and the lab. The TMS is connected to both the lab and the company's forty U.S. plants, where computer-driven devices designed by George Homan, company CEO, configure each customer's tailor-made detergent. The customer is largely unaware of the constant buzz of communication between the lab and the salesforce and the automation processes for making the customized cleaners. All the customer is really aware of is that ChemStation consistently delivers cleaning solutions that work. As a result, ChemStation's profit margins have skyrocketed into the double digits. Reports Homan, "The money we have been able to save by doing things this way is mindboggling."

But things weren't always this smooth. When Homan launched the company in 1983, industrial detergent was delivered to ChemStation customers in fifty-five-gallon plastic drums. But soaring prices for gasoline and plastics forced Homan to look for other options. To cut transportation costs by shipping more orders per truck, ChemStation soon began delivering concentrated detergent in smaller containers. This required the customer to add water on site to reconstitute the product. But soon Homan discovered another big problem. Because of variances in the environment, similar detergents weren't working equally well, even for customers in the same industry. What was really needed were detergents geared to a customer's individual cleaning needs. But that required more than just reformulation. Homan would have to make a serious commitment to technology to offset the efficiency lost by not manufacturing in bulk. What's more, he would have to turn his salesforce into an information machine. So that's exactly what he did.

Salespeople ask potential customers about their cleaning tasks, making sure to probe such issues as whether the detergent will be used in an area with a lot of people and how much the customer wants to spend. This information is captured and used to formulate the product needed. To help the sales process, TMS keeps every recipe ever used by a customer easily accessible by salespeople. Explains Homan, "If a salesperson is standing in front of a Budweiser plant wondering what the heck they use in there to clean equipment, he can look up what our other Bud plants are using."

Once the information is gathered from the prospect, it's fed over the salesperson's modem-equipped laptop into the TMS. With this information, Kathy Hansen and her fellow chemists can begin creating the formula for that customer. Once the formula is complete and the customer is pleased with the sample, the chemists enter the formula into the TMS and assign it a number. The technology kicks in with full force when it's time to manufacture the product. The TMS drives the machines at one or more of ChemStation's forty plants around the country as they make the specialized product. Except for the Chem-Station chemists, no one—not even the customer—knows what goes into each recipe. This makes it less likely that a customer will jump ship with the expectation that another manufacturer can duplicate the same suds. Say Homan of his secret recipes, "We're not as protective as Coca-Cola, but we're close."

What's next for ChemStation's customer information system? A device installed directly in the customer's detergent tank—actually the workings of a cellular phone attached to a float—that will automatically dial in to the TMS and set off an alarm when the detergent is running low.[1]

DEFECTION PROOF YOUR COMPANY WITH A CIS

Francis Bacon said that knowledge is power. Nowhere is that adage more true than in compiling and applying customer information. An effective, strategic use of customer information can help make a company highly defection resistant and often nearly defection proof.

Customer data collection, data warehousing, and data mining (see Figure 7.1) have become almost commonplace terms in the sales, marketing, and customer service lexicon today, thanks in large part to the dramatically lower costs now associated with obtaining and storing data. The greater availability of current customer data has, in turn, spurred the rapid development of sophisticated software to apply this information to customer loyalty and customer win-back programs.

Figure 7.1. Database Buzz Words.

Flat database	A database in which all of the information about an individual customer is kept in a single file. Flat databases are easy to manage because all the information is in one place. However, there is a limit on the amount of information that can be stored in a single record.
Relational database	A database in which the information about an individual is kept in several different files. Database users see a single set of data, such as a customer's record, but the information is actually coming from multiple sources. Information storage has an array of sorting and viewing options.
Data warehouse	An electronic storage facility where vast amounts of information are captured, housed, cleaned for accuracy, and sorted for later analysis. Although a data warehouse is principally software, a fair amount of hardware may be required for storage capacity, depending on the size of the company.
Data mining	The use of statistical processes to dig down through layers of data and identify customer patterns of behavior, emerging trends, and issues. Data mining helps companies look for the significant relationships or business opportunities hidden within stored customer information. Four of the most popular statistical modeling techniques in use for data mining are neural networks, decision tree models, rule induction, and data visualization.
Extranet	An extranet marries the benefits of Internet technology with the security of a private network (or intranet). Routinely used for intercompany collaboration, an extranet allows participants to keep their data safely behind a firewall, but authorized partners (inside and outside the participating companies) can access these data over the Internet.

Trying to manage customer retention or recovery without such data and the system to route and apply it is a lot like trying to find your way down a dark and bumpy path without a flashlight. A well-planned, companywide *customer information system* (CIS) can take much of the peril out of the customer loyalty journey. It enables your firm to integrate scattered customer databases containing different kinds of information and transparently tie together geographically and organizationally dispersed customer operations. Here are four illustrations of the ways in which a good CIS makes a difference.

Allstate Wraps It Up

Widely dispersed databases create problems that are common to most insurance companies. For example, every potential buyer who asks an agent for a quote on an auto insurance policy triggers a complex underwriting process that involves collecting and matching data on the applicant's driving record, auto registration, demographics, and even family risk (such as the presence of a teenage driver). Precious days can be lost in getting risk-related data from multiple external sources, converting it for use in an expert underwriting system, and delivering the final determination to the agent. But that's not all—if the individual's self-reported risk factors don't match what the external data show about that individual, the policy coming back may well bear a different price than the one the agent quoted.

That's why Allstate Insurance Company's successful push, begun in 1993, to create a comprehensive CIS for its fifteen thousand agents has had a profound impact on the company's ability to better serve its customers. The payoff has been substantial. Underwriting time has been cut in half, enabling Allstate agents to provide quotes within twenty-four to forty-eight hours. Policies can now be issued within three to five business days. And the behind-the-scenes data streamlining has eliminated $3 million to $4 million per year in unnecessary data costs. Data quality is so much improved that Allstate now guarantees that the rate an agent quotes is the rate with which the policy will be written. It's a far cry from Allstate's redundant data days in the early 1990s when each of its regional offices was purchasing state motor vehicle and auto registration data from six to eight sources. Through its CIS system, Allstate now gets one cost from each data provider and sets up the necessary conversion, deduplication (eliminating customer record duplication) and data processing procedures to ensure that incoming data are fed to Allstate's expert underwriting system and from there to the agent's desktop system.

But the CIS has also shown value well beyond underwriting. Although Allstate has been generating leads for its agents for years, these data warehouse capabilities now allow the company to prequalify leads using best customer profiles it has created from purchase history and other transaction data. By comparing incoming leads against that profile, Allstate can better identify those prospects with profitability potential or who are most likely to purchase a homeowner, life, or auto insurance product. Says Allstate vice president Steve King, "Our agents can increase their hit ratios—where you might call 20 people cold and get one lead, you can call 10 of our refined leads and get one or two possibilities from that."[2]

A companywide CIS can eliminate the problem of incomplete and outdated product and service information. Instead of relying on paper records or isolated computer profiles in customer transactions, the information can be put on-line and kept current on a continuous, real-time basis.

SunExpress Speeds Ahead

Creating close relationships with customers is a cornerstone of the customer care philosophy at SunExpress, the aftermarket company of Sun Microsystems. As the name implies, SunExpress places great emphasis on delighting its customers with speed and reliability. The company's TeleSalesDesk and the customer information system that supports it have proven critical to the firm's ability to provide exceptional customer care. Serving a client base of 100,000 users across eleven countries, SunExpress TeleSalesDesk reps serve a dual role for customers by performing both sales and service functions.

An on-line information system integrates order entry and leads management functions with customer profiles and an on-line product catalogue containing specifications on 5,000 products. This makes it possible for a telesales rep at a help desk anywhere in the world to access a customer's data file and assist that customer with a service problem or a sale. Whether the rep needs to access a customer's licensing requirements or system requirements or to provide information about a new product, the system complies. The information system enables the rep not just to deal with problems or inquiries but to sell add-on services as well.

This robust information system, coupled with intensive training and product knowledge, enables SunExpress TeleSalesDesk representatives to handle almost 100 percent of incoming customer calls in one conversation. If additional support is required, the rep can e-mail a message from the customer's profile screen to field product managers, who address the query within a few hours. These answers are fed to three SunExpress areas: TeleSalesDesk operations, the firm's Internet site, and the company's catalogue operation. This closed loop helps ensure that customer and product information files stay continually updated.

What's the payback for SunExpress? Since the TeleSalesDesk launch in 1992, the company has realized big improvements in sales and customer approval ratings. The average order size is up 100 percent, order volume is up 55 percent, call volume has tripled, and revenue generated by the TeleSalesDesk rep has doubled.[3]

A CIS allows a company to use every contact with customers as an opportunity to build and deepen customer relationships. That way, systematically captured information can be used to improve not just customer service, for example, but everything the company does. This information can be routed in real time not just to those who interact with customers but also to others in the company with a need to know or in a position to resolve design problems, create new products, or develop new marketing approaches.

Mercedes Keeps Watch

Many companies aspire to cradle-to-grave relationships with customers, but Mercedes has built a state-of-the-art CIS that makes that lofty objective a reality with many customers. Collecting marketing intelligence and customer feedback is serious business at Mercedes, so serious that opinions about product quality and suggestions about product improvements are routinely compiled from conversations with customers and fed back to the company's North American marketing and manufacturing operations—areas within the company that don't otherwise get a lot of customer contact from day to day. And how does the company react to customer feedback? Consider a favorite story of Bill Hurley, manager of customer information at Mercedes. On a winter day several years ago, dozens of owners of Mercedes called to complain about trouble starting their cars. Thanks to sophisticated technology for tracking call patterns and queries from customers, Mercedes quickly realized that the cars with problems shared similar vehicle identification numbers. Within twenty-four hours, customer reps were on the phone conferring with German engineers who isolated the problem and identified a solution. In response, road assistance crews were dispatched to owners' homes and offices to rescue cars in driveways and parking lots. Owners' reactions? Mercedes won big points with customers for expert problem solving and responsiveness.[4]

Perhaps the biggest advantage of customer information systems is that they give you the ability to get very close to customers to understand their needs and wants. A CIS can arm your company with the knowledge of customer preferences, giving it the speed essential to target customers and their needs precisely and then get the best products and services to them first. More complete and current customer information and the ability to access and apply it fast translates to greater and more sustained success. Just ask the Rio.

The Rio Wins Big

Want some real insights into the evolution of customer loyalty? Look no further than the gaming industry and the bright lights of Las Vegas. The first Vegas casinos, built in the 1940s, were little more than a sea of card tables, some dice, and a bar. Although it seems almost absurd today, the mazelike layout of these casinos was then the primary tool for keeping customers at the tables. Says Lee Cagely, director of Marnell/ Carrao Associates, a casino design firm, "The earlier casino designs tended to confuse people on purpose. They made it difficult to find the restrooms. They made it difficult to get out."

But fifty-plus years later, customer information systems have become the tool of choice for nurturing casino loyalty. In typical Vegas style, these data systems are enabling casinos to customize their glitz delivery according to an individual customer's preferences and profit potential. Take the Rio Hotel and Casino. Almost seven million customers a year play poker and baccarat, other games, and slot machines across the one hundred thousand square feet of casino floor.

The Rio's purple and teal colors are everywhere, and the round-the-clock Mardi Gras atmosphere has all the feel of gaming in a tropical carnival. But the real game at Rio is how the casino uses a CIS to track and keep the customers it wants. At the heart of the Rio system is a small corps of data analysts who monitor and evaluate the casino's vast warehouse of customer data. Everything to do with the customer, particularly how much long-term value each represents and how much in *comps* (or complimentary products and services) each will receive, is driven by the customer's CIS rating. This rating is about the customer's financial resources, how often she visits, what games she plays, how much she wagers per bet, and a full set of information on her leisure preferences.

As a result of its excellent record gathering and keeping, the Rio is able to develop programs to keep high-value customers coming back. The Play Rio program allows guests to register simply by presenting a photo ID. Says Dave Maritt, the Rio's vice president of marketing: "We'll ask them some things about what they like. Do they like auto racing, do they like books, do they like wine, do they like parties, special entertainment, etc., and we put all of this into the database." Less than a minute later, a player receives a plastic card encoded with his personal information. Each time the player inserts the card into a gambling machine, the customer profile is updated with the type of machine played, the location on the floor, how long he played, and whether he is up or down on his winnings. Sure, the house is always happy to take your money, but the information collected during play is almost as important as the cash. These information nuggets help the Rio refine its sales pitch to you, creating a relationship that is, the casino hopes, more than a one-night stand.

Players are segmented by dollars gambled per day. For example, those players who gamble a thousand dollars a day with the Rio, whether they win or not, receive the designation *hosted guest.* That accords them VIP status, with more comps and (not surprisingly) closer computerized tracking of their play. These customers are assigned a *host* by the casino, a person who pays attention and offers services to the customer. The data give the casino host the ability to monitor play among valued guests, cheering on the winners and cheering up the losers. The host is actually a highly paid, personal customer service representative. Hosts can bring in millions of dollars of business to a casino as a result of the relationships they have developed with the players over the years. Says Bill Hunt, director of player development, "They get to know the players, what the players like, so that ideally the VIP guests can make a five-minute phone call to let a host know they will be arriving on a Friday and that host can take it from there—front-row tickets to a sold-out show, a dinner seating at the best restaurant, the suite they want, etc."

But the Rio's highest level of accommodation and recognition is reserved for a few very special players—those with a million-dollar line of credit—known in the industry as "whales." At the Rio, this means a complimentary seven-thousand-square-foot suite where guests lounge around in a living room the size of an apartment and brush their teeth in sinks with gold-plated faucets or play keno via a TV that rises from the floor at the touch of a button. Ironically, all this extravagance is lavished on the high-rollers who spend very little time in the suite. Instead, they play baccarat and roulette with $100,000 chips in the Rio's secluded back room called the Salon.

In an industry where the level and cost of customer migration is very high, the Rio's state-of-the-art CIS is one of its most critical loyalty weapons. Without a doubt, having complete customer preference and activity information, and using that information to leverage optimum player value, is the ticket to a big house win.[5]

In the following sections of this chapter we'll look at designing a CIS and gathering the data that will make it powerful. We'll close with a quick look at a CIS development in the pipeline and at an example that shows nontechnical leaders that they can still acquire the knowledge to help their organizations take advantage of technological tools like CIS.

DESIGNING YOUR CIS

The initial and critical step in designing a CIS is to bring business users and information technology (IT) people together at the same table so they can work together to write down the business objectives for the data warehouse project. Because the user knows the business issues and the IT person knows what's technically feasible, this careful collaboration is essential. Norwalk, Connecticut–based data warehouse consultant Richard Creeth, president of Creeth, Richman and Associates, offers these important guidelines for the process:

• Avoid the *horizon syndrome.* If the user is not technically savvy, it may be difficult for him or her to know what is possible. The challenge for IT is to help the user see the horizon. "Identify a phase one deliverable you can get quickly, and once you give users something, they will have a clearer idea of how much more is possible," advises Creeth. Many business users are completely unaware of the possibilities available in a CIS. IT staff can work with business users to design a system that works and is expandable as the customer database grows and use of it becomes more sophisticated. The IT staff can also make sure that the user realizes there are limits to what technology can do and keeps expectations realistic. According to Creeth, "One of the biggest mistakes businesses make when starting a data warehouse project is treating it as a tech issue. The company's overall business strategy should dictate the technology needs, not the other way around. Only then can you decide what data needs to be included, what analytical tools should be considered and whether you're to build your own or buy off the shelf."

• *Put your objectives in writing.* As simple as it sounds, the very first step is to "write down what the objective is. What is the business need the CIS will service? Should it allow product managers to analyze sales by product, by salesperson, by region?" Such decisions are important, Creeth says, because "the issue then becomes how many data go in. If it were left to IT, likely all data would go in, and that would doom the project to failure. Define the business application, identify the data required to provide the analysis, and identify the tools you can use to provide the data to users."

• *Get major users involved right from the start.* When sitting down to determine what the application objectives are, Creeth says he likes "to see a project team with heavy user community representation. Without that, you risk not meeting users' needs."

• *Keep it simple.* Some companies get overly caught up in creating fields for customer information, resulting in complex records. The best rule is to keep it simple. Here are some of the most useful data fields:

- Customer identification (name, telephone number, title, company name, address)
- Rating (size or value level)
- Background (demographics, lifestyle characteristics)
- Communication record (contact with company, participation in marketing programs, types of information or services required, channels of contact used, requests for information, complaint frequency and recency)
- Purchase behavior (recency, frequency, monetary value, financing requirements, return activity)
- Share of customer (the proportion of money a supplier gets out of all the money that customer spends in a specific category)
- Credit worthiness
- Performance ratings and history (performance evaluation, loyalty, and likelihood to refer the company to others)[6]

Here are some more smart moves. When developing and maintaining your database, keep these additional tips in mind.

- Design the CIS so it can sort information in a variety of ways— customer purchase frequency, age, and dollar volume, for example.
- Do regular file cleaning to update customer status, creating a separate file for defected or lapsed customers rather than purging them.

- Back up your databases. For computerized databases, this should be done once or twice a week; and copies should be kept in a separate, secure area.

- Provide database security, such as passwords for different levels of use, to ensure confidentiality.

- When adding new information, merging one database into another, or making major changes in database content or architecture, copy the database, and work with the copy.

CAPTURING CUSTOMER DATA

Consider these knowledge nuggets discovered through data mining and their results. Although sports cars overall are involved in more accidents than most other cars, Farmers Group, an insurance company, discovered that as long as a sports car wasn't the only vehicle in the household, the accident rate for sports cars actually wasn't much greater than that for regular cars. By offering lower insurance rates to sports car households that also had other cars, Farmers determined it could almost double its sports car market.[7]

Custom golf club maker Chipshot.com discovered that although people who added comments to its Web site's guest book seldom bought clubs, people who did buy clubs from the site almost always clicked on the customer service area before buying. This information helped the company decide to put more resources into bettering the site's customer service area and fewer resources into the guest book area.[8]

Dell Computer found that people who went to its Web site first and then called its 800 number from the site were more likely to buy than were those who called the toll-free line first. Given this insight, Dell increased the number of reps who handle calls from customers who are calling the 800 number from the Web.[9]

These results from data improve revenues and customer value. How do you go about capturing the data that can give you these insights? In the world of database technology, there are almost as many ways to capture customer information as there are ways to use the information that has been gathered. The end goal, always, is to have an information system sensitive enough to understand the needs of every customer. Here are four widely used ways to capture customer data:

1. *Build the database one sale at a time.* When a consumer purchases batteries from his local Radio Shack and the clerk logs the customer's name and address into the computer, Radio Shack is building a database to help determine whether he should receive a follow-up catalogue and which products should be emphasized. When a customer swipes her frequent shopper card at the supermarket, she is helping the chain identify products and promotions of possible future interest to her. This detailed customer information provides valuable insights into future cross-selling and up-selling opportunities.

2. *Customer surveys.* Surveys are an effective, though sometimes misused, way of gathering customer information. The self-completion type often seen in hotel rooms, on rental car counters, in retail stores, on planes, or in supermarkets may provide misleading data because they tend to be completed by a small group of self-selected customers, not a large random sample. Surveys mailed or e-mailed to customers are similarly subject to bias due to this tendency toward low response and the lack of detailed information given by respondents. When using surveys for data collection, be sure you use data collection methods that are representative of customers or customer segments you want to learn about.

3. *Personal, in-depth interviewing.* One of the best and most accurate methods of collecting customer opinions and perceptions, as well as demographics and lifestyle information, is the telephone or face-to-face interview. Trained interviewers can generate detailed information by probing customers' specific reasons for answering in certain ways. Interviewing is also the most expensive method, but companies can get more relevancy and objectivity from interview data than from almost any other type. Again, given the worth of the information collected, interviewing usually justifies the level of expense. For example, a pharmaceutical company that has released a new drug might contact a cross section of doctors who have recently prescribed the product to gain valuable insights about prescription habits.

4. *Frontline dialogue.* When employees collect customer data as a consequence of routine contact with customers, the cost is extremely low. In addition, this dialoguing between staff and customers helps nurture relationships with the customers, showing them that the company takes a genuine interest in them. Because we know that one of the barriers to customer registration of complaints is a belief that the company isn't interested, this direct collaboration helps to demonstrate the necessary interest.

The goal of Charles Schwab and Company, the discount brokerage firm, is to get customers to consolidate their assets—with Schwab. The difficulty comes in learning how much those assets are, because new investors routinely test the waters by investing only a portion of the amount they have available to invest. To accomplish its goal, Schwab adopted these basic principles for conducting dialogue with clients and capturing the necessary data:

• *Ask detailed questions.* A new customer is asked several straightforward questions when they become customers. Included in those questions are "how much do you have to invest?" "do you use a computer?" "are you on the Internet?" The answers to the questions are used to build a customer profile.

• *Track behavior.* Each time a salesperson talks to a customer, information gleaned from the conversation is added to the customer profile.

• *Incorporate surveys and demographic information.* Schwab certainly doesn't reject general statistical information on customers. But rather than making these data the centerpiece of its marketing strategy, Schwab uses them to supplement the more personal, dialogue-based data it develops on each customer.

• *Translate correspondence into usable information.* Schwab records the essence of all correspondence, including e-mail, using software that reads and categorizes each message. For example, the software might record that a customer wants to change an account or has a complaint about a trade. According to Schwab, the software can successfully categorize 60 percent of correspondence into customer profile data. Humans must read and categorize the remaining 40 percent.

• *Make analytical deductions.* Customers may not be forthcoming about their assets, so the company has to deduce the potential value of the customer based on the information it has gathered.

• *Connect the data points.* Schwab is able to measure the true extent of a relationship by mining data. For instance, its system can call attention to multiple accounts owned by one customer—say, the person with a $200,000 IRA who manages $3 million in retirement funds at her privately held company.[10]

Nurture Your Data Collectors

One of the fastest ways to compromise a database is to forget to nurture the people who collect the data. Databases are only as good as the information fed into them. Both salespeople and frontline customer service reps are key information gatherers in most companies and both require special care.

HELP DATA COLLECTORS SEE THE BENEFITS. Salespeople can be very resistant to the idea of centralized access to account data. In many cases they fear that the process of entering data into the system will only slow them down by diverting valuable selling time into administrative tasks. They also fear that they will lose control of their customer accounts if others have access to their customer data.

The solution is to make sure that your integration effort will provide direct benefits back to the salesforce. For example, demonstrate how the integrated database can help identify the key decision makers at a site and get valuable presale information to them as a prelude to a sales contact. Plan on providing a communication loop back to the field to feed salespeople solid leads from corporate-level direct-mail or telemarketing campaigns. Train them by showing them how your new data capabilities can improve their yields and give customers greater flexibility for ordering via direct and Internet channels.

Particularly for departments like customer service, which may feel like forgotten citizens in their companies, gathering, helping evaluate and analyze, and then applying customer information greatly broadens the scope of their contributions. Moreover, it enables them not only to act on the information gathered but also to think about better ways of collecting, analyzing, discussing, and tracking data from customers.

DON'T FATIGUE YOUR COLLECTION SOURCES. Don't let your collection process turns sales and customer service people into data entry clerks. Kevin Burnette, database marketing manager for corporate accounts at Dell Computer, stresses the importance of giving frontliners clear direction about the type of information they are supposed to gather: "We don't want to overuse the field with requests for additional information. You can fatigue your compilers of data just as you can a mailing list."[11]

PROVIDE ADEQUATE TRAINING AND SUPPORT. For many companies, the integration process requires moving from a flat-file database to a relational database. From an end-user perspective, a flat-file system is extremely user-friendly and simple. Because a relational database adds a level of complexity for the user, up-front training helps people feel comfortable with the new system.

When computer-based instrumentation hardware and software products supplier National Instruments (NI) launched the first install-ment of a global salesforce automation effort, the Austin, Texas–based firm chose its Swedish sales office for the debut. NI corporate staffers Michael Beamer and Veneeta Fraser set up camp at the Swedish facil-ity approximately two weeks before the pilot went live. Being there in person to support the transition was critical, they explained, for set-ting up the system, doing preliminary training, and running numer-ous test scenarios so that the data collectors and other users could get comfortable using the system. "Questions will inevitably arise during this period that you didn't consider," Beamer says. "But if you get any problems fixed quickly, the end user sees that you're not just paying them lip service."[12]

Always remember: effective people plus effective data collection systems equal effective databases. Make your data collectors a critical focus in your database management plan.

On the Web: Recognize the Power of Personalization

Golfer Brian Beusoleil is a guy with a handicap—not so much on the course as in the golf store. This social worker by day and golfer on weekends stands six foot three—and he's left-handed. For years, Beusoleil has had difficulty locating clubs that were the right length and proper angle. But his luck has changed. With his most recent pur-chase of a set of irons, woods, a putter, and a driver, Beusoleil's wor-ries are over. What has changed? He purchased from the Web-based custom golf shop, Chipshot.com. And he doubts he'll shop for golf equipment anywhere else again. "They know all my measurements and I'm really happy with the quality, so why would I?"[13]

It wasn't too long ago that new Web-based retailers, or e-tailers, considered the number of visits to, or hits on, their site to be a good first-line metric of their performance in building customer loyalty. But with fewer than 10 percent of the visitors actually making pur-chases and less than 2 percent returning for a second purchase, on-line retailers and services have had to get smarter. To win the race for loyalty, some Web sites have invested heavily in both on-line and tra-ditional media advertising. Others have aligned with shopper reward programs that are the Internet equivalent of frequent flyer and supermarket loyalty clubs. For the best of them, though, smarter has equated to giving visitors a more relevant, personalized experience by anticipating their needs, giving them exactly what they want, and providing great value in exchange for their loyalty.

This personalization is accomplished through an intelligent application of in-depth customer data and the use of sophisticated data techniques such as clustering, collaborative filtering, and profiling, which enable firms to get increasingly smarter about customer purchase activities, product preferences and interests, Web site navigation habits, and the like.

Marketing experts often liken the potential of Web sites to understand their customers' needs to the ability of the small local retailer to know everyone in the neighborhood on a first-name basis. The most frequent application of data gathered from Web sites is to help develop marketing and communication programs aimed at driving user traffic to specific sites. In-depth customer data enable sites to develop an almost personal, albeit virtual, relationship with customers on a one-to-one basis. Amazon.com identifies each customer by name every time he or she enters the site. It also e-mails product recommendations to customers based on expressed customer preferences. Charles Schwab enables customers to personalize their account cover pages. GIST, a communications Web site that provides television content, enables users to create a customized television listings guide that reflects their viewing preferences.

Portal search engines like Yahoo!, Lycos, and AltaVista already collect a lot of information on their users, enabling them to target enticements and ads that increase visits to the individual sites they list. Lycos makes product suggestions. Excite has raised the stakes by providing a direct, personal shopping service to its users.

Search portals will soon be able to send alert messages to users' pagers and wireless phones. And customized portals are also rapidly approaching. Imagine going on-line and being greeting by a welcome page that looks a lot like Main Street—your Main Street—with a flashing marquee that says "Welcome [your name]." Populating your virtual Main Street are storefronts unique to you, reflecting your favorite product and service preferences. Gathering, analyzing, and employing customer data in increasingly sophisticated ways will be key to success for Web marketers. Let's take a closer look at how this information is gathered.

ONGOING RESEARCH. Collecting and continually updating information on customer preferences can be summed up in one word: research. On the Web, technology makes it possible to get the viewpoints of virtually every customer. On-line Web surveys typically are somewhat superficial with respect to depth of data and representativeness (most get feedback from only 10 percent to 25 percent of their population, which threatens their reliability); however, they can provide a great many general preference, attitude, and usage data very quickly.

Streamline, Inc., the Boston-based Internet provider of household goods and services, has built its business around busy, affluent suburban families who are looking to simplify their lifestyles and make them more time efficient. Streamline's customers can order food and videos and also laundry, dry cleaning, and other services on-line. Streamline considers itself a solutions company, having created its business model entirely around tightly profiled customers' expressions of needs, service, and value.

Over half of Streamline's new customers come as a result of referrals, and the company turns away prospects that fall outside its service parameters. One of the ways Streamline stays so close to its customers, offering them an ever-improving array of benefits, is that it also uses its Web site as a data-gathering device. Streamline conducts weekly user surveys via the Web to stay on top of customer needs and wants. Thirty percent to 40 percent of the customers participate in these mini-research studies, giving the company active updated insight into customer needs as well as input on Streamline's perceived performance, almost in real time.

NextCard tries to find out what prospects are thinking. When potential customers abandon their on-line application forms before completing them, NextCard uses a follow-up survey to find out why. Streamline and NextCard are just two examples from a growing corps of Web sites that regularly collect customer data from both regular and new users.

SIMPLE COLLECTION SYSTEMS. The good news is that customer data collection doesn't necessarily have to be sophisticated to be effective. A lot of the customer information gathering on the Internet is fairly simple. One good example of this is the practice of GrandmaBetty.com.

In 1998, Betty Fox was a sixty-seven-year-old grandmother in Queens, New York, when she lost her job as office manager for a billing company after it moved too far away for her to commute to work.

Having done various types of work since her husband died in the early 1960s, she was now looking for a way to both channel her energy and earn money. Her son, a computer technology officer for a bank, started her off on creating a site for seniors. In a short period of time, GrandmaBetty.com became a portal for all sorts of information and shopping opportunities, with over forty categories and links to thousands of sites of potential interest to seniors.

One of the impressive things about Grandma Betty, and GrandmaBetty.com, is the true simplicity of her site operation. Fox solicits very basic information from site visitors in order to, as she says, "add value to people's lives." She simply requests that site users—usually seniors—complete a brief interest profile to tell her what information they would like to know about. Fox answers personally the hundreds of e-mails she receives every week, directing her users to the message boards or sites that will be the most relevant. She also saves and collates this request information to help her decide what new service offerings and links she should add to her site and what she should include in her free weekly newsletter, available via e-mail to site users. Effective collection and use of customer information enables GrandmaBetty.com to be strategically different, to create community and interactivity, and most of all, to cultivate customers one by one and communicate with them one to one.

This wealth of knowledge is paying off for Betty Fox. In addition to being regularly featured in national on-line, print, and broadcast media as a niche marketing icon, Fox has become highly sought after as an authority on the needs of Americans aged fifty and older.[14]

WHAT TO COLLECT. Sometimes people and companies become so taken with the technological capabilities of the Internet and database management software programs that the purpose of the data is overlooked in the thrill of finding ways to collect and mine it. It may be possible for you to collect an immense amount of data, but always ask yourself, What exactly is the point? When designing a CIS system, you must keep your ultimate goal in the forefront at all times. Collecting data has to focus on collecting key, usable, and pertinent data, not just on collecting data for its own sake.

If a company designs its CIS system wisely, good data are collected and stored and irrelevant data are not. For companies both on- and off-line, data are needed that enable a company to identify its best customers, tailor missionary and promotional messages based on individual profiles, cross-sell related products and services, provide personalized customer service and follow-up, and conduct research. In short, having these detailed customer profiles gives companies the means to develop the kinds of value-based, long-term relationships that help ensure customer loyalty. Here are some options the Web site owner has in designing the information collecting aspect of the site in order to capture relevant data:

• *Track site traffic and usage.* This tells you things like how many people are visiting, how long they remained on the site, what pages they viewed, what information they downloaded, and what portal or other site they came from. There are several types of software available that compile this information, and these logs offer additional information on how shoppers use sites.

• *Track site preferences.* Sites will also want to know what customers like and dislike about the site so that future content and design can be more attractive. How customers use the site—their response to icons and graphics, how easy they find the site to navigate, and so on—is also important. This is the virtual equivalent of examining the effectiveness of store fixtures, layout, and display in traditional retail environments. It's been determined, for example, that many people who use the Internet to make product and service purchases would rather move rapidly between pages than have lots of graphics per page, no matter how attractive, to download.

• *Capture key customer data.* These data typically include site-specific information and purchase history, age, gender, e-mail address, other Web sites and pages visited, income, educational level, occupation, marital status, home location, telephone numbers, referral source (if available), ethnicity (for tracking average proportions of visitors to the site only), and lifestyle characteristics (hobbies and interests). In addition, sites will want to make sure that methods of collecting customer information are unobtrusive. This means that they should be well incorporated into the content or a promotion being offered. In the spirit of partnership and cooperation, it's a good idea to share with customers why the information is being requested.

• *Keep profiles updated.* Once these data are captured and warehoused, a means must be provided for keeping them current. For example, Web customers should be able to update their profiles whenever that is appropriate. Web site staff members should also frequently review the database and periodically check segments of it for accuracy.

• *Have a privacy policy.* Acknowledge clearly and publicly that privacy is an issue your company understands. State your privacy policy in clear language, and post it in a conspicuous place on your Web site. If you plan to use information only in the aggregate, say so. Allow anyone who does not want data collected to avoid data collection. Additionally, consider obtaining a third-party endorsement that guarantees your adherence to your privacy policy. Although no oversight organization has yet to penetrate the mass consciousness at the Good Housekeeping approval level, the Cupertino, California–based nonprofit Trust-e is trying for that status. Its *trustmark* privacy seal signifies that a site adheres to a range of privacy policies. Some sites are going the extra privacy step and profiling only those customers who formally and officially say yes to a profiling agreement.[15]

HITTING THE MARKETING BULL'S-EYE USING CIS

Let's learn from five companies that are using customer information systems to improve the way they do business and build customer loyalty.

FedEx

Real-time data competency has made Federal Express Corporation, the world's largest express transportation company, a monolith of operational excellence. Every night at exactly 2:07 A.M., a giant rumble begins at the Memphis airport. Over the next two hours, at ninety-second intervals, more than a million packages of all shapes and sizes leave the 2.4-million-square-foot FedEx superhub via 120 aircraft bound for destinations worldwide. Correct delivery of each of these packages requires an advanced information system that can pinpoint and affect the package's whereabouts and handling at any point in its journey. This real-time data competency that drives operation excellence is now being extended to FedEx's marketing organizations, thanks to the establishment of a sophisticated *data mart* built by the firm's marketing analysts and planning organization.

The data mart, which began as a modest database for promotions in 1993, has rapidly delivered the best in data-driven marketing techniques to the firm's marketing employees. Part of a larger plan for increasing FedEx's hold on the air express marketplace, the server-based data mart and related access and analysis technologies have helped the $11 billion shipper analyze its customer base and manage customized marketing campaigns.

According to Sharanjit Singh, director of the marketing analysis team that built the data mart, FedEx now has the marketing skills to support a customer-centric vision. "We reorganized many of our marketing functions and created new job descriptions in order to make best use of the people who understand both the business and the information technology," he explains. "Our analytical professionals now support teams focused on customer segments, rather than the product teams we had before. Each team targets customers and prospects based upon actual or suspected needs and potential profitability." A data steering committee staffed largely with user-group representatives helps the firm monitor data quality issues and stay abreast of changes in data requirements or definitions. The net result has been a four-to five-fold return on investment.

As we will discuss in Chapter Eight, targeting the right customers from the start is a fundamental first step in any company's plan to defection proof its customers. Without a doubt, FedEx's customer information system is making all the difference. Jeffrey Maddock, head of the company's Global Marketing Group, "was involved in the launch of an international service called 'Express Freight' back in 1994." The marketing campaign for that service featured a broad-scope, product-focused combination of print advertising and direct-mail promotions. "In essence, Maddock reports, "we talked to anyone who would listen."

But the company's recent launch of another international service was completely data driven, says Maddock. "Actual customer data was used to design seven levels of offers and five versions of the mailing for different customer groups." Transaction data helped identify the most likely prospects for the new service capabilities, and FedEx scored each of these individuals based on that customer's likely level of future business. Telemarketing was used to gain more profile information on each prospective purchaser.

What does FedEx have to show for its efforts? "We've seen significant improvement in every campaign since we started using the data mart capabilities," notes Maddock. "And we've seen a steady improvement in the productivity of our marketers in using it."

FedEx is now looking to expand the use of the customer information system to new communities across the company, including customer service and sales. Explains Singh, "Rather than just having marketing professionals tie into our marketing data, we want to become even more of an enterprise-wide engine. It [the data mart] will become more of decision-support system than just a marketing support system."[16]

Like FedEx, more and more companies are discovering how customer information systems are the critical key to smart marketing. From more effective channel partnering to saving marketing dollars through e-mail campaigns to establishing new revenue streams, CISs are in the forefront of exciting new marketing innovations, as these further examples show.

Ralston Purina and Sam's Club

Ralston Purina doesn't sell direct to consumers but through retail channels. To create demand and pull at the retail level, it has used marketing and promotional campaigns to build a large database of households with pets. By layering lifestyle information purchased from outside sources onto this database, Ralston-Purina can target newsletters, e-mail programs, and rebates to these households to encourage either trial or repeat purchases.

In addition to raising product awareness, Ralston Purina has also used its databases to team with its retail partners to make sales. Wal-Mart's membership warehouse club division, Sam's Club, partnered with Ralston Purina by merging Ralston Purina's file of pet owners with Sam's Club members. The database merge produced a list of Sam's Club pet product purchasers who had purchased Ralston Purina products and a list of those who had not. It also produced a list of Ralston Purina product purchasers who were Sam's Club members and a list of those who were not. This created an opportunity for Sam's Club to increase its membership by targeting individuals who might be looking for bulk pet food purchases. At the same time, it was an attractive opportunity for Ralston Purina to broaden its sales and deepen its relationships with existing customers.[17]

Neiman Marcus

Speaking of retailers, few do as effective a job of creating loyalty from their customer databases as Neiman Marcus does. Ranking among the top five department store chains in the United States in terms of revenue generation, Neiman Marcus carefully targets, and retains, affluent customers. Neiman's InCircle club, the industry's first credit-card-based loyalty marketing program, established in 1984, helps the retailer increase the lifetime value of 130,000 member customers.

InCircle functions like a frequent flyer program. When members spend in excess of $3,000 with Neiman Marcus (in the store or through telephone or mail orders) during a calendar year, they begin to earn points that can be exchanged for luxury products and services. In addition to the standard fare, like travel and leisure service coupons, Neiman Marcus reinforces its upscale image by making products like exclusive automobiles and cruise trips available to members when they have purchased at extremely high levels. Neiman Marcus also uses club membership as a means of staying in contact with these active and valuable customers. They receive exclusive offers, promotions, and club publications.

When the chain promotes certain store events to customers with specific profiles, it also offers sales support to staff. Each member of the sales and teleservice staff routinely has access to what is called *electronic clienteling* software, which enables staff to pull up each customer's buying profile on the point-of-sale register screen. In addition, if the chain is promoting, say, a new brand of women's sportswear by mail to customers who have purchased sportswear in the past, the names of customers receiving the mailing might be provided to the sales associates in that department. This enables the associates to both track how customers of that store respond to the promotion and to develop deeper relationships and cross-sales opportunities with these customers when they come to the store in response to the promotion.[18]

3Com

In 1997, 3Com, the multibillion dollar manufacturer of voice, data, and video technology, began a demanding, yearlong process of creating a single customer information system with standardized approaches to capturing data on customers worldwide. In the past, what few customer data existed were in disconnected and typically incompatible systems held by individual employees. Today, 3Com's database, called Direct Touch, is accessible by staff anywhere in the world twenty-four hours a day. The database is updated at least once every day, and is entirely Internet based. It is also flexible; records can be developed from information from a number of input channels—e-mail, direct mail, telephone, and so on.

Thanks to Direct Touch, marketing effectiveness has shot up dramatically at 3Com, reducing marketing costs by up to 85 percent for some programs. For example, Direct Touch has enabled the company to mount highly effective e-mail campaigns, including special promotions such as sweepstakes, at a substantial savings over the cost of traditional direct-mail campaigns. Moreover, these Web-based sweepstakes are generating higher-quality leads and more loyal customers than other campaigns do.[19]

Time Inc.

Time Inc. is the second-largest publishing company in the world, with close to twenty-five consumer magazines and book, music, and video clubs. Its household database of over fifty million names in the United States and two million names in Canada is used to target potential new customers, cross-sell to existing customers, tightly segment magazine offers around household characteristics, and customize messages to existing customers. Time is able to classify its customers' purchases into fifty different product affinities or areas of interest, which helps it define lifestyles and potential response to programs. In addition, the company layers additional demographic and socioeconomic data onto each record, such as birth dates of household members, presence of children and their ages, home ownership and market value, credit-card history, occupation, and estimated income of the head of household.

This depth of current and potential customer information in the database has created additional advertising revenue streams for Time Inc. It can customize magazine editions for subscribers, developing a targeted, high-impact advertising vehicle. One example of this was a promotion conducted in conjunction with the launch of a new model of a suburban utility vehicle (SUV). Time merged its subscriber files with vehicle ownership lists acquired from an outside company. The subscriber file then produced eight segments of SUV owners, depending on whether the subscriber owned a two-door or four-door competitive model SUV or the advertiser's brand. Eight different messages were printed on reply cards and bound into the magazines for the eight different segments, next to the advertiser's ad. The promotion generated five times the response that the advertiser normally received.[20]

KNOWLEDGE DISCOVERY—
THE NEXT GENERATION OF CIS?

The technology behind customer information systems, like all technology, is continually evolving. Here's what you might expect to see in the near future. Some database experts are predicting that knowledge discovery will start to eclipse data mining techniques in the next five years or so.

A knowledge discovery database (KDD) works like this. Instead of mining layers upon layers of customer transactional and lifestyle data for knowledge nuggets, a set of flexible knowledge-required algorithms is established and the available data are searched to find exceptions to this rule. For example, a firm establishes a discovery goal that says all regions must increase sales by 6 percent. The knowledge discovery software will then identify at the macro level only those sales regions that are under- or overperforming. Furthermore, the software will identify the root cause of this deviation at a more granular data level. For example, it might report that the central region is 15 percent below target for the XYZ product because females aged thirty-five-plus are buying the product at lower levels than forecasted. The KDD will provide a chart or report showing the exceptions and will suggest strategies for changing the situation. It might point out, for example, that a new communication protocol that includes e-mail coupled with direct mail at a estimated cost of $X per prospect has shown success in other regions and could be employed in the Central Region.

Of course, the success of KDD will be dependent on the firm's ability to provide clear goal statements that in turn can be formed into specific goal-searching algorithms. This cannot happen unless the firm has successfully captured, categorized, and monitored the right level of campaign knowledge and customer experience data. Like CIS power, the power of KDD is only as strong as the underlying data and methods for interpreting them and the commitment of staff to using and improving the system.

KDD is now very much on the drawing boards of corporate thought leaders. Much of the technical thinking is still ongoing in the halls of academia. But marketing user forums are increasingly embracing the concepts of this technology and looking for ways to speed its application to solving real-life marketing dilemmas.[21]

A NONTECH CEO'S JOURNEY
INTO TECHNOLOGY

For twenty years Doug Hyde has been managing an electric services business. Up until 1997, this meant keeping a cap on costs and satisfying regulators. As CEO of Vermont-based Green Mountain Power, Hyde managed within the traditional utility business model: electric companies operated within a particular geographical region, generated power, and sent it to anonymous customers who were billed at a monthly rate. But now, as founder and president of Green Mountain Energy Resources (GMER), Hyde finds his world has shifted dramatically. As a result of energy deregulation, Hyde is now at the helm of a retail marketer of electric services that relies greatly on technology and one-to-one marketing and mass customization.

GMER's strategy is tightly focused: sell branded renewable energy to environmentally conscious customers. The company buys its power wholesale from generators powered by wind, water, and solar energy. In turn, it targets customers who are environmentally conscious, brand loyal, and willing to pay a premium price for green goods.

At the center of this aggressive strategy is a process that gathers customer data through the GMER Web site and call centers and feeds it into a data warehouse. Information drawn from this data warehouse guides the company's marketing efforts. In essence, GMER's ability to capture customer information of very fine granularity and manipulate it to provide customized products is what makes the strategy possible. Jane Doe, for example, may prefer a energy package that is 60 percent wind and 40 percent solar, a flat-rate monthly bill, and a means of receiving and paying that bill over the Internet. With GMER's data-gathering process and the resulting products, Jane can have it her way.

Hyde and his team conducted extensive market research, looking closely at long distance telephone resellers, for example, to better understand the infrastructure required to deliver customer-centric services. It soon became clear that a far more sophisticated deployment of technology would be needed than any in the management team were used to, with a price tag of $50 to $100 million over a five-year period.

So how did Hyde, a fifty-something, lawyer-by-education CEO who was at best an occasional e-mail and PC user, grow into a guy who spends much of his time thinking strategically about technology? And what lessons can Hyde teach company owners who are now realizing that even businesses that offer things like financial services or insurance or educational products have to become high-tech firms? Here are his recommendations:

- *Educate yourself.* Hyde's immediate challenge was learning to manage outside contractors who knew more about information technology than he did. To help himself decipher this new frontier of electronic commerce and mass customization, Hyde plunged into an aggressive course of self-study, which included reading books and attending CEO think tanks led by IT thought leaders.
- *Get in the trenches when necessary.* After receiving dramatically different reports on systems development progress, Hyde was unclear on the appropriate course of action. His solution? He joined a group wrestling with issues related to the company's call center infrastructure and screen architecture. This hands-on experience gave him the insight he needed to reorganize some of the consulting resources, a relatively simple solution in the end.
- *Create a need-for-speed managerial style.* Hyde's day-to-day management style has shifted to a less formal, quicker response mode. Gone are the days of printed memoranda and formal appointments. Now much of Hyde's communication with staff is accomplished through zipping off e-mails and attending just-in-time informal meetings.
- *Appreciate knowledge as a valuable deliverable.* Coming from a culture in which the company's value was dependent on physical assets (transformers, wires, hydroelectric generators), Hyde had to shift into a business model requiring substantial investments to be made in creating and maintaining an information system designed to produce knowledge, not things. Moreover, it's Hyde's vision and commitment to knowledge and information systems that will allow GMER's energy resources to burn bright for its customers.[22]

SUMMARY

- Making your business defection proof requires information— information about your customers, information about their needs and preferences, information about your own business and its strengths and weaknesses.

- Gathering data is essential to serving customers and making them loyal.

- Getting on the information highway running past your door makes keeping and creating loyal customers easier than ever before.

- Customer information systems integrate customer data and make it available to every facet of the company.

- Every contact is an opportunity to build and deepen the relationship with the customer when a good CIS is in place.

- A CIS database can be built via direct human contact or the Internet.

- Sophisticated Web programs can capture and customize data, making every contact with customers a personal event.

- CISs are in the forefront of marketing innovation.

- New technology is available every day, but the success of any system is still dependent on the elegance of its design, intelligence of its users, and knowledge of the decision makers.

CHAPTER EIGHT

Targeting Prospects with Strong Loyalty Potential

Without question, the most important step any company can take for winning customer loyalty and reducing defections is to recruit high-potential prospects in the first place. But identifying the best prospects can be a challenging process. This chapter will examine six rules for targeting high-potential prospects and explain how to avoid common mishaps that can hinder the process.

RULE 1. ATTRACT THE BEST PROSPECTS

Learning to attract the right prospects is an often painful lesson that once learned can pay big dividends for any firm. Consider the experience of Susan Bishop, founder and president of Bishop Partners. When Bishop launched her New York-based executive search company in 1990, a shortage of cash weighed heavily on the new operation, as it does with most start-ups. And because client revenue was in short supply, Bishop and her staff thought almost any paying client would do. Why? Because they believed that making their clients happy through great service was the first priority. After all, they reasoned, happy clients would then lead to more business and with more business comes more revenue. Explained Bishop:

> [One client in that period] was the CEO of a large cable TV network with an important executive position sitting vacant—and he wanted to fill it fast. The search would bring much-needed visibility to our two-year-old operation, not to mention $30,000 in the bank. We knew that the CEO was ornery and could even be verbally abusive. We also knew that he refused to share financial and strategic data with us that could help us sell his company to candidates. And we were well aware that he wanted to screen the resume of every candidate we located and choose whom to interview himself—never mind what we thought. But these were small problems, we reasoned, given the enormous upside of the job.
>
> *Yes, we said, we'll take the business.*

Five years later, Bishop Partners had grown, but at a cost. The firm's happy client business model was now in doubt. Earnings remained flat, employees were stressed from working for demanding and difficult clients, and the company was conducting mostly middle-management searches.

But things were about to change. Attending Harvard Business School's boot camp for entrepreneurs inspired Bishop to redefine the company's mission to concentrate on high-level executive search consulting in selected industries. Returning to her firm, she was shocked to discover that her staff had highly disparate images of the business, none of which agreed with her definition. So they went to work as a team to develop a new business model, one that would make getting the *right* customers the company's first priority.

How did shifting the focus to the *right* customers change Bishop Partners' targeting strategy? Look no further than Bishop's description of a prospective 1997 client assignment and compare it to her 1992 decision:

> The client was the founder of a publicly traded Internet company looking for a new CEO. E-commerce was an arena we ardently wanted to enter, and the search would bring in at least $60,000. But this time, similarly "small" problems loomed large to us. The founder had already made up his mind that he wanted a CEO with a sales background and wouldn't allow us to analyze whether that made sense

from a strategic point of view. Further, he wanted us to find a CEO who would accept a salary 25% below the market rate, without equity. And finally, he refused to pay us our full fee until the new CEO had been in the job three months and as he put it, "I know if I like him."

No, we said, we won't touch your job.

Bishop and her team realized that being handcuffed from the beginning meant that the situation was likely to be difficult throughout. Rather than find themselves in a no-win situation down the road, they chose to decline the job in the beginning. Having defined the type of client that was desirable, the company was able to identify and refuse a client that would only mean trouble.[1]

How Streamline Hits the Target

As at Bishop Partners, a stringent target definition drives the marketing strategy at Streamline, Inc., the Boston-based Internet provider of household goods and services. Says Gina Wilcox, director of strategic relations, "We have a laser-like focus on busy suburban families (BSF). Everything we do involves them. Just because you can do business with someone doesn't mean that you should. It's easy to get customers. It's harder to get the right customers." Streamline defines BSFs as young and middle-aged couples with high incomes and at least one child. Today more than 90 percent of Streamline's customer base lies within the BSF bull's-eye, and about that same percentage has household incomes of $75,000 or greater.

Streamline's ruthlessly clear target definition is producing results. On average its customers place orders in forty-seven out of the fifty-two weeks each year. The average order costs more than $110 and consists of around seventy-five separate items. This brings the value of the average customer's total purchases to more than $5,000 per year. What's more, over half of Streamline's new customers come as a result of referrals from existing customers.

Streamline's services work like this: a customer pays a $30 per month subscription, and Streamline installs a delivery box in the customer's garage. The box is designed to store refrigerated, frozen, and dry goods. Next a Streamline field agent visits the home, equipped with a bar code scanner, and records what's already stocked in the pantry, refrigerator, and medicine cabinet. From this data, the agent creates a first draft of the customer's shopping list and posts it on the

Web where the customer can edit it and place weekly orders. Customers choose from over ten thousand grocery items in addition to other household services like film processing, laundry, and dry cleaning.

In contrast to many on-line start-ups with a get-big-now strategy, Streamline has the mantra "first, get it right" and then grow it big. Says Tim DeMello, Streamline's founder and CEO, "You have to get your business model absolutely perfect before you do a full-screen launch into the market. Because if you succeed on the Web, you succeed big. And you can't change a tire on a car that's moving at 80 miles per hour." But just like Susan Bishop, DeMello knows that choosing to acquire the right customers means also choosing to acquire fewer customers. "Everybody asks me the same question," laments DeMello. "How many customers do you have? That's the wrong question! The right questions are, 'How much business is each customer doing?' and 'How many customers are referring new people to you?' In the categories we serve, we get 85% of the money that our customers spend each year. And our referral rate is out of sight."[2]

How to Find Your Right Customer

Consider these six key factors as you work to target the customers that you can serve best and that will be loyal in return.

1. *Define your niche and develop your business model around it.* How you define your firm has everything to do with the customers you will attract. For Streamline this means defining itself not as an on-line grocery business like Peapod or NetGrocer, but as a lifestyle solutions business. Although plenty of Web companies operate on the cutting edge of technology, Streamline prefers to operate on the cutting edge of service. Its promise to customers is proof of this commitment: in return for $30 per month, Streamline will save the family three to five hours per week and will perform those chores with such detail that customers keep coming back and refer others to boot.

2. *Target clients and industries that match your firm's vision and expertise.* Having a true depth of knowledge in specific market spaces and then targeting clients accordingly can pay big dividends. Word of mouth and referrals can shorten your selling cycle and once you capture the new customer, your learning from past assignments helps you add value quickly. For Bishop Partners, for example, this means targeting entertainment and media-related market spaces, looking for

assignments from television, publishing, radio, and new media and e-commerce companies but turning away from assignments in financial services, banking, retailing, and so on. For Streamline, this means targeting busy, affluent suburban families who are looking to simplify their lives.

3. *Make sure the profitability is there.* Nothing is more disheartening to a company than to attract new customers who are ultimately unprofitable. Profit margin considerations should be implicit in any definition of target customers. Bishop Partners analyzed client profit margins and raised its minimum fee from $30,000 to $40,000. At a commission rate of 33 percent, this meant the firm would accept assignments only for executives earning a minimum of $120,000 a year. In Chapter One, we discussed what Garth Hallberg calls the *high-profit segment* and how, in many industries, one-third of the buyers account for at least two thirds of the volume.[3] For example, heavy users of fast food visit chains like McDonald's, Wendy's, and Burger King at least twenty times a month. These customers represent only 20 percent of their patrons—but 60 percent of all fast-food visits. Moreover, these high-profit customers generally deliver six to ten times as much profit as the low-profit segment. Look carefully at prospective customers and clients and how they rank in profitability potential.

4. *Take only new clients with strong opportunities for repeat business. Growability* of an account is key. For Bishop Partners, this means targeting companies that are already large enough to require senior level searches in the future or are on a growth curve that makes such searches likely. This is critical to the firm's success because the first search for any client teaches Bishop Partners a lot about the client's culture and this knowledge then helps the search firm conduct even better subsequent searches. For Streamline, this means collaborating with families who, because they want less hassle from routine chores, are willing to let the firm get closer so as to find more and better ways to serve them. That's why a whopping 30 percent to 40 percent of Streamline customers voluntarily participate each week in mini-research studies on the firm's Web site and why most new customers go on to add additional Streamline services throughout the relationship.

5. *Take new clients that hire you for your expertise and will let you do your job.* For Bishop Partners, this means having clients who will collaborate with staff in analyzing the requirements of the open position

and creating a job description that addresses it. For Streamline, this means having customers who grant delivery reps permission to enter their garages even when no one is home. It also means having customers who are likely to participate in Streamline's Don't Run Out program. Families identify their must-have items—such as milk, diapers, pet food—and authorize the company to replenish these items automatically. Today, almost every Streamline customer uses Don't Run Out.

6. *Be wary of bad press prospects.* Reputation matters. Difficult clients can damage staff morale and your bottom line. Make a habit of saying no to prospects who have received bad press for business or fiscal improprieties.

Ways to Spot the Ultra Customer

As we just mentioned, every industry has a fraction of high-profit, or *ultra,* customers. Let's analyze these right customers in more detail. Studies have shown that in retailing, for example, ultra customers outspend others by a ratio of six to one. At electronic retailer QVC, the ratio is ten to one. In the airline industry, the ratio is twelve to one, and in the restaurant business it's thirteen to one.[4]

Customer profiling and computer data modeling are enabling companies to get increasingly sophisticated in identifying and targeting high-value prospects. A host of demographic and lifestyle data suppliers are developing *conversion* model software to help firms identify new prospects. The newest prospecting software is helping uncover these ultra characteristics among prospects:

- They need less direct incentive to purchase.
- They are more resistant than other customers to competitive claims and lure away attempts.
- They are less price sensitive.
- They are more accepting of occasional value delivery lapses and less likely to accept alternatives if their brand or service is unavailable.
- They are apt to demonstrate more positive attitudes about "their" brand.
- They exhibit changes in level of supplier commitment prior to their declines in purchase behavior.

Jan Hofmeyr and Butch Rice of the South African firm Research Surveys have been developing leading-edge prospecting and targeting methods for identifying ultra customers. They have created a computer model that allows a client's marketplace to be viewed in terms of users and nonusers. Users can be divided into those who are truly committed and loyal and those who are *convertible*, that is declining or wavering in their loyalty. Nonusers (prospects and former customers) are divided into potentially convertible and nonavailable (because they are committed to their current supplier). Detailed analysis can then be developed for current customers and prospects. The percentage of current customers who are entrenched, or completely loyal, can be identified, as well as those who have moderate loyalty, shallow loyalty, or convertibility (true vulnerability). Nonusers (prospects or former customers) can be identified in similar categories: those who are available or highly receptive to a competitive offer and those who are ambivalent but who would switch with the right incentive. Other prospects who have average or strong loyalty to their brand or supplier are considered unavailable by the model.

This model is being used to plan the amount of advertising and promotional activity required for new customers and prospects according to their commitment level and potential value. It has been applied in over fifty countries and for scores of products and services. Hofmeyr and Rice have found, for example, that banks in the United States and South Africa have committed customer scores of 62 percent and 73 percent, respectively; however, the commitment score for United Kingdom banks is only 36 percent. This means that many UK bank customers are vulnerable to defection and ripe for acquisition. Hofmeyr and Rice's model is designed to both identify these high-value prospects and pinpoint the marketing message to which they will most likely respond.[5]

Segment the Right Customers

In addition to targeting the right prospects, you must place them into manageable segments as part of growing them into long-term customers. And this means more than looking at demographics. As Frederick G. Thompson, president of Kerr Kelly Thompson, a marketing communications firm, notes, "I have two neighbors in Connecticut who, according to commonly available demographic data, would appear to be virtually identical. They're both fifty-one years old, live in the same zip code and each earned more than $1 million last year. One is an Ivy-League-educated investment banker. The other is Keith Richards, the rather eccentric chain-smoking lead guitarist of the Rolling Stones."[6]

As the Keith Richards/banker example illustrates, effectively segmenting targeted prospects can be a challenging process. We looked at segmenting customers by customer lifetime value in Chapter Three and at the importance of using LTV to allocate marketing and product development resources. Here are some additional things to consider as you segment your targeted prospects.

- Select a manageable number of segments.
- Ensure that each segment addresses explicitly different people or businesses.
- Make sure the people or firms in each segment are similar enough to respond well to the same positioning and advertising appeals.
- Ensure that each segment description evokes for the marketer a clear, intuitively sensible customer picture.
- Choose only segments that have enough stability and longevity to warrant a long-term contact strategy.
- Capture and use evolving behavior, attitude, and needs data to deepen customer profiles and test segment validation as relationships mature.
- Make sure customer migration from one segment to another makes sense when it occurs.[7]

RULE 2. KNOW HOW TO SPOT THE CUSTOMERS YOU DON'T WANT

Although it's important to define and target the right customers, it can be equally critical to spot those prospects you don't want as well. It's a strategy more and more firms are practicing. Just look at Big Five accounting firms like Arthur Andersen and Price Waterhouse. They have stepped-up their scrutiny of prospective clients, asking them to submit information ranging from financial condition and internal financial controls to management structure and changes. Although this has meant some near-term revenue loss, overall these accounting firms have come out ahead because many had been spending more than 15 percent of their auditing and accounting revenue on professional liability coverage. How about clients who have a track record of disputes with former auditors? It's often a reason to say "no thanks," according to Pat McDonnell, vice president of business assurance practices for Coopers & Lybrand's Chicago office: "Now, we won't take on a client that has fired its previous accounting firm over an accounting dispute because it indicates a greater risk."[8]

More and more companies are finding that learning to say no can actually be a growth strategy. Companies should also always be on the lookout for prospects who could contribute more problems than value. We've identified five types of customers you should try to avoid:

• *Price grinders.* Beware of new customers who pressure you to low-ball your price on an initial sale and in return promise you loads of long-term future business. You'll likely never see more business in the future. The automotive retailing industry has more than its share of price grinders, prospective customers who will beat on a dealer to get the lowest price or the most attractive loan or lease terms. These prospects will often fabricate an offer from another dealer and play it against the legitimate offer. All the while the price grinder is also remarking that his wife is ready to trade, his son turns sixteen soon, and his mother-in-law needs a new car. Some innovative dealerships are now practicing one price–no hassle vehicle pricing, which a number of customers—especially women—prefer and which has the benefit for the dealer of removing the possibility of price grinder behavior from the car purchase process.

• *Chronic defectors.* These are customers who regularly pull their business from suppliers without explanation. Their volatility and refusal to communicate make them undesirable. Chronic defectors are the bought away customers we profiled in Chapter Three. They are particularly prevalent in industries that are highly competitive on price and other sign-up incentives, such as long distance and cellular phone companies and credit-card issuers. When credit-card companies, for example, offer low initial annual percentage rates, high credit limits, and minimal balance transfer fees, they tend to attract customers who pay off their balances every month and then move on when the low APR period is up.

• *Discourteous dorks.* These are chronically rude and verbally abusive customers who often show their stripes at the first meeting with any new supplier. One warning sign is that the prospect doesn't practice simple courtesies such as saying "please" and "thank you." These customers are routinely hard on staff and undermine a company's morale and operations. What's more, these tough-to-take behaviors often manifest themselves in other discourteous actions such as not paying invoices on time, further burdening staff and profit margins.

• *Pushers.* These are quick-fix customers who want to find new suppliers with great haste. And they are often more trouble than they're worth. For example, a red flag goes up for veteran real-estate broker Kathy Doyle, of Boston-based Doyle, Hennessey and Evergreen, whenever she gets a call from a new client who desperately wants to go out that very day to look for office space. "Anyone who has to move immediately makes me nervous," she says. "Usually they either didn't pay their rent or they don't plan very well or they don't make efficient decisions."[9] Will prospects like these return big profits? It's doubtful.

• *Misfits.* Finally, beware of new customers who have needs that may not align well with your firm's ability to perform. For example, if 99.9 percent of your firm's deliveries to customers are made during normal business hours, and the new customer wants delivery in the middle of the night, tread carefully. Unless this customer represents a great deal of high-margin business, it's probably an account not worth taking.

Internet marketing strategist David Siegel believes that, because today's customers are so demanding, no company can serve more than five target groups, or segments, well. Companies must be extremely selective, as a result, about the customers they want. As Siegel says: "The customer is always right, but not all customers are always right for you."[10]

RULE 3. BUILD YOUR PRODUCT OR SERVICE WITH THE RIGHT CUSTOMERS IN MIND

Having a clear understanding of your customers' likes and dislikes and then designing your products and services to match these needs is essential for successful targeting. A one-size-fits-all strategy is a recipe for disaster, and smart companies have learned that the most successful products and services are those designed, from the start, with the right customer in mind.

How Target Corporation Built
Its Own Field of Dreams

"If you build it, he will come." In the hit 1989 movie *Field of Dreams,* these were the mysterious words that Iowa farmer Ray Kinsella heard echoing from his cornfields. The words inspired Ray to turn his ordinary cornfield into a place where dreams could come true.

That very same year, that same phrase could just as aptly have applied to the expansion strategy of Target discount stores. The original strategy, that is. After some painful misses in 1989, the chain of more than 620 stores learned the true motto for success required adding one more, but very important, word: "If you build it *right,* they will come."

That's the lesson Target, owned by Dayton Hudson Corp., discovered during the launch of its first Florida stores in the fall of 1989. These stores were opened while the chain was conducting a national marketing effort with Will Steger, the first person to cross Antarctica on a dog sled. And like all other Target stores, the shiny new Florida stores were brimming that autumn with snow parkas, gloves, and sweaters. The inventory didn't sell. And that's when Target began its journey into what retailers call *micromarketing,* a strategy in which each store's array of products reflects those items most desired by shoppers in the store's immediate trading area.

Target micromarkets by stocking products in each store according to local demographic and lifestyle characteristics. For example, one suburban community's profile may be high-income young families with an interest in leisure products and sporting goods. For a Target store in this area, kids' soccer outfits and in-line skates might sell very well. Contrast the suburban store to an inner-city Target store, surrounded by lower-income customers with strong religious ties, where items like first Communion dresses and candles could be big sellers. Says Robert Giampietro, the Target vice president who leads the micromarketing effort, "it comes down to having the right merchandise in the right store at the right time."

But like most changes in strategy, internal challenges plagued Target's entry into the new world of micromarketing. At first, buyers resisted the micromarketing approach because they believed that their success lay in making big, profitable purchases that would deliver big volume and brisk sales chainwide. They quickly came around, however, when they saw the success of selling athletic apparel with the logos of local teams. From almost nothing in 1991, this athletic apparel business grew to $100 million in 1996, and this watershed event helped the buyers see the potential for doing business this new way. Today, Target's 150 buyers are required to visit the stores for which they buy as well as surrounding competitive stores. In addition, Target also gives its stores the authorization to add other merchandise without the buyers' approval.

The other tool in Target's micromarketing tool kit is a complex, computer-driven combination of planning, buying, and store operations. First, buyers develop merchandise assortments to appeal to customers segmented by ethnicity and by age. Next, planners look at each individual store and fill its merchandise needs according to a community profile. Store managers then tweak the model, drawing from their personal knowledge about local tastes and practices. The old retail adage that "retail is detail" is especially true for micromarketing. This attention to detail means that Target ships more one-piece bathing suits to Florida's west coast and its older customers and sends more bikinis to the state's eastern shore and younger patrons. It means carrying local favorite Jays potato chips in Chicago stores and stocking Saguaro branded chips in Phoenix.

Currently, the sum of different products carried by each store is only about 15 percent to 20 percent of the total, but the result is a different mix in almost every Target store. Target's goal, however, is to increase the amount of goods contoured to local preferences to 30 percent. And Target's micromarketing strategy is right on target, according to Al Meyers, retail consultant in Price Waterhouse's Management Horizons division. Says Meyers, "The high performance retailers of the future will be those who carry products specifically selected for their own customers. The days of retailers being all things to all people are over."[11]

Building a Brand On-Line and Off

If you're Michael Kahn, vice president of marketing for Art.com, a well-defined target definition is more than words on a whiteboard. It's the company's guiding light to a successful future. Launched in 1997,

Art.com aspires to become a household name or as Kahn puts it, "the Crate and Barrel of art." But the folks at Art.com have a feet-on-the-ground mentality about their path. Says Kahn, "We may be an on-line business and reached through a modem or T1 line, but at the end of the day, we are still another retail brand selling through a new distribution channel." Moreover, "We need to 'own' a really tight definition of who our target is, what our positioning is and what our personality will become." That's why Art.com has distilled its branding strategy into three key points, as reported by Kahn:

- *Target:* female consumers and other art buyers (men, recent movers, newlyweds, gays and lesbians, college students)
- *Positioning:* to be the inviting and fun destination for discovering and buying art and art-related products that the consumer has never had before . . . not in 2,000 years of civilization
- *Personality:* cool and sophisticated, yet simple and accessible[12]

Having a tight target definition is key to successful branding. It's the crucial starting point for creating those all-important things that ultimately *brand* a company and its products and services in the mind of a buyer. But successful branding is more than a logo and advertising copy. It's the feeling that prospects and customers get when they walk into your store or log on to your site. It's why early in the history of Wal-Mart, Sam Walton stationed those nice senior citizens at store entrances to greet you. It's why Amazon.com's brand includes those surprise gifts that get shipped along with your order. It's why Saturn has those polo-shirted salespeople with their no-haggle approach to car selling. You get the picture.

Whether you are building a business on-line or off, pay attention to the entire range of your user's experience because, in the end, that's how you are remembered. Make no mistake—your brand is the sum total of how your customer is touched by your organization. It's about the way your receptionist answers the phone, it's about how quickly your products ship, it's about the accuracy of your invoices, it's about the way your firm is portrayed in the media, it's about how fast your help desk solves problems. The bottom line is that your branding begins the first time your prospect comes in contact with your firm. And as our mothers told us growing up, "You only get one chance to make a good first impression."

RULE 4. STAFF YOUR FIRM WITH EMPLOYEES WHO MATCH YOUR CUSTOMERS' NEEDS

Does targeting the right customers mean letting go of staff whose skills no longer match customer needs? The answer is often yes. And it can be a gut-wrenching process for everyone, especially when staff feel like family and the dismissals feel like divorce. Remember Bishop Partners' shift to a right customer strategy? That forced right employee issues as well. Explains Susan Bishop, "We couldn't position ourselves as industry experts if our staff was composed of junior-level people doing work in haphazard ways. The time had come to raise the bar for our employees and to build an infrastructure that could support them."

Four staff members were let go over a period of months, and these dismissals did more than rupture the company family; they sent a strong signal that Bishop's role was also changing. "I had long been seen as friend, mother, mentor, chief cheerleader, and member of the crew," Bishop says; "it was time to become the boss." Personnel policies about such issues as sick leave and work hours were tightened. An employee manual was written. Many staff members complained, and some staffers left—including some Bishop wished had stayed. But these resignations gave her further opportunity to begin hiring more skilled employees. She also built a reporting structure that relieved her from having all employees as direct reports and enabled her to spend more time selling business rather than managing internal operations. In addition, staff training and education went into high gear. In-house mini-MBA programs were created, and attendance by staff at key industry conferences and trade shows was encouraged. The result of this staff realignment around the right customer business model is that Bishop Partners now enjoys the largest staff, revenues, and profit margins in the company's history.[13]

A similar issue surrounding the right employees arose during Streamline's early days, as well. At a time when the start-up company was desperate for more help, Tim DeMello looked at his six-person frontline staff and dismissed three of the employees in one day, because, as he said: "They didn't seem like people I wanted to do business with. It's about longevity. It's about creating a genuine service culture." Streamline marketing vice president Frank Britt echoed this sentiment: "When you're inventing a new business model, one critical question is: What kind of team do you put together? We're pursuing a 'best available athlete' strategy. It's like when a pro football team drafts a college sprinter and turns him into an All-Pro receiver. It's not about what you've done. It's about what you can do."[14]

RULE 5. AVOID THE CASANOVA COMPLEX

Ask almost anyone what they associate with the name Casanova, and you'll likely get some smiles and smirks and references to a man who lived long ago whose female conquests are legendary. Born Giovanni Giacomo Casanova in Venice, this eighteenth-century Italian adventurer was a soldier, a preacher, a secretary, an alchemist, a gambler, a violinist, a lottery director, a spy, and a member of the court of Louis XV. But few know these details. It's Casanova's reputation as a love 'em and leave 'em ladies' man that has captured our imaginations.

Not so very different from Casanova, many companies devote considerably more energy and resources to winning or capturing customers than they do to keeping them. In fact, if you listen closely, you will find the term *conquest* is a frequently used description of the new customer in many industries, automotive retailers for one. Companies often focus on chasing down the next sale, competing on price, and compensating employees for winning new accounts—at the expense of keeping existing customers happy and loyal. Many companies perpetuate what we call the Casanova Complex and drive it through their organizations in several key ways. Let's look at two critical problem areas for many companies:

• *Sales compensation programs.* Compensating salespeople, and sometimes other staff, for the new customers they bring in and not for the customers they keep and build is a common practice in many organizations, and it can result in costly, counterproductive behaviors by both customers and sales reps. For example, a home and business security systems company we know rewarded its top annual producers of new customers with free trips to luxurious resort locations. These people were feted and presented with plaques of achievement at a special awards dinner. Most of these salespeople revealed, however, that many of their customers left one year and returned the next, demonstrating little loyalty and only coming back when the salesperson offered some small additional element of value. On the company's books, these reclaimed accounts were shown as new. Both customers and salespeople had learned to work the system to their advantage. The situation we described in Chapter Two for the South African telecommunications provider MTN points to a similar result. Customers and salespeople ended up rewarded when customers disconnected and reconnected to the service.

• *Promotional programs for attracting new triers.* These offers will bring in some folks that will stay for the long haul, but they also attract many bargain shoppers, people you've bought away from someone else. They are with you only for the benefits of your promotional deal, and then they'll move on to yet another offer. Recognizing such patterns led New Zealand Telecom to take a progressive approach to generating new customers and recovering lost customers from competitors. It developed Talking Points, a rewards program aimed at high-spending new, current, and former customers. Customers earn points based on the volume of their long-distance activity, and then use these points to select products and services such as free toll calls, movie passes, multimonth call-waiting services, and even cordless phones, pagers, fax machines, and travel packages. Such a program is designed to be self-selecting, culling out customers who are light users and frequent switchers. New Zealand Telecom included a detailed and highly comprehensive lifestyles and demographics questionnaire with the mailing that launched the program. Submitting the completed questionnaire gave participants extra points toward their rewards, and New Zealand Telecom, remarkably, received in excess of a 90 percent response. Questionnaire information has helped with Talking Points continuity and helped the company discover which elements of the program are likely to yield the most productive new and converted customers.

Here are some ways to help your firm avoid the Casanova Complex:

• *Audit your sales and promotional programs and policies with the Casanova Complex in mind.* You don't want to target love 'em and leave 'em customers or to behave that way toward your customers yourself. Instead, you want high-potential prospects that are solid opportunities for partnership and long-term relationship building. Revise any policies that attract and reward only short-term relationships. Think quality over quantity.

• *Track the loyalty of customers recruited through sales and promotional offers.* Your success metrics should include response rates (number of people who say yes to an offer as a percentage of all who receive the offer) as well as repeat purchase rates, cross-purchase rates, referral rates, and so on. Most firms simply measure initial response rate and then Casanova behavior often goes undetected. As a result these very same sales or promotional programs are continued, often with the same unproductive results.

• *Practice out-of-the-box thinking when designing sales and promotional offers.* Recognizing that promotional offers were a fact of life in the telecom industry, New Zealand Telecom conceived a reward plan that sought out and locked in high users.

• *Look for ways to reward retention selling.* For example, at your next sales banquet consider giving out rewards for these selling milestones:

> • Sales rep who has made the largest sale to an existing customer
>
> • Sales rep who has the most customers cross-purchasing lines of your company's products
>
> • Sales rep who has the biggest increase in existing customer sales over sales one year ago

• *Make referrals from existing customers the undisputed preferred way to gain new business in your company.* Use such means as employee rewards and customer success stories to make referrals a prized commodity in your organization.

RULE 6. WORK FOR REFERRALS— THE BEST WAY TO GET THE NEW CUSTOMERS YOU WANT

In the customer research studies we conduct for clients, we consistently find the scores for likelihood of recommending a product or service to a friend, relative, or associate are lower than the likelihood that the customer would purchase that product or service herself. Why? Because the referring customer often feels reluctant to risk her own reputation by recommending the product or service. Customers will often say something like this: "I use that company's services and I like them, but it took me awhile to learn their system. I'm not sure my buddy would be quite as patient."

In fact, this resistance to recommending makes recommendation an even more prized commodity. When customers do refer, the referral carries some clout. That's why referral is the best and most reliable method of generating attractive new customers. It is *permission-based* marketing of the strongest order. For example, studies have shown that a referred prospect has an 80 percent likelihood of making a decision to buy. Studies also show that a referred prospect is more likely to remain loyal than is a new buyer who comes to you any other way.[15]

Leveraging word of mouth has been a key success driver for San Jose–based auction site eBay since its launch in 1997. As other Silicon Valley start-ups wrestled for market awareness through expensive TV and print campaigns, eBay spent almost nothing on advertising and marketing. Instead, eBay's marketing team chose to make the rounds at collector trade shows where they could demonstrate their offerings to high-value prospects. This pound-the-pavement strategy paid off big. Traffic to the site exploded and so did word of mouth. Early users spread the word by posting glowing praise on collecting newsgroup sites and e-mail chains. All of this has made eBay earnings something to talk about as well. Net earnings for the first quarter of 1999 were $34 million, a 469 percent increase over the $6 million reported for the same period the previous year, establishing eBay as the undisputed leader in the on-line trading community.

The company is showing no signs of abandoning its commitment to nurturing word of mouth. At this writing, two eBay-branded Fleetwoods are crossing the country so that site users can talk face to face with company staffers in a campaign with the motto "From our homepage to your hometown." Says the eBay vice president of marketing, "We learned early on, if you listen to your customers, they will become your greatest evangelists."[16]

The Internet has opened up a new dimension in word-of-mouth marketing. When Steven Jurvetson and his partners at the venture capital firm Draper Fisher Jurvetson coined the phrase *viral marketing* in 1997, they were describing the way Hotmail, one of their portfolio companies, was targeting customers through a message at the bottom of every e-mail. In its first eighteen months, Hotmail, a free e-mail service for Web users, signed up over twelve million subscribers with a marketing, advertising, and promotion budget of less than $500,000. It's now signing up more than 150,000 subscribers every day, seven days a week. "[The process is] like an adaptive virus," says Jurvetson. "We defined it initially as network-enhanced word of mouth."[17]

Quite simply, viral marketing can be defined as any technique that induces Web sites or users to pass on a marketing message to other sites or users, potentially creating exponential growth in the message's visibility and impact.

It's a concept that's making a big difference for many companies including catalogue retailer Boston Proper, which estimates that 30 percent of the traffic at its new Web site, Bostonproper.com, is generated by viral marketing. Boston Proper advertises its on-line address only in its mail-order catalogues, yet its Web site gets new customers everyday. Where are they coming from? From the company's E-mail a Friend program. It's a viral marketing campaign that Boston Proper is using to turn on-line shopping from a solo activity into a more social experience shared with family and friends. The company's research had long shown that women like to shop with their friends and enjoy the "how does this look on me?" experience together. So when Bostonproper.com revamped its Web site, a viral marketing feature was created. Consumers are encouraged to e-mail product listings from the Web site to relatives and friends. Sales figures soared the quarter the viral marketing campaign was introduced, with on-line sales jumping 100 percent over the previous quarter's sales. The Web site is now generating 8 percent of Boston Proper's total sales, compared with 3 percent before the marketing campaign was launched. Trend data suggest an increase to 20 percent for the coming year. Boston Proper is confident its viral marketing program along with the Web site's customer-friendly features will continue to attract more ultra customers—defined as affluent, baby boomer working women.[18] Other companies putting viral marketing to effective use include the following:

• At Chicago-based Anthem Corp.'s BarsOnLine.com, a visitor to the site can "buy" a friend a beer, and the friend gets a coupon redeemable at an affiliated bar. The person receiving the e-mail bar coupon also has the option of sending a coupon to a friend and so on. The *beer mail* campaign, along with sponsored events at affiliate bars, participation in street fairs, and radio ads, has increased traffic to the site ten-fold in about a year's time.

• Internet financial services company X.com, has built proprietary software to conduct its Refer-a-friend program among its customers. Every time a current customer recommends someone who is then approved to become a customer, the person who did the referring receives a $10 credit in his X.com account up to a maximum of $1,000. All of X.com's marketing is being conducted among current customers; the bank is not conducting any external e-mail marketing.

• SmarterKids.com, is an on-line educational store for parents with children three to fourteen years of age. This marketer of learning-oriented toys, games, books, and software for children employs a team of teachers who evaluate each product on more than two hundred attributes, including appropriateness, grade, major and minor skills required, and learning style. SmarterKids.com generates new customers through its referral incentive program. For every prospect referred by a customer, SmarterKids sends both the prospect and the customer a $10 coupon. SmarterKids sends a personalized e-mail to the prospect, which the customer has initiated on the SmarterKids site. The e-mail contains instructions to go to a special site that gives the prospect the discount.

Almost any company can benefit from viral marketing tactics. Don't think that referral programs are just for dot-com companies. With e-mail becoming a mainstream communication tool, any company's existing referral program can be power charged with e-mail oriented viral marketing applications. Let's look at two quick examples: a firm we know that provides computer system consulting offers referral incentives to existing clients in the form of days of professionals services, at a value of $1,500 per day. The number of days awarded is based on the number of new customers referred. There is no limit on the number of days that can be earned. Likewise, an Internet service provider we know gives a month of connection service to any customer who refers a new customer who stays with the ISP for at least three months. Both of these companies could increase participation by sending this offer to their customers via e-mail. In addition, they could post this offer on their Web sites and add a "send to a friend" button to the page that would quickly send the offer along to the e-mail address provided. Such strategies are something to think about when you consider the power of referral and the fact that e-mail messages cost $.01 to $.25 per message compared to $1 to $2 per direct-mail piece.

BEYOND TARGETING—TURNING PROSPECTS INTO TRIERS

As we've discussed, companies should be cautious and disciplined about targeting the right prospects. But there is another reality to consider. Until high-value prospects are converted into buyers their profit potential remains untapped. As Robert Louis Stevenson once said, "Nothing happens 'til somebody buys something," and the only way a firm can recoup prospecting costs and create profitable relationships is to consistently win sales. But turning high-value prospects into first-time buyers is harder than ever and requires patience and diligence. From the loyalty studies we conduct for clients, we have found that customers are much more wary and selective than they were even five years ago, and this caution will continue to increase. Several factors are contributing to this trend.

• *Information availability and access.* Customers are better educated and more experienced as buyers than at any time in the past. Couple this with the rapid increase in available information (through the Internet, cable television, and standard print and electronic media), and you have a consuming population that makes more in-depth, considered decisions. Because this readily available information invites comparison shopping, it's important that your company's frontliners stay better informed than your customers. Employee sales training and information updates, research, and so forth are requirements for competing in the information age.

• *Time pressure and the need for speed.* Not only is information available in greater abundance, but ever-higher levels of technology are delivering it with ever increasing speed. We have become the *hurry-up society* as a result of such instant tools as e-mail, faxes, and digital phones. Speed has become one of the most important and visible areas of performance, and it's often a make-or-break issue for new prospects on-line and off. One big culprit is *barriers to click.* Web usage studies[19] suggest that the typical user is using a mental model that says, "I'm assuming the next page I click on will take about the average amount of time to download as the average of all the pages I have already clicked on in this site thus far." If the first three pages took "forever," then the user will often resist clicking on other links. This barrier to click can greatly dampen the user's willingness to explore and ultimately become attached to your site. Off-line customers get irritated with time-wasters such as slow-moving cash register lines, ill-fitting merchandise, and returns that waste time and money. Screw this up with a prospect and you can kiss your conversion opportunities good-bye. That's why upscale supermarket chain Wegman's Food Markets, headquartered in Rochester, New York, continues to find innovative ways to cater to its hurry-up clientele. With directly delivered locally grown produce and stores with up to thirty-five checkout stations, some Wegman's stores earn over $1 million in weekly revenue, several times the national average.

• *Overpromise and underdelivery intolerance.* In this age where instant gratification is the norm, it's easy for customer expectations to soar. It's a chain reaction that can keep your prospects from converting into buyers. Here's how it happens: your advertising or promotional message makes a promise to a prospect; that promise, in turn, creates a certain expectation. Expectation, in turn, translates to accountability. The performance of your product or service must match or exceed, in the mind of your prospect, this accountability, and it's often a gold standard, that is, one that's hard to meet. Recognizing the prospect's tendency to escalate the expectation, tread carefully with your marketing messages. The best strategy is always to underpromise and overdeliver. Some sales trainers call this the *and-then-some* approach, advising companies to deliver value at least slightly greater than what was promised.

SUMMARY

- Business is moving faster and faster as technology speeds up movement of information.

- Start-up companies often make the mistake of thinking any customer is a good customer.

- Successful businesses do not waste time wooing the wrong customers.

- Successful companies define the kind of customers they want and focus on serving those customers' needs.

- Successful companies develop methods for keeping appropriate customers.

- Learning to spot undesirable customers is almost as important as learning to spot desirable ones.

- Tailoring your products and services to the customer creates a lucrative and satisfying match.

- Staffing your business with people that match the focus of the company and the target customers will help you find and keep the right customers.

- Focusing on developing long-term relationships with the right customers is a better strategy than focusing on winning many new customers.

- The best customers will come from referrals from existing good customers.

CHAPTER NINE

Leveraging the Power of Customer-Focused Teams

S everal years ago employees at technical computing software supplier The Math Works voted on the area of the firm that was the biggest hassle. The winner? The operations department, and for good reason. Customer orders at the Natick, Massachusetts–based company took up to ten days to turn around because of an overly complicated fulfillment process involving lots of steps and staffers. The vote confirmed what operations vice president Elizabeth Haight already knew: things had to change. Haight pulled her management group together and attempted to reinvent the order fulfillment process. It didn't work. That's when Haight and her associates went to the executive group with a dramatically different proposal: turn the traditionally styled hierarchical department into teams.

The executive group agreed, and Haight and her managers worked collaboratively to map out the transition plan. Recalls Haight, "We decided it was going to happen on a Monday. On Friday, I called the whole department together and explained the plan, what the new structure was, what their job title was, where they would sit, how what they did was going to change, and how we were going to do it."

By Monday morning, all forty people in the operations department were organized into six teams. The old systems were thrown out, and the department plunged headfirst into the land of teams. And within thirty days, orders that once took ten days were shipping in twenty-four hours.

How could so much improvement happen so quickly? Explains Haight, "We [made a commitment] that the management team, for the first month, would be a triage unit. The team would diagnose problems and offer suggestions for new ways to solve them. They'd be in the hallway and answer questions, encourage, and make sure the old ways were no longer in operation. We took away all the backlog so the operations staff had no excuse for falling back." But that didn't mean the staffers didn't have support. Managers were available at all times to help them with the new plan. Looking back, Haight says the triage—helping staffers diagnose what step to take next—was the most important part of getting the firm to quickly embrace the new working style.

The operation department's results ultimately launched the entire company's shift to a matrix-based organization in which staffers participated in cross-functional teams (see Figure 9.1 for definitions of these terms). This means, for example, that a software engineer assigned formally to the research and development department might also serve on a number of project teams, which could, for example, be focused on retooling the orientation program for new hires or developing a companywide customer database. Says Haight, "We pretty much have a matrix-run organization. Title doesn't mean much here. Everything we do is through cross-functional teams, at every level. So, the goal is to get the right people with the right knowledge into the room, not to get the people with the right title in the room."

For any company, the ultimate cross-functional partner is the customer, and The Math Works organization also involves customers directly with staff teams, especially in the areas of new product development and user training. Haight explains, "They actually come in and work with our engineers, and they sit in on cross-functional team meetings, as well. When we bring customers in for training, we get people from various parts of the company to sit with them while they use the product. Then, we work with the feedback they give us to get a better design."[1]

Take a look at companies that are successfully building customer loyalty, and you will often find widespread use of teams. Some of these

Figure 9.1. Terms to Know.

Team	A group of people whose work is interdependent and who are collectively responsible for achieving an outcome.
Cross-functional team	A group of people from different disciplines across an organization working together to achieve a mutually beneficial outcome.
Cross-trained team	A team whose members have been trained in several skills and can carry out multiple tasks.
Matrix organization	An organization in which team members report to both their project and functional or hierarchical managers (such as a sales or manufacturing manager). The organizational hierarchy is greatly flattened, allowing employees to get much closer to their customers. The company retains some functional (vertical) management structure, but the work accomplished through the team-based (horizontal) structure on behalf of the customer drives the organization. (The Math Works, discussed in this chapter, is an example of a matrix organization.)
Lattice organization	An organization in which employees are organized purely around projects. Unlike matrix organizations, lattice organizations have no major functional hierarchy within their structure.
Flat organization	An organization with less organizational hierarchy and more functional and employee autonomy. Most flat organizations use cross-functional teams to solve issues. Status comes from the mastery of problems, situations, and skills across boundaries.
Hierarchical organization	A traditional command-and-control organization, with multiple layers of management and strong boundaries between management and staff. Decisions are centralized and tightly controlled.

firms are pure team-based organizations where teams perform the core work of the organization—turning knowledge and raw materials into products and services that customers value. In these firms, work is done laterally: people work with their peers in a team, and teams work with other teams to accomplish tasks and make decisions.

In other successful organizations, teams may be more ad hoc, used for short-term purposes such as solving a specific customer service problem. The core work of the firm continues to occur through its line-and-box hierarchy. These are not team-based organizations. They are organizations that use teams. Suffice it to say that teams can be effective in a wide range of organization styles. In this chapter we'll look at how to assemble, train, and manage teams for maximum productivity, particularly in customer retention.

THE VALUE OF CUSTOMER-FIRST TEAMS

Without a doubt, some of America's best companies are proving that teaming is a vital way to structure work and meet business demands. But that is just part of the story. Take a team-based culture and overlay it with a keen focus on customer needs, and you've created customer-first teams. Then step back and let your teams lead the way. Those are some of the many lessons learned by the following companies as they have leveraged the power of customer-first teams. Read on.

How Teams Put a Hospital on the Road to Recovery

In 1995, Baptist Hospital, one of five hospitals in the Baptist Health Care System in Pensacola, Florida, was in trouble. Patient surveys ranked it near the bottom of all hospitals nationally, the patient census was dropping, and staff morale was dismal. Today, the picture is much different. Customer service surveys rank the hospital among the top 1 percent nationally. Market share has jumped 4 percentage points, and annual revenues are up $4.5 million and costs are down $3.5 million. Patient malpractice claims have dropped from ninety-four in 1994 to twenty-two six years later. Staff morale has significantly improved, and staff turnover is lower. What accounted for this remarkable turnaround? Employee teams.

In 1996, Baptist Hospital began forming cross-functional employee teams to examine every aspect of value delivery to patients and their families. Today, more than 150 employees out of 2,117 serve on teams annually. Team membership is diverse—cafeteria workers serve alongside corporate vice presidents—and teams explore a wide range of issues, from visitor parking to patient privacy. The result? These teams have developed hundreds of seemingly small improvements that together have made a huge impact on patient care. Here are just three of them:

- Arriving visitors are greeted with huge signs directing them to complementary valet parking.

- Scripts have been developed to help staff better interact with patients. For example, after cleaning a room, janitors now ask, "Is there anything else I can do? I have some time to help you." Patient requests often include closing a window shade, changing the volume on the television set, or opening or closing doors. Calls to nurses for such chores have declined by 40 percent.

• Nurses carry wireless phones so doctors can contact them without paging them over the intercom. This reduces noise and helps patients rest.

These changes and others like them have made a real difference for patients and their families. Said the daughter of one patient, "We got lost when my mother was a patient here, and a cleaning lady, instead of pointing, took us where we needed to go." And the happier the patients and their families, the stronger the customer loyalty. For example, a mother commenting on the care her son received in the emergency room said, "The kindness, care and compassion exhibited by these people were incredible." She went on to say that she didn't like Baptist Hospital before this encounter, but now plans to seek them out for future health care.

Pleased with the results at Baptist Hospital, its corporate parent, Baptist Health Care, has expanded the use of employee teams to its four other facilities in southwest Florida and southern Alabama. Commenting on what the employee teams have accomplished, Baptist Health Care vice president of marketing Pam Bilbrey, says, "Teams have led the way for our organization. They'll continue to be our beacon for improving patient care and winning customer loyalty."[2]

How Teamwork Is Changing IBM

Louis Gerstner walked into IBM on April Fool's Day 1993 as CEO, but the state of the company was anything but a laughing matter. Long known for lifetime employment, the company was in the process of cutting nearly half of its 406,000 person workforce. It had taken a write-off of $20 billion, and its stock price had plummeted. A daunting culture of perfectionism stymied the development and release of new products, causing Gerstner to remark to some technical people, "You don't launch products here. They escape."

But Gerstner saw through the company's problems to its strengths and opportunities. Because of its wide breadth of offerings, IBM, unlike many of its competitors, had the ability to provide clients with a comprehensive array of data management and manipulation solutions. In its quest to make perfect products, customer focus and a sense of urgency had been compromised. But that was about to change. As Gerstner said, "I came here with the view that you start the day with customers, that you start thinking about a company around its customers, and you organize around customers." And he did just that. Gerstner went to work to create a more customer-focused, team-based architecture. Ignoring tradition, he dismantled the company's geographical fiefdoms and ordered a reorganization of all functional areas from development to sales along industry lines. He ordered project teams to get close to customers and make things happen.

Perhaps no one at IBM took Gerstner's direction more to heart than David Gee and his team of twelve staffers whose mission was to reinvent how Big Blue does business. As Gee says, "Part of our job is to shake up the status quo. We want to get in trouble. We bend the rules." In the basement of IBM's Almaden Research Center in San Jose, Gee and his teammates oversee alphaWorks, IBM's on-line laboratory, created to change how the company commercializes products and communicates with customers. They have assembled an impressive network of over sixty thousand users who try out and experiment with IBM prototypes and new product ideas. This combination of customer focus and team orientation is paying big dividends. Within a few months of the team's formation, alphaWorks introduced five new Internet-based products in succession, a track record hardly imaginable within the structure of the old IBM. Says Gee, "I'm not going to tell you that we've changed the world. But, we are making a difference. And in a company this size, even a small win is a huge victory."[3]

Reaping the Advantages of Teamwork

Teams can offer a substantial advantage for firms intent on earning and keeping customer loyalty. And they can operate in various structures. Whether your firm operates as a line-and-box hierarchy like IBM or Baptist Hospital or a team-based matrix organization like The Math Works, teams can offer many advantages over individuals working independently:

- Teams can focus attention on results and away from those functional activities that divert energy away from customer value delivery.

- Motivation, commitment, and ownership can be higher when teams are at work. That's because teams can be given responsibility for a whole piece of the business and held accountable as a group.

- Quality is higher and cycle time lower when decisions are made by team members with relevant information and perspectives.
- Innovation and improvement can occur more readily in teams because diverse perspectives are working together to find better ways to do things. (Matrix organizations, with staffers from various disciplines serving on multiple teams, may offer the most opportunity for the cross-fertilization that results in innovative ideas.)
- Professional growth can occur more rapidly when people work in teams because team assignments provide them with opportunities to develop broader and deeper skills and responsibilities.

Moreover, companies looking for ways to use teams to improve customer loyalty have many options about the focus of such teams. Here are a few ideas:

- A product or service team can analyze the firm's products and services for customer loyalty weaknesses and for determining ways to reduce them.
- A make-it-fun team can look for ways to lighten the company culture while deepening the firm's commitment to customer loyalty.
- A communication team can focus on all the ways a customer is touched by the company and how to make these touch points and interactions more loyalty driven.
- A complaints team can search out customer complaints in a particular area, drill down to root causes, and make recommendations for ways to eliminate them.
- A new technologies team can search out new methods for getting close and staying close to customers.
- A customer loyalty team can look at the company's customer reward programs, comparing them against other firms' points-based plans, for example, to find ways to improve them.

Of course teams are not the answer to all company woes. There are plenty of situations in which teams are not the best solution for completing work. Some tasks may be better accomplished by having individual employees complete various parts of them, and then having another staff member put the parts together. Teamwork, in contrast, is about doing work together when complementary team members' skills can be used to advantage. If they are not necessary, teams should not be formed. As one teamwork expert said: "When teams are made the flavor of the month, they fail. If there's not a group performance issue, there's no reason for teams."[4]

In the remainder of this chapter, we explore what it takes to mobilize employees into high-performance teams. We'll look at how to get teams *ready, willing,* and *able* to solve problems and create solutions for winning the battle for customer loyalty.

READY—GETTING PREPARED FOR TEAMS

Teams thrive when they are conceived in organizations capable of supporting them. For some firms, this means shifting the organization to better accommodate teams. We'll look at how one firm in Great Britain is taking this leap and at guidelines to consider when making these organizational changes. In addition, we'll examine the critical steps in forming a team and how to make the most of this early stage.

Finding the Right Organizational Structure

Team-based organizations don't just happen. They're developed and nurtured over time. Consider the Legal & General Assurance Society, one of the United Kingdom's largest insurance and investment management companies with operating groups in the United States, France, and the Netherlands. A few years ago the company set out to transition itself from a traditional hierarchical organization to a customer-focused firm with a team-based architecture. This was no small feat for a 150-year-old company whose 1,200+ employees were deeply entrenched in multilayered operational and reporting structures where, as Frank Hoffman, customer service director, describes it, "those potentially able to do the most for the customer were, in fact, the least able to do so."

To accomplish its goal, Legal & General took drastic measures. For example, the company inverted and flattened the structure of its customer service division so that its 150 call center reps were more closely aligned with customers and only one layer—customer service managers—separated the call center manager and the front line.

Moreover, to better assist reps in taking a service-driven approach when interacting with customers, the division was reorganized around a structure of self-managed teams, with ten to fifteen people in each team. Says Hoffman, "Humans generally work better in teams. You can't ask someone to identify with 1,000 colleagues, but you can with a team of ten or 12 people. Team working provides an environment of mutual support which can empower according to the maturity and confidence of individual teams."

Legal & General's efforts are beginning to pay off. Since the company began its team-based restructuring, ratings on customer surveys are up 14 percent. Staff bonuses, now based on teamwork skills and customer focus, are healthy, with 97 percent of staff receiving performance-related bonuses in the latest review period.

Now Legal & General is systematically rolling out this team-based restructuring to other divisions. *Transition Day* or T-Day, is a division's official day of cross-over, and experience has taught Legal & General to stay close to newly formed teams as they find their way. From conducting focus groups of team members, internal customers, and suppliers to providing steady communication and regular team member training, Legal & General has learned that ready support and coaching is the key to helping new teams develop confidence and maturity.[5]

Shifting to a Team-Based Structure

As Legal & General and The Math Works will attest, moving from a traditional, hierarchical structure to a team-based structure is not easy, and companies unprepared for the transition can easily fail. Organization development experts Jacalyn Sherriton and James Stern, coauthors of *Corporate Culture/Team Culture,* offer a practical, six-step model for aligning corporate culture and team culture.[6]

STEP 1. CONDUCT A NEEDS ASSESSMENT. Most companies are unable to describe either their existing culture or the one to which they aspire. In many cases, senior management assumes the existing culture is supportive of teams, and employees experience just the opposite. Yet neither group can effectively describe the current culture or how it should change. Data gathering is needed to answer six key questions:

- How do employees feel about changing to a team based structure?

- What organizational processes and systems are currently in place?
- How will these processes either support or hinder the new culture?
- What are the missing processes or systems necessary to support the change?
- What are the obstacles to implementing the new culture?
- What aspects of the current culture deserve preservation?

STEP 2. SET A CLEAR DIRECTION. It's essential that organizations be sharply focused on where they are going with the new team-based culture and why that culture is important. A hazy focus will be interpreted by employees as ambivalence about goals or, worse yet, as a sign that the organization doesn't know where it's going or what it's doing. When leading the change to teams, senior management needs to produce strategic statements of policy that can serve as guidelines for team performance. Two such tools are a *statement of philosophy about teams and teamwork* (which functions as the basis for defining new organizational expectations) and a *standards of success statement* (which describes measurable outcomes that the teams will monitor and evaluate to determine their success). These directives will help those making the change to align the infrastructure and will provide input for the training and evaluation phases of the changeover process.

STEP 3. ADDRESS INFRASTRUCTURE CHANGES. The third step in the change model requires attending to the firm's infrastructure. The infrastructure is composed of all of a firm's processes and systems, including performance management, recognition programs, the recruitment system, and so on. All these systems must be realigned around a team-based structure. For example, a firm that espouses teamwork yet rewards the individual rather than the team sends the wrong message. It's amazing how often a company will announce (and even train employees) on an exciting new concept, yet maintain the old environment and, in doing so, remove any possibility of real change. Identifying and making the essential infrastructure changes is a critical step toward creating a true teamwork culture.

STEP 4. USE A COLLATERAL ORGANIZATION. A fourth element of the change model is the use of collateral organizations: temporary organizational structures that have a specific assignment of assisting the cultural change by focusing on parts of the infrastructure that need particular attention. Collateral organization members also serve as ambassadors of cultural change within the firm. When IBM's Quality & Information Technology Unit was transitioning to a team-based style, a subset of the senior management team, dubbed the Culture Club, was the collateral organization that worked on its infrastructure. Culture Club members also bought in other ad hoc teams to work on specific infrastructure issues.[7]

STEP 5. PROVIDE TRAINING. The fifth step, training, is typically the area that firms pay most attention to when moving to a team-based culture. But training may be wasted when the first two steps of providing executive direction and addressing infrastructure have not occurred or have been only partially carried out. In addition, avoid general classroom training on how to work in a team, and instead provide intact teams with real-time, relevant tasks that teach team members how to work as a team. This way real team issues rather than generic issues can be addressed.

STEP 6. EVALUATE AND MEASURE OUTCOMES. The sixth and often most neglected step of the change process is defining and measuring outcomes. Evaluation and measurement will provide a means to assess results and also indicate where intervention and special assistance are needed. The standards of success prepared in the first step of the process should contain the desired results against which team outcomes can be monitored and measured. Over time, team measurements can be expressed as trends and reported periodically to all cultural change stakeholders.

Right from the Start—Close-Up on a Veteran Team-Based Organization

Some organizations are just born lucky (or smart). They adopt from day one a sophisticated team-based style focused squarely on customers. W. L. Gore and Associates, the manufacturer of Gore-Tex fabric and other materials, is such a company. Its flat lattice structure (see Figure 9.1) helps it sustain a unique corporate culture predicated on no decision-making hierarchies, no predetermined channels of communications, and no defined jobs confining associates to particular tasks.

Bill Gore founded this remarkably successful company forty years ago with a vision that emphatically embraced fairness, freedom to create, commitment keeping, and peer respect. These same core values are reflected today in a firm that remains free of functional management hierarchy, where teams form around customer-driven opportunities, and where team leaders emerge based on their demonstrated skill, commitment, and coaching and coordinating abilities for advancing a business objective. With 6,500 associates in forty-five locations worldwide and $1.4 billion in annual sales, the company has made its mark in electronic products, fabrics, industrial products, and medical products. Growth has come to the company because of continual innovation by Gore associates. And Gore's unique culture has made this customer-driven innovation possible.

But before you totally redesign your organization in favor of the Gore model, hold on. As we saw earlier with 150-year-old Legal & General, it's possible for any company to become more customer-focused by making its structure flatter and more team-based. But W. L. Gore, having always been a lattice-style company, can sustain a more self-directed culture than most. Says company human resource leader Sally Gore, "I'm afraid any existing organization would find it difficult to transition from a more traditional, hierarchical structure to our Lattice. People who are thinking about applying our approach in their own business tell us that newly forming companies have a much easier time creating our Lattice-like environment than established ones. It's a structure that requires constant reinforcement and widespread support to be successful, and that's not easy to develop in companies with a history of traditional management."

Regardless of your current organizational structure, or where you want to take it, a lot can be learned from Gore. Just follow the path of a prospective employee from interview through earliest days on the job, and you get a sense for how the culture nurtures employee empowerment and customer proaction. For example, interviewing questions go well beyond technical skills and focus on team skills ("Tell me about a time you had a conflict with a team member") and communication and problem-solving skills so necessary for success in the Gore culture. When a person is hired, it's for a particular commitment, rather than a job. Says Jackie Brinton, a human relations team member and twenty-two-year Gore veteran, "We don't have narrowly defined job titles that limit people, but instead, we have general expectations within functional areas." For example, someone hired into the accounting department may work initially on payroll but the expectation is that he will eventually make broader contributions in such areas as accounts payable, general ledger, and cost accounting. That's because the company has learned that people take greater ownership of something they have volunteered for and committed to as opposed to something they're instructed to do.

Each new Gore hire is assigned a sponsor—an associate who has made a commitment to get the new recruit to what Brinton calls the "quick win." This means the sponsor provides the new associate with a basic understanding of his commitments and how to reach them. And as the associate's commitments change over time, the sponsor may change as well.

Don't think that just because there is a great deal of support in the Gore environment, there are no demands on employees. Just the contrary. Says Brinton, "People have a misconception that this is a soft corporate culture, but this is a pretty tough environment for people to be in. We put a lot of responsibility on individuals to be personally successful and to work toward business success." Yet, adds Sally Gore, "We believe the associate satisfaction and spirit of innovation that results from our culture more than compensates for its challenges."[8]

Forming Teams, Setting Objectives

Team formation can be tricky. Members may come to the team as strangers or know each other only informally. Trickier still, members may share some past negative experience with one another. That's why effective teams must begin with a clear set of goals. In fact, research has shown that clear, overarching goals are what distinguishes high-performing teams from all others.

To get more insight on how to set team goals for shared commitment, consider a perhaps unlikely source—the construction industry. In an industry where litigation fees on a building project sometimes exceed the design fees, McDevitt Street Bovis, one of the country's largest construction managers, makes team formation the very first order of business on any new project. For instance, on a recent project to build a $1 million addition to an office owned by Kaiser Permanente, Bovis assembled eight representatives from Kaiser, one person from the architectural firm, one from the engineering firm, and seven from Bovis's own general contracting firm. Bovis facilitator, Monica Bennett, specially trained in team formation and process, used the following three steps to turn this group of contractors, designers, suppliers, and owners into a team.

STEP 1. CREATE A TEAM MISSION STATEMENT. Make sure the mission is a product of discussion and involvement by a broad range of team members. In this instance, Bennett divided the members of the would-be team into three groups—Kaiser people in one area, Bovis people in another, and the architect and engineer in a third. She asked each group to list its project goals. For the most part the goals were remarkably alike—bring the project in on time and bring it in under budget (although this goal mainly benefits Kaiser and Bovis). All three groups said they wanted the people using the building to be happy using it (although this was a benefit mainly for Kaiser). Most revealing of all, each of the three groups stated that they wanted this project to lead to long-term relationships among their respective organizations. This broad agreement on goals enabled the group to write a team mission statement.

STEP 2. TRANSLATE THE MISSION INTO MEASURABLE AND SPECIFIC PERFORMANCE OBJECTIVES. With the mission statement in place, Bennett asked each of the groups to list what it needed from the other two groups in order to make good on its end of the mission. The point of this step is to define a set of specific and measurable performance objectives. Kaiser stated it expected Bovis to not only keep to the schedule but shave time off it. Bovis, in turn, promised to focus on improving the schedule. Kaiser also said it expected Bovis to be available at all times, responding immediately to beepers, voice mail, and e-mail. Bovis agreed. For its part, Bovis, said it needed Kaiser to make prompt payments so it, in turn, could pay subcontractors in a timely fashion. The engineer and architect asked for quick responses to design contingencies. And so it went. Each promise was recorded on a chart Bennett called a performance agreement matrix, and a measurable action standard for each promise (such as a definition for timely payment in terms of days from invoice) was agreed on.

STEP 3. MAKE SURE TEAM MEMBERS CONTINUE TO MEET AND FOCUS ON THESE OBJECTIVES. This kick-off meeting enabled the three parties to negotiate respective duties with each other. This human give and take is what places a team on the path of accomplishment. It's important that the candor and directness experienced at this stage continue throughout the life of the project (and the team). In the case of the Bovis project, these team meetings were regularly held, right through to a postmortem.[9]

Keeping Teams on Track

Keeping a team on course after its launch has its own set of challenges. Consider these guidelines for maximizing productivity and keeping the team headed where it needs to go:

• *Set meeting norms early on.* As petty as it may sound, lack of agreement about team meeting logistics can lead to major conflict among team members. Particularly in cross-functional teams, where members are often not used to working with one another, it's common to hear comments like, "You know those salespeople, they're never on time!" Head off these issues by making the establishment of meeting norms an early priority for the team. Team members must decide upon the frequency of meetings, how they will meet (face to face, via conference calls, or some other way), the length of meetings, typical agendas, and so forth.

• *Identify team member roles.* To achieve the goals of the team, members must achieve clarity about their roles. Although these roles can vary by team, typical roles that team members assume include facilitator or team leader, planner or coordinator, communicator or liaison person, training coordinator, and specialist (the person who performs team tasks like recording meeting notes). Members should work together to assign roles among themselves.

• *Set reporting norms.* How will information about team progress be shared among team members? With management? With other employees? Like meeting norms, these issues should be agreed upon early in the team life cycle.

• *Recognize team player styles.* Just as different team members bring different information and expertise to the team, they also bring different team player styles. In 1990, teamwork expert Glenn Parker conducted a useful organizational leadership study that identified four types of team players: contributor, collaborator, communicator, and challenger. Parker has found that teams can increase their performance by learning each member's personal style and how to work effectively with people using each style.[10]

• *Resolve conflict.* Because teams are composed of people with different skills and expertise, conflict among team members is sure to arise. Team members need to expect that differences will occur, and learn how to resolve these differences in an effective manner. Training in conflict resolution skills is essential.

WILLING—GETTING EMPLOYEE BUY-IN

Team training professionals agree that people who serve on teams won't produce more because they're told, required, or asked to. They will do so only when they are motivated by team loyalty, understand the performance criteria at the outset, and are given incentives to succeed.

Best Practices

Let's look at a couple of best practices for keeping team members motivated and ready to serve.

MAKE TEAMWORK A SHARED, CORPORATE VALUE. The only real way to ensure that teamwork thrives in an organization is to make teamwork a practiced, embraced value from the top down. The old adage "A picture is worth a thousand words" is applicable here. Employees are smart and they know lip service from the real thing. You'll recall Elizabeth Haight and The Math Works from earlier in this chapter. Commenting on employee buy-in to the team concept, Haight says, "We rolled out values that people live by. We went through a process of discovering what our values were, and we invited people throughout the organization to help define them. We've now folded values into everything we do, whether it's management training, people's vocabulary, how they act, and even what they're rated against. The [company] president lives these values, and I think that's where a lot of companies go wrong. They discover what they are, they roll the values out, and then the executive group goes off and behaves in any manner that they want."[11]

Who better to test a company's commitment to teamwork than a new employee—say, one that's been with your firm less than six months? That's how Hatim Tyabji, CEO of VeriFone, sees it. VeriFone is a worldwide leader in providing the hardware and software that enables retailers to swipe credit cards for authorization. Its total revenues have more than doubled to $300 million since 1990, and Tyabji credits his company's virtual team orientation (in which employees align temporarily to complete a task) and obsessive customer focus as key reasons. When a relatively new VeriFone employee got into a major dogfight for a new account in Greece, the company's virtual team was put to the test. Says Tyabji, "My guy went in to close the deal, and the customer was objecting by saying: 'This Canadian company just came to visit us. They say you don't have any expertise in debit cards. You don't have any PIN pads installed, and they are the world leaders in debit. So we're not really sure we want to go with you.'"

Fully expecting to consummate the deal, this eleventh-hour objection was a shock to the rep. What did he do? He asked for twenty-four hours, went back to his hotel room in Athens, and put out an e-mail to all VeriFone sales and marketing personnel worldwide. He reported what had happened and how the account was in real jeopardy. And he said, "Please tell me what kind of debit installations we have, what kind of equipment is in place and any reference accounts I can use to go back and fight the case."

Within twenty-four hours, says Tyabji, the worldwide team of VeriFone people provided him with sixteen responses and ten account referrals. But true to the company's team orientation, how the rep presented the information is just as impressive. Says Tyabji, "Rather than paraphrase the e-mails, he went out, rented a printer, connected it, did a screen print. Then he went to the customer and politely laid out the e-mails. 'Sir, you can read for yourself. And oh, by the way, the e-mails include the names and phone numbers of our customers. And oh, by the way, we have 400,000 PIN pads installed.'" VeriFone won the order. And the rep learned firsthand that his teammates were only a click away.[12]

USE INCENTIVE PROGRAMS THAT SUPPORT TEAMWORK. To keep employees willing to work as team members, you must send them a consistent message that teamwork is valued in the organization and will be rewarded. The right incentive program can help you send that message. But the wrong incentive program can do just the opposite.

That's what Seph Barnard found out when he decided to energize his sales staff by creating an incentive plan in which a commission would be calculated on top of the sales staff's salaries. But this decision almost destroyed the esprit de corps at Barnard's firm, Tapes Resources, Inc., a distributor of blank audio- and videotapes for production companies and television stations. Barnard recalls that "cracks started to appear in morale. There was resentment over it. Tension appeared in the office that we'd never had before."

The commission system caused a number of problems that damaged teamwork across the twelve-member staff. Telephone salespeople who had once cooperated with one another, helping each other out on various tasks, were now resistant to spending time away from the phones. They also weren't happy when another employee serviced a customer they had assisted earlier, thereby earning the commission. What's more, employees who were in areas like shipping that were not included in the commission plan felt totally left out.

The light bulb came on for Barnard when he observed how his entire sales team pulled together to win a sales contest sponsored by tape manufacturer BASF. All the reps rallied together around one common goal: winning a trip to Cancun. So Barnard began designing an incentive program that would reward teamwork and include all employees. He also wanted it to work in tandem with the company's existing reward structure, under which employees receive an extra month's pay at the end of the year if the company's financial targets are met. So he added a monthly bonus for all employees, offering 10 percent additional pay if monthly sales are 20 percent higher than they were one year ago, 15 percent additional pay if sales are 30 percent higher, and so on. The new plan has worked. Sales increased 20 percent in four out of six of the first months of implementation. With all employees included in the bonus, teamwork has greatly improved, and cooperation problems have evaporated.

To continue to promote teamwork, Barnard has changed some reporting procedures as well. A daily sales report is now circulated to every employee, enabling all to see how the firm is doing today compared to how it was doing a year ago. This step has improved staff proactivity. Says Barnard, "On a slow day, people will say, 'We haven't gotten an order from these customers in a while. Why don't we call them?'"

Creating an incentive system that rewards teamwork rather than simply sales superstars has made Barnard a believer. He is convinced that by supporting teamwork, he is pushing sales and service to higher levels. He adds, "It has provided me with tremendous peace of mind that the whole machine is working well."[13]

Consider the lessons offered by three more examples of companies in which compensation programs help drive teamwork. Cigna Corporation has worked with its teams to establish twelve team performance criteria, and each criterion has a certain number of points. At the end of the year, points are totaled, and team members receive their incentive compensation based on the points the team has accumulated. That incentive helps to determine how the team functions. Says Cigna compensation manager Claire Leidell, "There's no confusion among employees about what their teams should be doing. Once a measure has been established, it will generate behavior."[14]

Emulex Corporation, a leading developer of fiber technology for the computer industry, has created the Focus Report, a one-page document that summarizes six key performance measurements. For example, one measure is "warranty repair turnaround time." High performance on this metric has proven to be a substantial driver of competitive advantage and customer loyalty. These six performance metrics are the center of the report on each team's monthly progress. They help determine all rewards and recognition for both teams and individuals, including merit increases and promotions.[15]

At Louisville Gas & Electric Company a team incentive award was designed to reflect both increases in performance levels as perceived by customers and expense control. Customer research is ongoing, and performance scores are reviewed every month. Data regarding team expense control are provided by the finance department. By exceeding their monthly goals in these areas, teams can earn as much as 50 percent increases in base salary per month.[16]

Make Team Recognition a Priority

No plan for motivating teamwork is complete without a recognition program. Team recognition is very important to keeping team members pumped and reinforced in the belief that their work matters. Although there are many recognition programs past and present to consider as models, it is clear that firms must design programs that meet their unique needs. Some teams prefer recognition that is external and appeals to what psychologists call extrinsic motivation. One example of this kind of recognition is a celebration event to honor team accomplishments; placing a picture and story about the team in the community newspaper is another example. Other teams are more motivated by intrinsic rewards, which appeal to the team members' inner selves. Examples include asking the team for its opinion on a new business opportunity or giving the team new tools or other resources.

As you plan your recognition program, also keep the following two considerations in mind.

- *Make it special.* People like to feel special and have fun. One of the most creative applications of external team recognition that we have seen is from teamwork expert Glenn Parker. He suggests a team awards meeting at which "Oscars" are presented for such things as

  - Most Valuable Player in a Supporting Role
  - The Ralph Nader Award for Challenging the System (and living to tell about it)
  - The US Air On Time–Every Time Award (for showing up on time to every meeting)
  - The BFMA—Best Functional Manager Award (to the department manager who fully supported the work of cross-functional teams)[17]

- *Whenever appropriate, get customers involved.* This can be particularly effective for both staffer and customer. For example, a service team at a business services company had successfully saved an important client on the brink of defection. The client, extremely appreciative of the extra effort and renewed commitment, made a special trip to the team's location to join with management to take the team members out to dinner. The recognition from both client and management that this dinner symbolized further galvanized the team commitment to high performance.

Give Team Members Fresh, New Challenges

Sometimes one of the best ways to keep performance high is to give employees a breather from one team assignment by asking them to contribute for a while to a different team. It's a practice that Portland, Oregon–based Hanna Andersson, a highly successful catalogue and Internet marketer of quality children's clothing made in Sweden, uses with success. The company employs sixty-five to seventy full- and part-time customer service representatives who take approximately six hundred thousand customer calls annually. Recognizing that taking call after call can be monotonous for a rep, Andersson gives reps time away from the phones to work on one of five specialty teams alongside other employees from different areas. These specialty teams all focus on keeping the call center running at top effectiveness; their areas are products, incentives, marketing, training, and the Internet. Says Call Center Leader Heidi Brewer, "Often, reps don't get to see the big picture. Specialty teams allow reps to interact with other areas of the company and see how all parts of the company come together. When we involve them in the operation in this way, they're more effective at decision-making and are able to provide better customer service."[18]

ABLE—GETTING EMPLOYEES PREPARED

It's not enough that teams be ready and willing, they must also be able—that is prepared—to perform in an environment that is demanding and often uncharted. If you think about it, teamwork is not a natural event, it's a learned behavior—and one that most people need a lot of help in mastering. Even in sports where teams compete with one another, a premium is placed on individual excellence. It's the home run king in baseball or the high scorer in basketball or the running back scoring touchdowns in football who makes the headlines. In school, attention goes to the kid with the top College Board scores, and in business, it typically goes to the sales rep with the highest close rate. Little wonder that people come to teams ill equipped for the challenges of teamwork. This makes learning how to be team leaders and team players important for team success. Following are a few tips:

• *Learn how to be a team leader.* One of the myths about teams is that teams don't need leaders. Wrong. Leadership is required in all teams. Sometimes, more than one team member is a leader. Being an effective team leader is demanding. For starters, consider the role of leaders in team meetings. A leader must prepare the agenda and set the tone at the formation of the group and the start of each meeting. She must keep the team on track and interactive but avoid micromanaging the group dynamics. Before meetings, she must help prepare any team member or outsider who is presenting information to the rest of the team, and after the meeting, she must guide discussion and review of the presentation in the context of session and overall team goals. During the meeting, she must either record the proceedings, or assign someone to do it. She must prioritize the information to be generated, help team members articulate ideas or key points, and make sure all the points are covered. She must keep the group energized and both detect and manage any dysfunction that may occur. Finally, she must know how to close the meeting, so that there are no remaining issues, no loose ends, left on the agenda. She must seek consensus on conclusions, help define next steps, and ensure team member commitment to decisions made during the meeting. Team leader training focusing on such needs as leadership skills, motivation, presentation and communication skills, and negotiation methods is a real asset for members of almost any team.

• *Learn how to be a team player.* Teamwork experts report that more training is focused on team leadership than on preparing people to be effective team players. Yet the more that team members understand about how to be a team player and how to increase team player effectiveness, the better. Other preparation important to excelling as a team member is training in communication skills, listening, assertiveness, conflict resolution, and time management.

• *Don't forget the customer.* In any team member training around customer loyalty or customer recovery projects, it's very helpful to have customers directly involved. Some companies have team members intern or just spend time with customers on site. This gives them real-world exposure to the customer's environment, and it also adds credibility to information the member brings back to the team. Companies like Chrysler, Southwest Airlines, John Deere, and as we saw, The Math Works regularly bring customers into the team environment to share their experiences and contribute to decision making.

• *Let performance gaps point to training needs.* Whether it's skill building for being a team player or a team leader or acquiring more customer knowledge, training needs should be identified whenever gaps are found between member capabilities and team objectives. Discovering what these gaps are and then training to close them is the most prudent use of resources. Effective managers and teams carefully track team progress and let team experiences help determine what training is required.

• *Capitalize on team learning.* Trial and error can be a great teacher. Sometimes it is the best team training mechanism, as teams learn from past individual or group mistakes. Remember Kathy O'Neal, the marketing executive at ClubCorp? A few years ago, O'Neal was on a management information system (MIS) team whose task was to upgrade customer relationship and service technology, and she represented member services. The software the team came up with to help with this effort was a positive collaboration, and individual clubs were eager to have the capabilities it provided. When team members had tried to develop similar software several years before, the effort failed because of a lack of internal training and knowledge. Comparing the two experiences, O'Neal said that the first time, "We had technical people trying to roll this out to membership people, and they spoke two different languages. The tech folks didn't understand the membership people's jobs and vice versa. Learning from that experience, we now have a team in which we have taught tech skills to membership and membership skills to tech folks."[19]

• *Give teams the benefit of best practices.* One way to make a team better is to search out its members' best practices and make these methods available to everyone in the group. For example, General Electric Mortgage Insurance reps handle close to ten thousand loan delinquencies every year. The company relies heavily on its reps to make the right decisions regarding mortgage foreclosure, customer financial guidance, and so forth. Some reps, GE has found, are much better at making financially sound decisions than others. GE management determined the company could save millions of dollars if it could take what the best reps were able to do and create a step-by-step decision protocol that every other rep could follow. To accomplish this, GE formed a full-time, eight-person team comprising high-performing reps, and gave the team the mandate to identify team members' best decision practices. The results? A computer-based program that enables all reps to be equally proficient in making decisions more quickly. By inputting data such as demographic variables, the borrower's willingness to pay, current debts and assets, and so on, reps can more accurately predict which borrowers are more likely to default and which are more likely to pay. Using the team's computer model, rep performance dramatically improved. GE's foreclosure rate was reduced by almost half, saving millions of dollars for the corporation and its mortgage lenders.[20]

SUMMARY

• Team building is a complex process that has to be tailored to the individual company.

• There are many ways that customer-focused teams can be integrated into a company for multiple benefits.

• Once in place, teams can often make dramatic and positive differences in a company's culture and bottom line.

• Teams can be integrated into businesses either in place of or along with hierarchical systems of organization.

• Teams often work better and faster than individuals given the same task.

- Teams offer advantages over individual effort when diversity of skills, experience, or information is important to the task at hand.

- For teams to be successful, the entire organization must support the effort.

- It is easier to organize a business around teams at the outset than to institute teams later.

- Clear goals are essential to successful team efforts.

- Keeping teams on track leads to success for teams, individuals in the teams, and the company as a whole.

CHAPTER TEN

How to Build a
Fiercely Loyal Staff

A aron Feuerstein will always remember his seventieth birthday. Not so much for the loving family and friends who gathered to celebrate or the big cake or the thoughtful gifts. Instead, the day is memorable because on that day in December 1995 a fire ravaged his Lawrence, Massachusetts, textile mill, severely injuring eight workers, destroying three buildings, and threatening his company's survival. Feuerstein could have taken the $300 million in insurance money and retired a very wealthy man. But he did just the opposite. The day after the catastrophe, Feuerstein pledged to keep all the fourteen hundred employees displaced by the fire on the payroll and to rebuild Malden Mills on its charred remains in the economically depressed community.

It was the logical decision for a CEO who had operated the family-owned business, founded in 1906 by his grandfather, with the fervent belief that building a loyal workforce was key to success. Over the last four decades, when most of the local textile mills had fled south or abroad in search of cheaper labor, Feuerstein had decided to stick with the local, unionized workforce and invest heavily in research and development, marketing, branding, and industrial engineering. When the company almost went bankrupt in the early 1980s, Feuerstein refused to blame the problems on his $10 an hour labor rates and Asian manufacturers with cheaper labor costs. "We had tough times, not because of the cost of labor, but because of decisions we made here in this office," says the CEO.

It was during those dark days that building a loyal workforce paid off. Desperate to find a new product, his engineers and workers, who had an intimate knowledge of his machines' capabilities, came up with Polartec and Polarfleece—fluffy polyester fabrics with the thermal properties of wool. These products were winners. Widely used by apparel marketers such as L. L. Bean, Patagonia, and Eddie Bauer, Polartec and Polarfleece now account for $400 million of the company's $450+ million in annual revenues.

A sense of mutual dependency was what sustained Feuerstein and "his people" through the devastating fire. For Feuerstein, Malden Mills was dependent on its highly skilled and loyal workforce for the complex manufacture of highly specialized products that customers demanded. If the mill was to survive, reasoned Feuerstein, employees had to be well cared for while facilities were being rebuilt. For the employees, many coming from immigrant-filled neighborhoods in Methuen and Lawrence, the mill was their ticket to the middle class. If their jobs paying $10+ dollars an hour disappeared, many would end up in lower-paying service jobs.

"Me, I depend on this job because I don't have a professional career," explains Idalinda Herriquez, a shearing machine operator. She typifies the loyal worker Feuerstein says is key to the mill's success. Although Idalinda wasn't immediately called back after the fire, she still showed up on her own to pitch in anywhere she could. "I wanted to show appreciation to Aaron Feuerstein," she said. "He's a good man. I'm a good worker. He needed our help."

Malden Mills is thriving today with sales fast approaching the $500 million mark. It's an especially impressive record considering the company's near bankruptcy in the early 1980s and the devastating fire in 1995. A less resilient firm would have foundered, but strong leadership and a loyal, committed workforce pulled the company through. Feuerstein concedes that if Malden Mills had been publicly held and answerable to shareholders at the time of the fire, he could not have been as generous to employees. But he's quick to point out that for any company, publicly held or not, loyal workers are critical. Says Feuerstein, "Everything rests on our ability to produce quality products for our customers. That's the ball game. And that quality, when you're done with your state-of-the-art buildings and your engineers and your research and development, depends on that worker on the floor."

Aaron Feuerstein was fortunate. He grew up in a family business where staff loyalty was always a key value, and in continuing the practice, his textile mill prospered. Other companies are forced to learn such lessons the hard way. For example, in 1998, the advertising agency Wells BDDP was fired by its client of thirty years, Procter & Gamble, because of unmanageable agency turnover. Over a two-year period, Wells had lost half a dozen agency veterans who had served P&G. This staff turnover cost Wells a heavy price: $125 million a year in ad outlays on leading brands like Oil of Olay, Gain detergent, Pringles potato chips. Said Bob Wehling, P&G's top ad executive, "an agency is about people. All of the people who we had grown up with and who knew us well . . . and had a real sense of our brands . . . one by one were gone." Wells had been warned by P&G executives about the need to create a stable environment, but staff turnover continued. Not only did the turnover cost Wells its most prestigious client, news of the agency's dismissal sent the share price of Wells's British parent company, GGT Group, plunging 40 percent.

From Malden Mills to Procter & Gamble, companies are coming to realize that talent is the most important factor in a company's long-term success. Having employees (and suppliers' employees) who are smart, well trained, and operationally agile drives success like nothing else. Talent has become more important than capital, strategy, or R&D. Why? Capital is available today for good ideas and well-conceived projects. Strategic advantages don't last—even if you have a smart strategy, others can easily copy it. And with the speed of technological change, R&D advantages can become obsolete overnight. This makes people a firm's most sustainable competitive advantage.[1]

The bottom line is this: to have loyal customers, you must first have a talented, loyal staff. This chapter will examine the state of staff loyalty, the real costs of staff defections, and the best practices for attracting and maintaining fiercely loyal employees. Lastly, when a staff departure is inevitable, we'll examine how to make the most of it.

THE STATE OF STAFF LOYALTY: FORCES, FACTS, AND TRENDS

Staff turnover is near twenty-year highs for many companies. Two research firms recently joined forces to conduct a nationwide employee loyalty study. The results confirmed that staff loyalty is in short supply. Here is a sampling of findings:[2]

- Only 24 percent of employees consider themselves truly loyal, committed to their organizations, and planning to stay at least two years.

- Thirty-three percent of employees are high risk, not committed and not planning to stay.

- Thirty-nine percent of employees are classified by the study as trapped. They plan to stay but are not committed to their organizations.

- Among those who felt they worked for an ethical organization, 55 percent were truly loyal. For those who didn't feel they worked for an ethical organization, the loyalty figure was 9 percent.

But lack of loyalty isn't the only thing hampering staff retention. Changing demographics are already causing turnover and shortages for many firms as well. For example, by the year 2020, there will be 15 percent fewer Americans in the thirty-five- to forty-five-year-old age range than there are now. People in this age range have historically filled the management ranks of many companies. Assuming the U.S. economy grows at 2 percent to 4 percent per year, the need for bright, talented thirty-five- to forty-five-year-olds will increase by, let's say, 25 percent, while the supply will go down 15 percent. This collision of high demand and low supply will cause fierce talent wars in almost every industry.

But changing demographics are just half the problem. Many companies don't even realize the depth of their staff retention problems. While at the senior level, turnover may be only 4 percent to 5 percent, the real drain of talent is typically among those employees who are aged twenty-five to thirty-five and have been at the same firm three to ten years. These staff members are often among the most productive and represent the highest long-term contribution potential for any company. Yet most companies don't track defections among this important group. This silent defection is particularly prevalent in large, decentralized companies with twenty to one hundred divisions. On a single division basis, the defection numbers among staff aged twenty-five to thirty-five may not seem problematic. But when viewed across all divisions of a company, they are often alarmingly high.

Nowhere is the worker supply versus demand problem more pronounced than in the technology sector. The Bureau of Labor Statistics reports that the five fastest growing occupations through the year 2008 are in information technology. McKinsey & Company director Bruce Robertson shares these findings and insights from McKinsey's numerous studies of technology workers:[3]

- The supply of managers thirty-five- to forty-four-years-old in technology firms is expected to decline by 15 percent by 2020.

- One-third of all "hard" technology jobs (code writing and so on) could be permanently unfilled before 2010.

- Smaller technology firms can't expect to lure technology workers out of big companies. Over half the technology workers graduating from 1991 to 1996 joined companies of less than five hundred (compared to 23 percent of graduates in the years 1971 to 1990).

- Many technology firms are running "high-growth temp agencies." Although only 20 percent of new hires graduating in 1971 or earlier left their first employer in two years or less, over 40 percent of the 1994 to 1996 graduates left their first employer within two years. Two-thirds of respondents who graduated after 1990 expect to leave their current employer within three years.

- The average technology employee is getting thirty new offers a year.

THE REAL COSTS OF STAFF DEFECTIONS

Firms pay a big price for staff defection. For starters, when staff members defect, customers soon follow—just as Wells lost Procter & Gamble because of staff turnover. Staff turnover greatly affects customer loyalty. Recent customer defection studies have shown that roughly 70 percent of the reasons customers leave can be traced back to issues related to staff turnover. And staff turnover often leads to more staff turnover. The departure of a valuable employee can send shock waves through a company culture, leaving remaining staff demoralized and disillusioned.

Moreover, replacing the departed employee is expensive. Human resource executives estimate that when all factors are considered—the recruitment fees, the defector's lost leads and contacts, the new employee's reduced productivity while he's learning the new job, and the time coworkers spend guiding him—replacement costs are approximately 150 percent of the departing person's salary.

And direct replacement costs are not all the costs. In our information-driven economy, a company's wealth is increasingly driven by its intellectual capital—whether it's the top-secret ingredient in a firm's best-selling product or an important customer's favorite wine—this information most often resides in the minds of a firm's knowledge workers. This fact worries many companies, and they are responding in varying ways. From documenting stories from original participants about past corporate triumphs to using exit interviews to capture critical how-to's, the most enlightened firms are coming to realize that nothing compares in value to a veteran employee who takes care of business, likes his job, and has no plans to leave.

Unfortunately, failure to recognize intellectual capital as a valuable asset is still the norm. Says Maury Hanigan, founder of New York City–based Hanigan Consulting Group, "If a $2,000 desktop computer disappears from an employee's desk, I guarantee there will be an investigation, a whole to-do. But if a $100,000 executive with all kinds of client relationships gets poached by a competitor, there is no investigation. No one is called on the carpet for it."[4]

Lately, a warning bell has finally begun to sound in many firms. An incredibly tight job market and a shortage of workers is slowing productivity and expansion plans for many companies. To make matters worse, many firms are finding that unpleasant memories from the not-so-long-ago downsizing years still linger in the minds of many employees, who remember being told, "This is not personal. This is a business decision." Today, these same employees, now more assertive and fiercely in demand by other companies, are saying, "You are so right. This is not personal. It's simply business, and I have a better offer so I'm leaving."

NINE BEST PRACTICES FOR BUILDING STAFF LOYALTY

Building staff loyalty to retain good workers and build a culture focused on customer value requires laying a strong foundation that helps preempt employee defection issues before they even occur. It means creating a culture in the organization that nurtures staff loyalty from the moment the new hire walks through the door and throughout the employee life cycle. The good news is that employees, like everyone else, desire to be part of something bigger. As *Fortune* columnist Thomas Stewart says, "Human beings want to pledge allegiance to something. The desire to belong is a foundation value, underlying all others."[5]

We've identified nine best practices for building staff loyalty. We examine each of them in the remainder of the chapter.

1. Build a climate of trust.
2. Train, train, and cross-train.
3. Make sure each employee has a career path.
4. Provide frequent staff evaluations and reviews.
5. Seek to inform, seek to debrief.
6. Recognize and reward initiative.
7. Ask employees what they want and give it to them.
8. By all means, have fun.
9. Hire the right employees in the first place.

Best Practice 1. Build a Climate of Trust

Ask top performers what they look for in deciding where to work, and they'll tell you a "great company" and "great job." Drill deeper, and you'll find the companies that get these high marks are excelling in what many call the *touchy-feely* attributes, such as a showing staff care and concern, trust, respect, and fairness. The loyalty study cited earlier in the chapter found trust-related issues a problem in many firms.[6]

- Fifty-six percent of employees surveyed said their employers fail to show concern for them.
- Forty-five percent said their companies failed to treat them fairly.
- Forty-one percent said their employees fail to trust them.

And trust may be getting weaker, rather than stronger. In a survey of 215 companies, 75 percent of the executives surveyed said trust in the workplace had declined. Only 15 percent said it had improved. Employees surveyed felt they had little input into major changes affecting them nor could they consider their companies places in which to "invest" their future. The level of trust was found to be highest between frontline staff and their immediate supervisors and lowest between frontline staff and senior managers. This same study found trust to have a direct impact on staff morale, productivity—and loyalty.[7]

For most employees, trust is shown in one important way when they can manage their own time and resources. The Home Depot store manager who said, "This [store] is my $50 million business. I can double it, or I can run it into the ground. Where else could I get that kind of independence and that much of a challenge at age 33?" is typical of today's workforce, which wants jobs with elbow room, where they can exercise some control and decision making and know they are trusted.[8]

Conversely, an employer's lack of trust can be a deal breaker. Just ask Debra Young who had an interesting job as a marketing manager for an Internet start-up. Young liked most everything about her firm with one big exception: Every week, all employees had to fill out a time sheet accounting for every hour they had spent working and turn it in to the CEO. The lack of trust this implied eventually drove a lot of employees, including Young, out the door. Young found a new post, as a marketing manager for a mechanical services firm where employees work together to set goals and are trusted to arrange their work hours.

Many firms are finding that with employee trust and empowerment comes profits. Several years ago, Southwestern Bell Yellow Pages increased the billing adjustments call center representatives could make on their own from $150 to $500 per customer. Any service rep can issue an adjustment voucher up to $500 without any manager's ever approving it. What's more, virtually all customer complaints, which used to require up to five days for resolution, can now be resolved the same day. Though some people in the company were concerned this $500 adjustment limit would cause costs to skyrocket, adjustments showed only a modest increase of 6 percent. What have increased, however, are the company's revenues, which have shown continual improvement of 8 to 10 percent annually.[9]

To build more employee trust and empowerment into your company culture, consider the following:

- Ensure staff trust and empowerment are key values in the firm's mission and vision statements.
- Practice effective storytelling (discussed later in the chapter).
- Create company rites and rituals that reinforce the rewards of employee trust and empowerment.
- Maintain a free flow of information between management and staff to reinforce trust and help prevent negative communication and gossip.
- Teach senior managers the importance of "walking their talk" and inspiring employee trust.

Best Practice 2. Train, Train, and Cross-Train

When we ask employees about training and what it represents to them, they tell us that by offering training, their company is sending them a message that says, "We think you are valuable, so we are making an investment in you." This sentiment reinforces the fact that today's streetwise employees know that their only real security in the marketplace is their job skills, and many are intolerant of employers that will not help them stay current. Employees know this, but employers are still learning. For example, a recent employee retention survey among close to four hundred senior human resource executives showed that of twenty-three employee retention strategies, technical training was ranked first in effectiveness. Unfortunately, only half the companies surveyed offered it. Other kinds of training, particularly nontechnical programs to make employees more proficient in their jobs, despite ranking second in effectiveness, were offered by only a third of the companies.[10]

Several years ago, Advanced Microelectronics, a growing computer services company in Vincennes, Indiana, let its employee training programs lapse. Within a matter of months, employee productivity sharply declined and staff defections significantly increased. "I'm out of date" and "I'm not keeping up" were the reasons for leaving most frequently voiced by departing employees. This feedback surprised company founder Steve Burkhart, who had underestimated his sixty-member staff's deep desire for training. Burkhart went into action and not only reinstated the training program but broadened its scope. No longer was the training effort targeted just to the firm's computer repair and network service technicians. Now administrative staff could take evening classes to learn word-processing and spreadsheet software programs. The result? Morale increased and turnover declined. Says Burkhart, "Training is just about a seven-day-a-week process around here now. It seems to be almost a demanded benefit, or people don't feel like they have a valuable job."[11]

To further increase staff loyalty, consider training opportunities beyond employees' immediate job requirements. Recent staff loyalty studies have shown that employees place a particularly high premium on training that addresses skill areas beyond those that are directly job related. Cross-functional and nonbusiness training are two types to consider.

- *Cross-functional training.* Giving employees exposure to multiple areas of the business fosters cohesiveness and involvement and helps create leadership in the ranks. For example, MetLife Healthcare Network of Arizona provides cross-training for customer relations staff members in one another's territories. This expands their understanding of needs in different parts of the state and enables them to provide higher quality service. Some managed care companies have also seen positive results from regularly rotating customer service staff with employees in sales, marketing, communications, operations, and other functional areas.[12] Southwest Airlines CEO Herb Kelleher, widely regarded as one of the country's most effective chief executives, admits that he makes his human resource department "crazy" because he insists on an active program of functional rotation and cross-training for as many employees as possible. With a staff enrichment program like this, it is not surprising that Southwest is at the top of the airline industry.[13]

- *Nonbusiness training.* Companies that allow staff to partake of nonbusiness training, learning such things as foreign languages and personal financial planning, end up with well-rounded employees. Companies like State Farm Insurance, for example, actively promote diversity learning. A customer service supervisor in a State Farm office in Concordville, Pennsylvania, might lead a group of employees who are learning about life in Botswana.[14] Surprisingly, firms offering nonbusiness training often report improved on-the-job productivity

among participating staffers. In addition to creating more knowledgeable and well-rounded employees, these kinds of opportunities
tell your employees that you care about them and their interests
beyond their jobs. With the growth of Internet and corporate intranet
sites, training possibilities are rapidly expanding.

Best Practice 3. Make Sure Each Employee Has a Career Path

Companies that are proactive in assisting employees to chart career
paths and then reach their goals earn greater staff loyalty. Developing
career paths for staff was one of the key ways IHS HelpDesk president
Eric Rabinowitz dramatically lowered staff turnover rates in his $13
million firm. As a supplier of on-site contract staff for internal telephone service technical support at companies like Johnson & Johnson, Rabinowitz knew staff turnover in the industry ran high, usually
50 percent per year. But when the company's turnover grew to 300
percent, six times that industry norm, things had to change. In talking with staffers, Rabinowitz realized that employees wanted a path,
a sense of direction, for their careers at IHS that led beyond the telephone support function. Staffers wanted reassurance that even though
they had temporary assignments at client help desks, their jobs at IHS
were more permanent. In response, Rabinowitz created career tracks
for the help desk employees—including a managerial route and a
technical path that allowed them to become full fledged technology
consultants. Annual check-ins were established with each employee
to help set the employee's short- and long-term goals within the company. Incorporated into each career path is a two-year timeline, with
benchmarks to click off at certain intervals. An employee mentoring
program has also been established to help staffers achieve career goals.

The results of these career path initiatives have been impressive,
with staff turnover dropping from 300 percent to 25 percent. The percentage of new hires who leave the company after ninety days has
dropped from 30 percent to 12.5 percent. The number of employee
referrals is up as well.[15]

Here are some additional techniques to use in establishing employee career paths:

• Develop career paths for every employee—send the signal "there
are no dead-end jobs here."

- Encourage employees to move into other areas of the company. Vantive Corporation, a customer relationship management software provider, encourages its customer service staff to move into other corporate areas including training, marketing, sales, and human resources.

- Provide tools, such as aptitude testing and manager feedback, with which employees can inventory and access their talents. (We discuss evaluations in the next section.)

- Make information about job opportunities in the company easily accessible.

Best Practice 4. Provide Frequent Staff Evaluations and Reviews

Effective feedback systems play a big role in keeping staffers productive, happy, and committed to their jobs. Research studies consistently find employees are emphatic in their requests for as much feedback from management and peers as they can get. Yet most companies are trapped in the old ritual of once-or-twice-a-year performance reviews, leaving most employees wanting and needing much more. Here are some suggestions:

- *Practice just-in-time feedback.* Look for ways to build feedback into daily interactions. E-mails, voice mails, routine meetings, and short memos, for example, are all opportunities for giving a staffer constant and ongoing input about performance.

- *Teach employees to recognize feedback.* Sometimes employees don't recognize that feedback is being given. That's what Anne Saunier, a principal at consulting firm Sibson & Company, learned when a staffer in her group who had been on the job three months complained to a unit coach that he wasn't receiving enough feedback. "I couldn't believe it," says Saunier. "We walked back together from the client's office every day. And every day we discussed what we could do better. Just because I didn't sit him down in my office doesn't mean I wasn't providing feedback. The next time we walked back from the client's, I began our discussion by saying, 'Now, here's some feedback.'"[16]

- *Create bottom-up feedback.* Dorothy Gill, the human resource executive of Parkview Medical Center in Pueblo, Colorado, a 286-bed hospital, found that traditional reviews using checklists, ratings, and official forms weren't working. The process had become dreaded by both staffer and supervisor, rather than being seen as a constructive and valuable tool for assessment and improvement. Gill and her team came up with a new approach. Instead of top-down appraisals, they designed bottom-up annual reviews. Employees are asked things like, "What can the leader do to make employee's job easier?" and, "What gets in the way of accomplishing the job?" These upside-down reviews no longer focus on simply telling employees how they're doing. Instead, they are open-ended opportunities for managers to learn how they can help employees do a better job. This revamped review model puts emphasis on having both the manager and employee describe and then act on things that can be done to make work go more smoothly and efficiently.[17]

Think about using these additional ways to make staff feedback a valuable tool for building staff loyalty:

• Conduct feedback sessions no less often than once a quarter.

• Provide employees with feedback from multiple sources—peers, bosses, and subordinates–and ask for self-reports as well. This 360-degree-feedback approach results in a far more effective assessment than does information from a single source.

• Give staff feedback with care and sensitivity. The goal is to strengthen the bond of trust between managers and staff. If an emotionally charged event has just occurred, it's often wise to delay feedback on it by a day or two (but not more than a week) to help ensure a productive dialogue.

• Give employees as much self-direction and say as possible in how agreed-to changes are implemented and carried out. Such empowerment is essential to employee motivation.

• Make sure staff get the coaching, encouragement, and support needed for behavior modification. Remember, new habits take time to form.

Best Practice 5. Seek to Inform, Seek to Debrief

Employees often complain that even though they are working harder than ever, their contributions or thoughts about anything beyond their immediate jobs are rarely sought. Says an employee in a communications company, "I have lots of ideas for how my company could move into the Internet, but I'm not one of the inner circle of people making those decisions and don't know how to approach them. They all sit in adjacent offices and seem to talk more to each other than anyone else. There's little reaching out to a broad array of employees for ideas and input."

As we discussed earlier, employees who feel underutilized or ignored become unproductive and often seek jobs elsewhere. That's why Michael Bonsignore, chairman and chief executive of Honeywell International, spends two days a week traveling to Honeywell plants and offices in the United States and abroad to meet staff. Though time consuming and often exhausting, these meetings are a crucial way, as Bonsignore sees it, to keep employees motivated. In a typical week Bonsignore will travel to one or two sites and hold a general town meeting followed by another meeting with twenty "high potential" employees, answering questions and listening to their thoughts. It's at the smaller gathering where this CEO's real learning often happens. Says Bonsignore, "Since no other executives but me is present at those small meetings, there's an atmosphere of candor and a chance to get a unique perspective I would never get if I stayed in my office."[18]

Floors, not miles, are what separate employees of The Richards Group, an ad agency based in Dallas, and that fact worries founder Stan Richards. In 1997, when the company grew big enough to occupy two floors, Richards began worrying something special would be lost: "Everything changes when you move to multiple floors. People become tribal. Communication becomes more formal—and less effective." So Richards devised a unique solution. He began holding regular meetings in the stairwell between the two floors so that staffers could learn company news directly from him. Today, those stairwell meetings continue, only now the staff number more than four hundred and occupy four and half floors. Recognizing the importance of staff intimacy and open communication, Richards notes, "Agencies can be hotbeds of paranoia. The best way to combat that tendency is simply not to keep secrets from each other."[19]

To foster effective communication with staff, consider the following tactics:

- Practice radical inclusion—arranging for people to hear news at exactly the same time sends a signal that everyone is valued and everyone is in the know.

- Practice spontaneous communication. Stan Richards strives to communicate with his employees within fifteen minutes of receiving important information. His philosophy: people should hear the news, good or bad, right away. This also minimizes rumors.

- Keep larger group meetings short and sweet. The larger the group, the smaller the attention span.

- Be engaging. Make e-mails, newsletters, intranet sites, bulletin boards, and the like fun and interesting to read. Employees love to see their names and pictures in print, and this inclusion increases readership.

- Be on the lookout for novel ways to communicate with staff. From panel discussions to town meetings to special messages on payroll checks, use a variety of forums to connect with staff.

Best Practice 6. Recognize and Reward Initiative

An L. L. Bean customer called on Christmas Day from Bangor, Maine, with a problem. She needed to exchange a jacket she had given her boyfriend as a present. The challenge was that he was departing from Portland, Maine, for Australia the next morning at 7 A.M. The agent taking the call checked the inventory on the computer but found the item out of stock. But knowing the Freeport, Maine, warehouse occasionally had some items in bins even when the computer screen said none were available, he went over to the warehouse personally and found the jacket in an otherwise empty bin. He called the customer back and asked when she and her boyfriend would be traveling through Freeport on their way to the Portland airport. "At 3 A.M.," she responded. Which is the precise time the customer service rep was stationed at the store entrance to complete the exchange.[20]

Best-in-class companies don't just do the expected for customers. Instead, they delight customers through uncommon performance. And it's proactive, frontline staff that make this possible. How do you create loyal, committed staffers who routinely go beyond the call of duty? By fostering a culture that recognizes and rewards initiative. Let's look at how two companies in very different industries do just that.

Prudential Relocation Management (PRM), of Valhalla, New York, handles staff relocation services for hundreds of U.S. and international companies and tens of thousands of its own employees. The organization is highly focused on customer relationships and retains over 99 percent of its clients. Each quarter, hundreds of PRM staff members and teams are nominated for the company's President's Quality Award, which recognizes outstanding proactive efforts to serve clients. Anyone can be selected. Accountants, secretaries, and administrative assistants are just as likely to be chosen as client contact staff and company officers. They are singled out and honored for client relationship building, creative solutions, cross-functional involvement, and empowered actions—all with the outcome of providing superior customer value. Quarterly winners become eligible for the Chairman's Circle, an annual formal award ceremony. PRM understands that going the extra mile is crucial to customer loyalty and that what gets rewarded gets done. Says PRM President and COO Steve Gross, "Ideas aren't enough. Only those who take action will contribute to our ultimate success."[21]

Like PRM, Price Automotive in New Castle, Delaware, rewards staff initiative. The dealership, under the leadership of General Manager Michael Price, has created an innovative staff recognition program with an interesting twist: peer-to-peer recognition. Nominations can be submitted on-line via the dealership's intranet, and there is no limit to the number of employees who can be nominated. Each nomination carries with it award points for both the nominator and the nominee, and there is a monthly sweepstakes and drawing for more award points. Award points are redeemable for area restaurants, theaters, sporting events, concerts, museums, and charitable contributions. Employees register on-line by entering their own name, nominating a peer, and giving a brief description of what the peer did to help Price Automotive achieve its vision of being a value-based company that works to keep both customers and staff.[22]

Robert Half International, a worldwide staff recruitment company, reports that lack of praise and recognition is the number one reason people leave their jobs. To reinforce initiative and staff loyalty, design recognition and reward programs with the following features in mind.

• *Avoid the "we can't afford it" trap.* The biggest obstacle to installing effective recognition and reward programs appears to be employers' belief that these programs will be too expensive. This is rarely the case. Frequently, the most important elements of such programs are nonmonetary. The best programs will reflect company mission and values, actively include staff in development and execution, and be known and seen as important by all company employees.

• *Make a clear distinction between* recognition *and* reward. Make a place for both in your loyalty arsenal. Rewards and incentives on the one hand tend to be inducements with monetary value and are typically designed to get staff to do something management wants, such as be more proactive. Rewards can be effective; however, if companies use only programs with a financial base to encourage employee initiative, they are likely to find that staff tire of them or find ways to subvert them to their advantage. Recognition on the other hand is the company's opportunity to publicly say "thank you" to employees for their cooperation, positive attitudes, or special behaviors on behalf of each other and the customer. Criteria for recognition should be open, creating maximum opportunity for each employee. For example, the accountant who expedites a complicated bill for a customer should be just as qualified as the group secretary who anticipates coworkers' schedules and effectively interfaces between her boss and staff or the customer service representative who has cut through miles of red tape for a customer. The recognition should be special, a real token of appreciation that singles out the employee for his or her contribution. Again, the cost is far less important than the good feeling the recognition creates in the employee and the rest of the staff.

Best Practice 7. Ask Employees What They Want, and Give It to Them

The only way to earn the deepest staff loyalty is to give employees what they want. How do you know what they want? You ask them. It sounds so simple, but few companies do it well. For one thing, staff are often reluctant to tell you what they want. For example, employee forums that invite staff to discuss issues affecting their work, career opportunities, compensation, and so forth seem fraught with risk to many employees. Employees may not feel free to speak in front of management or other staff members. One-on-one feedback sessions between manager and staff can ease some of this discomfort, but even so, staffers are often reluctant to really speak their minds.

That's why the anonymous written survey is the tool of choice for many firms seeking to understand the true state of staff morale. Results can be sobering for many firms. Just ask Springfield Remanufacturing Corporation (SRC), which conducted a staff loyalty study to identify how employees felt about their jobs, their working conditions, and the company itself. The responses both surprised and disappointed many of the company's managers. Says Springfield CEO Jack Stack, "Our Heavy-Duty Division, for example, came in with abysmally low scores on three issues. People were asked to agree or disagree with the following statements: 'At work, your opinions count'; 'Those of you who want to be a leader in this company have the opportunity to be one'; and 'In the past six months someone has talked to you about your personal development.'" Reports Stack, "43 percent of the people disagreed with the first statement, 48 percent with the second, and 62 percent with the third." Without question, the survey results gave Stack and his managers insights they otherwise would not have. Says Stack, "The truth is, those types of problems are easy to miss, especially if you're doing well. . . . It's a trap that even the best managers fall into. The only way to avoid it is to conduct audits from time to time."[23]

Employee loyalty study results are often mirror images of what's going on with customers. For example, one of our clients was known to have a highly ineffectual regional director. In that director's region, both customer and staff defection were quite high. On a staff loyalty study we conducted for them, regional employees rated teamwork and staff communication dramatically lower than staff in other regions did. Likewise, the customer loyalty scores for that same region were low, showing the region had particularly poor performance on communication with and responsiveness to customers. Staff problems ultimately become customer problems.

Of course, be sure you measure staff loyalty, not staff satisfaction. As we pointed out in discussing customer loyalty research in Chapter Six, getting valid results from such research may be complex. You'll want to seek the help of an outside expert to design and implement your research. Here are some guidelines to keep you on track:

- *Avoid measuring employee satisfaction.* Instead, ask questions that measure your firm's performance as an employer (for example: On a scale from 1 to 5, where 5 is excellent and 1 is poor, how would you rate our performance as your employer?).

- *Measure your employee's likelihood to remain your employee.* Also measure your employee's likelihood to recommend the company to other potential employees (for example: On a scale from 1 to

5, where 5 is excellent and 1 is poor, how likely are you to recommend the company to other potential employees?).

• *Ask for importance and level-of-agreement ratings on company performance attributes in the following six categories:*

> *Cohesion:* these attributes address teamwork and communication between and within groups, work quality and effectiveness in groups, and staff-management interaction.

> *Morale and culture:* these attributes address the *fabric* of the organization, its consideration of staff needs, and its desirability as a place of employment.

> *Career security and personal growth:* these attributes address employees' sense of shared destiny with the company or belief that the company will support their employment tenure and personal and career development.

> *Business alignment:* these attributes address the extent to which employees are partners and participate in the company's vision, mission, and strategic objectives.

> *Customer focus:* these attributes address employees' perceptions of the company's proactivity with and responsiveness to customers and their views on how the tools they are provided help them deliver customer value.

> *Management effectiveness:* these attributes address employees' views of how well people and processes are managed.

• *Report survey findings in a timely manner to staff.* Asking staff for their feedback implies a management commitment to action based on findings, so at the same time provide an action plan for addressing key concerns. Do this and you will increase employee trust and involvement and, in turn, strengthen loyalty. Don't do it, and employees are likely to blow off your next staff survey and undermine new initiatives proposed as a result of the research.

Twenty percent annual turnover and survey results that showed staff at high risk of defection are what prompted Ernst & Young chairman and CEO Philip Laskawy to take firm action. Laskawy was well aware that these issues were costing the company not only valuable staff but continuity with clients. And E&Y was spending hundreds of thousands of dollars to replace lost staff. With the help of an outside consultant, the E&Y Office of Retention was established, with a charter to reshape the working lives of Ernst & Young's thirty thousand professionals.

Ernst & Young recognized early on that asking employees what they most wanted was key to success. To implement this knowledge, *solution teams* tasked with the challenge of improving staffers' balance between work and personal life were formed. Based on the suggestions of the staff teams, innovative changes were soon initiated, including time limitations on on-site consulting assignments, increased telecommuting, a review team, or *workload patrol*, to make sure that no staff member is overwhelmed with work, and an on-line best practices database, called the Life Balance Matrix, which enables each E&Y office to share and learn from the company's efforts in this area. Working closely with staff to understand their needs has taught the firm to follow five principles in making the E&Y culture more staff friendly:

- Staff retention support must start at the top with senior management.

- Executives have to set life balance examples for their staff.

- Solutions to balancing work and personal life will vary by office and group, so flexibility is necessary.

- Life balance rules must be simple and easy to follow.

- Life balance needs and client service needs must coincide.[24]

Best Practice 8. By All Means, Have Fun

In today's harried marketplace, employees and managers alike need to blow off steam and have some fun. Here's how a few companies help staffers do just that:

- Once a quarter, Firmani and Associates, a public relations firm in Seattle, closes early for the day and the president takes all the firm's employees to a movie matinee.[25]

- Clif Bar, Inc., an energy-bar maker in Berkeley, California, provides a twenty-two-foot-high artificial rock wall for climbers in the company gym, plus aerobics classes, weightlifting, and other workouts each midafternoon.[26]

• Ben & Jerry's, the Vermont ice cream maker, has a "Grand Poobah of Joy" who gives entertaining daily messages over the office intercom, accompanied by harmonica music.[27]

• Prudential Resource Management celebrates all the major holidays of the year with a special event. On Halloween, for instance, all employees are invited to come to work in costume; and in addition to a party (during working hours), there is a contest with a valuable prize—such as a week's vacation in the Caribbean—for the most creative costume.[28]

• David Kaufer, cofounder of Seattle-based Kaufer Miller Communications, periodically rents a bus and, without advance notice, takes his staff to a Mariners game or other outing. (Kaufer has learned, however, that mystery events should be kept nonthreatening. He once took his staff on a surprise parasailing outing, a type of parachuting that requires being airlifted by boat. He watched with dismay as one staff member turned increasingly white with fright while awaiting his turn.)[29]

• MicroStrategy of Vienna, Virginia, hosts the Friends and Family Weekend each April, in which each employee is given a stipend to bring in—even fly in—family members for an open house so they can gain a better idea of the reasons staff members spend so much time there. The event often features notable entertainment, such as the Temptations or Penn & Teller.[30]

• Wells Fargo Bank in California has developed In Good Company, a program that combines fun with reward and recognition. Employees first get to award a $35 certificate to the coworker of their choice for any initiative considered outstanding. Then Wells Fargo further honors employees who receive the most certificates with "wild and crazy" prizes. For example, an employee can have one of the senior bank officers do his or her job for a day or have a company cafeteria menu item named in his or her honor.[31]

More and more, staff loyalty studies suggest that staff that play together stay together. The more a firm can inject fun into the workplace and lighten and brighten its culture, the happier its employee. Here are some additional ideas for making work more fun:

• Make meetings more comfortable and less tension-filled by starting with a fun icebreaker. For instance, have each person finish this sentence: "Wouldn't it be fun to . . . ?" In some cases, this question may be a bit risky, especially if the group has members with David Letterman–type humor! As a precaution, when starting such exercises, it often helps for the leader to go first with an answer, setting the tone for other responses. Whichever icebreaker you use, be aware that employees may be confused at first, but soon they will like the change in mood and atmosphere created by these gestures.

- Give conference rooms and common areas fun names and let employees name their offices or cubicles.

- Sponsor a bring-your-pet-to-work day.

- Hold guessing contests. For instance, have employees try to identify one another from childhood pictures.

- Start or end e-mails or memos with funny quotations.

Best Practice 9. Hire the Right Employees in the First Place

Without doubt, the best way to keep an employee is to hire one that fits in in the first place. Here are some of the ways companies are meeting the challenge of hiring smart:[32]

- *Profile top performers first.* A firm's best hires typically have a lot in common with top performers. That's why Select Comfort Corp., a mattress manufacturer in Columbia, South Carolina, uses information about its best-performing employees as a guide for hiring. The firm invites top performers to participate in focus groups to talk about what makes them successful. These same employees are asked to take a standard personality profiling test to identify behaviors that are most and least like their behaviors. Computerized scoring generates a twenty-page personality profile that is then used to develop interview questions for prospective employees.

- *Make recruiting top talent a key corporate value.* Even though a company is not always hiring, it should always be recruiting, filling its prospective employee pipeline with the best and brightest candidates. Lou Hoffman, president of a public relations firm in Silicon Valley, insists that everyone in his firm participate in the recruitment effort. Members of the management team are required to engage in two high-profile activities each year and make no less than two recruitment-related phone calls every week. At the account executive level, Hoffman measures recruiting idea generation and team hiring input to ensure that recruitment stays on everyone's radar screen.[33]

• *Get customers and staff involved in selection.* Who knows better how to spot high-potential applicants than those people who will work with them? That's why, in addition to standard testing and screening, Southwest Airlines uses teams of staff and customers to interview and select individuals for employment, seeking candidates who are personable, demonstrate creativity and loyalty proclivities, and are energetic. It hires only about 3 percent of all applicants. Likewise, Bob Cooper, founder and president of Frontier Media Group, a Malvern, Pennsylvania, interactive marketing agency, has job candidates talk with as many as a half-dozen employees in as many as three different trips to the agency.

• *Reward staff for successful hires.* Staff loyalty studies show that prospective employees referred by existing staffers make the best new hires. Linda Blaser, a contract recruiter for Exchange Applications, an information technology company in Boston, rewards referring employees with $3,000 for most positions and $5,000 for "hot jobs" that Blaser needs to fill immediately. The company offers a $2,500 referral reward to vendors and customers as well. At AccuData America, an employee referral is worth $2,000—with $500 paid out immediately, a second $500 paid after three months if the hire is still with the company, and the final $1,000 given six months after the hire.[34]

• *Make the salary competitive.* Don't let low-ball salaries block you from top candidates. McKinsey's Bruce Robertson "had a client that used the analogy of buying a car. It's not that he selected his car based only on price, but he did set a price that had him looking at Lexus and Mercedes rather than Luminas. If you're not willing to pay in the appropriate compensation range, you're going to get Luminas, not Mercedes, coming in the door."[35]

• *Collect feedback on your recruiting process.* Even the best recruiting program can always be improved. Hiring smart means identifying recruitment weak points and making them stronger. Beverly Kelly, human resource manager at Robert Charles Lesser & Co., a real-estate consulting firm in Los Angeles, asks candidates about other companies they're interviewing with and what makes a particular company attractive. She also queries current employees about what they liked and disliked about the hiring process. She sends an e-mail inquiry to people who declined an employment offer, asking why they did so.

Kelly has changed the company's Web site based on this feedback; it now features more attention-getting graphics, an overview of the company's interview process and training schedule, and samples of client work.

THREE TECHNIQUES TO USE ACROSS THE PRACTICES

Here are three further suggestions that can improve your ongoing retention strategies.

Manage the Employee Life Cycle

It's been suggested that companies should apply a marketing perspective to the challenge of attracting and keeping employees. The logic goes like this: you have a product called a *job* that is being sold to a customer called an *employee*. When you think about employee loyalty as a marketing challenge, the question to ask is, What actions should be taken to turn prospective employees into new hires? And once you have hired them, the question becomes, What actions are required to turn new hires into longer-term employees and, ultimately, staunch company advocates? This is similar in concept to the customer life cycle discussed in Chapter Six. Now we are applying the progressive loyalty stages to employees.

In every employee life cycle there are predictable crisis points when the defection risk is greatest. The better a company can predict and plan for these likely stress points, the better chance it will have of preventing defection and retaining the employee. These are the three common crisis periods for employees:

1. *New-hire hysteria.* This condition can be brought on by a number of new job circumstances including underwhelming assignments, friction with a new boss, or an unexpectedly heavy workload. It doesn't take much for the new employee to call a headhunter or even the old employer and say those four deadly words: "I made a mistake."

Solution. Pair the new recruit with an experienced associate who can help guide her through this difficult transition time. In addition, provide new hire orientation to acclimate every new employee to the company.

2. *Promotion peril.* An employee is vulnerable to defection when he is ready for a promotion but a slot is unavailable. Ambitious,

upwardly mobile employees waiting for promotions are ripe for the picking by competitors who are only too happy to give them that next step up on the ladder.

Solution. Buy some time by putting the employee in a special project role for a few months, one that recognizes his or her achievements. In the interim, find that promotion slot.

3. *Boredom blues.* The most productive employees typically don't tolerate boredom well. No promotion on the horizon? No new project to look forward to? New jobs outside your company will look more and more attractive.

Solution. Find out what specific areas most interest the employee, and find ways to tailor at least some of the bored employee's assignments around those areas. Here's where staggered stock options can help. Schedule a chunk of those options to vest about six months after the period when your new employees seem most prone to boredom blues.

Make Staff a Part of Every Customer Research Study

If you want to reinforce a number of staff loyalty best practices—such as demonstrating staff trust, training staff, informing and debriefing staff—all at the same time, it's easy. Include staff who touch the customer as one of the groups to be sampled in your customer loyalty research studies. It's a method we have practiced for years and with great results. Here's how it works. We survey staff using the same customer loyalty questionnaire used with customers. The twist is that we ask employees to respond to the questions the way they anticipate customers will respond. Staff frequently have very different perspectives from customers on how, and how well, the company is delivering customer value. Therefore, comparing customer perceptions against staff perceptions can be very revealing. What's more, sharing these gaps with staff creates a real awareness about what is and is not working with customers. Need more convincing? Here are three key reasons that you'll want to make staff a part of every customer survey:

1. Including staff in customer loyalty research enables staff to have a voice. It tells staff their opinions matter, which in turns helps trust to grow between the company and staff.

2. Surveying staff as part of the customer loyalty research process enables management to learn about specific process areas where there is a disconnect between what staff perceive and what customers perceive. These revelations can open the door for needed changes in how customers are served.

3. Surveying staff as part of the loyalty research process helps pave the way for staff buy-in and support of new initiatives and changes on behalf of customers that may affect staff.

Be a Good Storyteller

A few years ago, we did some customer loyalty training for Residence Inns. As part of our assignment, we interviewed a host of employees from across the country including general managers, assistant general managers, front-desk personnel, sales reps, and housekeepers. In many of these one-on-one interviews, we heard essentially the same story: how a young woman joined an RI property as a housekeeper and ultimately made her way to general manager of the property. The story carried an implied lesson: "In this company, hard work is rewarded and there are no limits to what you can achieve."

This is what Howard Gardner, professor of education at Harvard University and author of *Leading Minds,* calls a *story of identity.* It conveys value, builds tribal loyalty, and reveals how things really work in an organization. More influential than mission statements or memos or newsletters or policy manuals can ever be, stories, says Gardner, "constitute the single most powerful weapon in the leader's literary arsenal."[36]

Great leaders instinctively rely on stories to connect with their followers. From George C. Marshall to Ronald Reagan to the Bible, storytelling has always been the principal tool by which leaders help groups remember. Want to build a culture that truly values staff loyalty? Empowerment? Initiative on behalf of customers? Learn how to use the everyday teaching power of stories. Dig into your firm's collective memory, and find some inspiring narratives. Then start your next meeting with one. You'll be amazed at the results.

MAKING THE MOST OF AN EMPLOYEE'S DEPARTURE

Even the best of companies loses staff. And just as lost customers can offer valuable insights for a company, so can departing employees. Exit interviews and knowledge bounties are two tools for making the most of an employee's departure.

• *Exit interviews.* Whether the employee is leaving voluntarily or not, an exit interview can provide useful information about company culture, morale, staff attitudes, policies, supervisor abilities, and so forth. But tread carefully! Mishandled, an exit interview can damage rapport with the departing employee and, in the worst of cases, contribute to a lawsuit. As you plan an exit interview, you'll need to make some decisions about timing and responsibility. Consider your available resources and specific objectives when deciding the following:

When should the exit interview be conducted? While the employee is still on site, or a couple of weeks later when the departing staffer has had more time to reflect on the experience?

Should the interview be totally oral or should a brief written questionnaire be used to supplement the interview process?

Should the interview be done in-house by a human resource staffer, or should it be done by an outside firm to help instill respondent trust in the process and maintain confidentiality?

When structuring an exit interview, include lots of open-ended, nonthreatening questions. Such questions allow for rapport building between the interviewer and employee and enable the departing employee to fully express his or her views. Consider asking questions similar to these:

What did you like most about working in the company? What did you like least?

What did you like most about your job? What did you like least?

What did you like most about the department to which you were assigned? What did you like least?

What are the working conditions in which you do your best work? Compare them to your most recent assignment with this company.

How did the training you received as a new hire prepare you for the work you were doing six months later?

How do you feel about your pay at this company? How do you feel about your benefits package?

When you were deciding to join this company, what most impressed you? Has your impression changed? How has it changed?

What are the reasons for your departure?

What type of job are you going to? What attracts you there? How does it compare to what this company offers?

What could have been done to encourage you to stay?

What would you most like top management to know about your impressions of this company?

As we conclude, what did I not ask you that I should have about your decision to leave or your impressions about the company?

• *Knowledge bounties.* Debra Speight, vice president and chief information officer of Harvard Pilgrim Health Care, has added a novel element to the inevitability of staff turnover. Recognizing that her firm could not always keep the *person,* she devised some steps to at least retain some of the *knowledge* that the departing employee had gained while working for the company.

Harvard Pilgrim began offering what it terms *knowledge bounties* for exiting staff. When people give notice that they will leave, the departing employee fills out a job workbook that has questions about the special information or insights he or she has gained. Then a panel of peers and senior managers reviews the information and determines its monetary worth, anywhere from $1,000 to $5,000. Harvard Pilgrim is pleased with the results and the fact that the process reinforces to staff the importance of employee knowledge.[37]

Of course, departing employees may not be gone for good. There's a hot new trend on the job front—boomerangers. These are workers who are returning to their former employers after quitting. Most don't leave with the intention of returning. But then they find they don't like their new jobs or their family situation has changed or their old boss has left, and for these and other reasons they come back. Many companies are discovering that boomerangers can be great morale boosters. Hiring a known entity who can acclimate quickly to a job and a culture is a shot in the arm for other staffers. It sends a clear signal that the firm's a great place to work and that the grass is not so green elsewhere. Boomerangers also often cost less to hire than brand-new workers because of reduced training costs and nonexistent recruiting fees.

But there is a possible downside. Personnel managers concede that there are risks involved in rehiring former employees, particularly if they are given promotions or substantial raises. In short, it can send a message to loyal employees that the best way to get ahead is to leave and come back later. But most companies say the rewards far outweigh the risks. So remember these suggestions:

- *Never burn bridges with departing employees.* A San Francisco high-tech firm gives departing employees a grand sendoff and a real boomerang. One end cites the date of departure; the other end is a blank for date of return.

- *Keep in touch professionally and socially.* Bain & Co., a Boston-based consulting firm, goes all out to keep in touch with its two thousand alumni. It holds social events and sends out newsletters.

- *Check your ego at the door.* Let the ex-staffer know he or she is valued.

- *Consider wading back in slowly.* Short-term contract work is sometimes an easy way for both parties to begin the reengagement process.

- *Don't assume every ex-employee is a fit the second time around.* When necessary, conduct rigorous screening to gauge current skills and the risk that the person will leave again.

SUMMARY

- Hiring, retaining, and building a loyal staff requires dedication and attention, but can be the most important effort of any company trying to stay ahead of the competition.

- When a company finds the right people for the job and then encourages, empowers, and validates those people, the workplace is an enjoyable place to be and staff and customer loyalty flourish.

- Talent is more important than capital, strategy, or research and development.

- The job market is tight now and promises to become tighter in the future, with more jobs opening up and fewer people to fill them.

- Intellectual capital in the form of good, hard-working, and loyal employees is the most valuable asset a company can have.

- Consider the steps that make a good customer and apply those same steps to making good employees.

- Use every tactic you can find to build loyalty.

- Pay close attention to employee opinions, feedback, input, and ideas.

- Respond to information gained from staff, or you will never get information again.

- If an employee does leave, make the best of the situation by parting on good terms and trying to learn from the event.

To maximize customer loyalty, start today to create plans for winning back lost customers, saving customers on the brink of defection, and making your company defection proof. Use the checklist in Figure 10.1 to help you jumpstart your process.

Figure 10.1. Getting Started.

✔ *Make this fact known throughout your firm: the only thing worse than losing high-value customers is neglecting the opportunity to win them back.* Compare your firm's knowledge and initiatives for winning back lost customers against national averages (see our national survey). Examine the three key reasons why defections go unmanaged in most firms, and see which are affecting your company. Learn to recognize the substantial benefits of win-back—such as a much improved bottom line, better word of mouth, and improved staff morale—and make these benefits widely known across your organization. (Chapter One)

✔ *Learn from the purchase data in your loyalty lab.* Carefully analyze your purchase data to pinpoint and monitor customer defections. Use purchase data trends to spot at-risk customers. Likewise, use purchase data to monitor the success of your acquisition and retention programs and make these efforts stronger. Avoid the mistake of treating acquisition, retention, and win-back (the Big Three) as separate and unrelated processes, and instead, use their interconnectivity to strengthen all of them. (Chapter Two)

✔ *Develop lifetime value formulas.* Develop working formulas for estimating the customer lifetime value for current customers and prospects and the second lifetime value for lost customers. These formulas give you the all-important common denominator for determining which customers to attract, keep, and recover. (Chapters Two and Three)

✔ *Create win-back processes and protocols.* Create a comprehensive plan for winning back lost customers including a communication plan for rebuilding customer trust. Make your win-back frontliners a high functioning team by focusing on people, place, and process issues. (Chapters Three and Five)

✔ *Create save processes and protocols.* Create a comprehensive plan for saving customers on the brink of defection by using the CPR process (comprehend, propose, respond). (Chapter Four)

✔ *Assume no customer is ever safe from defection.* Use the Kano model and the Customer Loyalty Compass to uncover and deliver value according to customer priorities. (Chapter Six and Appendix A)

✔ *Defection-proof your firm using five essential loyalty tools:*

1. Leverage the customer lifecycle using wondrous entanglement strategies that turn first-time buyers into repeat customers and loyal advocates. (Chapter Six)

2. Build a customer information system that enables you to serve customers one to one. (Chapter Seven)

3. Create a targeting plan that attracts high-value prospects. (Chapter Eight)

4. Make customer-focused teams a key part of your organization. Get teams ready, willing, and able to function on the behalf of the customer. (Chapter Nine)

5. Make staff loyalty as much a priority as customer loyalty, and put processes in place to create and sustain it. (Chapter Ten)

Appendix A: The Customer Loyalty Compass: A Proven Process for Finding Customer Value

Identifying the values that motivate customers requires a disciplined and repeatable research process carried out by an unbiased third party. We have developed such a process, one that has worked well with our own clients. We call it the Customer Loyalty Compass because it is a proven process for finding customer value. It consists of four interconnected steps—prepare, assemble, comprehend, and employ (PACE).

STEP 1. PREPARE FOR THE RESEARCH PROCESS

Before conducting any customer research, it's essential that the research supplier first understand the organization's culture and processes and how they function on behalf of customers. The supplier gathers this information by interviewing a cross section of staff, from executives to frontliners, and reviewing prior research and data such as sales reports, complaint information, and the like. Two key questions require answers in this preparation step: (1) What does the company currently know about its customers and competitors? and (2) what insights are missing? For example, in staff interviews, the research supplier may probe issues regarding customer relationships, product or service quality, and customer communication and also may attempt to determine what the company believes it already knows about customer perceptions in these performance areas. From this learning, a set of customer questions for Step 2 can be developed.

STEP 2. ASSEMBLE CUSTOMER NEEDS AND WANTS

Using the questions about customers uncovered in Step 1 as a guide, the research supplier employs one or more types of qualitative research to gain a sound general idea of customer needs, expectations, problems, and complaints. In-depth customer interviews, focus groups, and mini-groups (hour meetings with three to four participants) are a few of the methods used to access this information. Key learning objectives include determining (1) what customer requirements are not being addressed, (2) what complaints are not being registered, (3) what areas of performance customers consider most and least important, and (4) how performance may have changed over time. The more classes of customers that can be debriefed—current, former, internal, and competitive—the clearer the insights will be. There are two outcomes from this research step: an in-depth understanding of the customer's definition of value and a survey questionnaire for use in Step 3.

STEP 3. COMPREHEND CUSTOMER PRIORITIES

In this step the supplier moves into the quantitative phase of the research process, in which the statistical details about the insights arrived at in Step 2 are uncovered and analyzed. What are the actual dimensions of the good news and the bad news?

 • *Customer survey.* To effectively dimensionalize and prioritize the performance factors driving customer loyalty or customer attrition, the survey questionnaire should collect, at a minimum, customers' ratings on the following information: attribute importance (of attributes identified in Step 2); attribute performance and reasons for low performance; competitors' attribute performance, if available; best-performed attribute and attribute most needing improvement; overall performance and the performance change experienced from period to period; likelihood to repurchase and reasons for low repurchase likelihood; anticipated volume of future purchase activity; likelihood to recommend; and areas of complaint, expressed and unexpressed. Other useful information, such as customer demographics and the response to new or modified product or service concepts, may also be collected.

• *Staff survey.* As with qualitative research, it is valuable to have information from as many customer groups as are applicable to the company's business. This, of course, also includes staff, or internal customers. Although many companies feel that staff insights are best learned through such traditional techniques as employee satisfaction studies, often more is learned about the level of customer focus in a company by having staff complete the same questionnaires as customers. Staff are instructed to complete the survey as they feel customers would respond. The perceptual differences, or gaps, between customers and staff provide insight into what companies are seen to deliver by customers versus what staff believes is being delivered.

• *Data collection method.* Telephone surveying is often the preferred method of data collection for a number reasons, including ease of probing with follow-up questions, the added information supplied by the customer's vocal inflection, and the ability to ask qualifying questions and select customers that match quota requirements. One of the most important elements of customer information developed in this step can be anecdotal, verbatim feedback regarding (1) areas of performance considered less than excellent, (2) reasons for low likelihood to continue purchasing or to recommend, and (3) specific areas of complaint, either previously registered or not. Many customer studies, especially those conducted by self-completion methods such as mail or Web-based surveys, either fail to generate this information or collect it in a random rather than a systematic manner. The importance of such feedback cannot be overstated; it adds depth and clarity to performance issues that may be contributing to customer attrition or defection.

• *Data modeling.* Once the information has been collected, data analysis and modeling can be conducted. The best way to deliver customer loyalty findings is with actionable, user-friendly graphics and models such as Motivation Windows, Action Windows, and Gap Profiles. (To see examples of these graphics and models visit our Web sites at www.loyaltysolutions.com and www.customerloyalty.org.) It's important that data analyses reveal both improvement needs and opportunity areas. For example, on a recent loyalty study we conducted for a service vendor, customers rated the vendor very high in several areas of customer contact. Yet our analysis found that this contact, though exemplary, was not perceived as important by clients and therefore was not leveraging customer loyalty. The client was able to use these findings to modify communication with customers, better defining for customers why this vendor contact was important and beneficial.

STEP 4. EMPLOY YOUR FINDINGS

With a clear understanding of what is driving customer value and loyalty, the company can develop action plans for improving its own performance and thus its customers' loyalty. Depending on the research findings, these plans may address initiatives at the group, department, or company level and may include such areas as these:

- Product, service, or operations quality improvement
- Communication, marketing, or promotion programs
- Staff customer loyalty and relationship training
- Staff customer loyalty reward and recognition programs
- Infrastructure modification or cross-functional team training
- Senior and middle-management customer loyalty leadership training
- Customer information system development

Developing a customer information system (CIS) may be among the most important outcomes of the research process. We find that most companies do not have well-developed, current, fully shared information on what drives customer value and loyalty. Yet a dynamic CIS is critical to both achieving customer loyalty and winning back lost customers. In addition, many companies do not debrief staff and customers on a regular basis, yet this is a key discipline in gaining the information that allows you to strategically create customer and staff value.

Appendix B: Estimation of Second Lifetime Value (SLTV) Investment and Profitability

The win-back analysis chart in Chapter Three (Figure 3.2) reflects the number of customers lost in 2001 and regained in 2002. In the case of ABC Product Company, regained customers are defined as customers who were considered defected in 2001 (meaning they produced revenue in 2000 but did not produce revenue in 2001). These defected customers were screened for win-back appeal. In Deciles 1–3, 300 customers, 900 customers, and 1,200 customers, respectively, were selected and a win-back effort was initiated. Figure B.1 summarizes the investment and profitability of these regained "best" customers.

• *Customer lifetime value (LTV).* For purposes of this example, the average customer lifetime value in Deciles 1 to 3, prior to defection, was \$25,000+, \$18,000, and \$12,500. (For more details about estimating customer lifetime value, see Chapter Two.)
• *Second lifetime value (SLTV).* SLTV, the estimated second lifetime contribution from a customer once that customer is regained, is total revenue less total costs. Total revenue includes base revenue; in this example, base revenue is the collective revenue generated by a customer over a three-year period from the purchase of ABC's core products and services. In addition to base revenue, there are three other possible revenue sources: (1) revenue from cross-selling the regained customer products and services over and above core products, (2) revenue from referrals from the regained customer, and (3) revenue generated from the data regained customers provide to the company as well as revenue gained because the company understands these customers' needs well from the information about them that already exists in the company's database. Together, base revenue and revenue from cross-selling, referral, and information value make up SLTV revenue.

Figure B.1. SLTV Investment and Profitability.

	Decile 1	Decile 2	Decile 3
Average CLV	$25,000+	$18,000	$12,500
Lost customers qualifying for win-back	300	900	1,200
Base revenue (years 1–3)	$16,000	$12,500	$8,000
+ Cross-sell	$2,400 (15%)	$1,875 (15%)	$1,200 (15%)
+ Referral value	$1,600 (10%)	$1,250 (10%)	$800 (10%)
+ Information value	$1,600 (10%)	$1,250 (10%)	$800 (10%)
= Total SLTV revenue	$21,600	$16,875	$10,800
Costs			
Direct cost	$7,560 (35%)	$5,906 (35%)	$3,780 (35%)
+ Retention cost	$1,080 (5%)	$844 (5%)	$540 (5%)
= Total SLTV costs	$8,640	$6,750	$4,320
Potential profits 100% win-back success rate			
Potential per customer profit	$12,960	$10,125	$6,480
Potential profit rate (Revenue/Cost)	(250%)	(250%)	(250%)
Potential group total profit	$3,888,000	$9,112,500	$7,776,000
Potential group total profit at actual win-back success rates	$1,944,000 (50% success)	$3,645,000 (40% success)	$2,592,000 (33% success)

Total potential profit all deciles	$8,181,000
Win-back budget/investment ($750 per customer for all deciles)	$1,800,000
Potential net profit	$6,381,000
Win-back budget as percentage of *total* potential profit	22%
Return for every $1 of win-back expenditure	$4.55

Likewise, SLTV costs are twofold: direct costs (costs of serving the customer) and retention costs. In this example, direct cost is estimated at 35 percent of revenue. This percentage is significantly lower than the 60 percent direct cost assumption used in the SLTV example in Figure 3.2. Likewise, retention costs are estimated at 5 percent of revenue rather than the 10 percent assumed in Figure 3.2. Direct and retention costs are fixed on a per-customer basis; and this example addresses top decile customers, while Figure 3.2 addresses volume delivered by the average regained customer. As we have discussed, research on differential marketing by Garth Hallberg and others show that for most categories, one-third of the buyers account for two-thirds or more of the volume and profitability. Customers in this high-profit segment generally deliver six to ten times more profit than customers in the low-profit segment. This example, therefore, assumes lower proportionate costs for top decile customers.

• *Potential profit rate.* This is calculated by dividing total customer revenue by total customer cost. It is a measure of the rate by which costs are recovered from profit generated. For example, for customers in Decile 1, $21,600 in profit divided by $8,643 in costs yields 2.50 or 250% potential profit rate.

• *Win-back rate.* This is the percentage of defected customers qualifying for win-back who are regained in each decile (as shown in Figure 2.12). This percentage reflects the level of success ABC has had in applying various methods (effective communication, more attractive terms, better service, or other improved performance) to regain customers.

• *Win-back budget as a percentage of profit.* This is one of two key methods presented for measuring win-back success. This metric is calculated by dividing the win-back investment ($1,800,000) by total profit potential ($8,181,000) for a yield (or rate) of 22 percent. In this example, even with a fairly costly win-back program, the investment is only one-fifth of the projected profit from the former customers in Deciles 1 to 3. Another way to consider these results is that ABC generated $6,381,000 of "found profitability" that it would not have received without a win-back program to recover high-value former customers.

• *Return on profit for every $1 of win-back expenditure.* This is another method for measuring win-back success. This metric is calculated by dividing total potential profit ($8,181,000) by the win-back investment ($1,800,000) for a yield of $4.55. This means for every dollar spent by ABC on win-back initiatives, over $4 of profit was generated.

• *Decile regain rate comparison.* Regain rates will vary by decile, and in ABC's case, the return from Decile 3 win-back initiatives is the least profitable of the three deciles. With a 33 percent recovery rate for Decile 3, ABC would have to spend $900,000 with a potential profit of $2,592,000. This is a considerably lower profit return versus $1,944,000 (on a $225,000 investment) and $3,645,000 (on a $675,000 investment) for Deciles 1 and 2, respectively. Bottom line, ABC should give win-back priority (dollars and time) to lost customers in the top two deciles before turning attention to Decile 3 customers.

~~ Notes

Chapter One

1. Toni Neal (president, SoHo Consulting, Austin, Tex.), telephone interview conducted by Jill Griffin, Jan. 2000.
2. Bill McCausland (former assistant vice president and general manager, GTE Telecommunications Services), telephone interview conducted by Jill Griffin, June 2000.
3. McCausland, telephone interview conducted by Jill Griffin.
4. "The Hidden Costs of Losing a Customer," *The Customer Connection,* [http://www.customer-connection.com/hidden_cost.html]. Accessed Aug. 28, 1998.
5. F. Reichheld, *The Loyalty Effect* (Boston: Harvard Business School Press, 1996).
6. D. Pruden, "How to Win Back Lost Customers," *Direct Marketing to Business Report,* Oct. 1995, p. 7.
7. Catherine Sheeran (director of sales and program management, MCI Corporation), telephone interview conducted by Jill Griffin, Jan. 2000.
8. Christine Foschetti (vice president of Retail Resources, Lynhurst, N.J.), memorandum, "Reactivating Lost Customers," Aug. 6, 1999.
9. "Winning Back Lost Customers," *Agency Sales* (magazine of the Manufacturers' Agents National Association), July 1997, p. 41.
10. B. Stauss and C. Friege, "Regaining Service Customers," *Journal of Service Research,* May 1999, pp. 347–361.
11. Bruce Grench (owner, HDIS, Olivette, Mo.), telephone interview conducted by Jill Griffin, Aug. 1999.
12. Paul Lukin (banking consultant and president of Barry Leeds Associates, New York), telephone interview conducted by Jill Griffin, Sept. 1999.
13. Lukin, telephone interview conducted by Jill Griffin.
14. M. Winleman, "The Right Stuff," *Chief Executive,* May 1999, p. 79.
15. G. Hallberg, *All Consumers Are Not Created Equal* (New York: Wiley, 1995), pp. 27–28.

16. R. Brooks, "Alienating Customers Isn't Always a Bad Idea, Many Firms Discover," *Wall Street Journal,* Jan. 7, 1999, p. A-1.

Chapter Two

1. G. S. Bilchik, "Keeping the Customer Satisfied," *Healthcare Business,* Sept.–Oct. 1999, pp. 34–36.
2. Margaret Sheridan (former MTN group marketing executive), telephone interview conducted by Jill Griffin, Aug. 1999.
3. *Regained customer* is a term used by B. Stauss and C. Friege, "Regaining Service Customers," *Journal of Service Research,* May 1999, pp. 347–361.
4. Some of the most insightful data analysis we've found comes from Hunter Business Group, a Milwaukee, Wisconsin–based business strategy firm led by business-to-business guru and author Victor Hunter. We've created a case and accompanying data using formats from a number of Hunter data charts. This case is adapted from Nick Poulos, "Hunter Case Study," e-mail and attachment sent to Jill Griffin, Oct. 1999. Data templates (format) for Figures 2.4 to 2.11 are modeled after charts prepared by the Hunter Business Group.

Chapter Three

1. Mike Booth, interview conducted by Jill Griffin, Chicago, Ill., Sept. 1999.
2. B. Stauss and C. Friege, "Regaining Service Customers," *Journal of Service Research,* May 1999, p. 351.
3. Stauss and Friege, "Regaining Service Customers," p. 353.
4. M. Barrier, "Ties That Bind: Wise Small Business People Aim for Long Term Relationships That Benefit Buyer and Seller," *Nation's Business,* Aug. 1997, *85*(8), 12.
5. K. Freiberg and J. Freiberg, *Nuts: Southwest Airlines Crazy Recipe for Business and Personal Success* (Austin, Tex.: Bard Books, 1996), p. 268.
6. S. Woolley, "Get Lost, Buster," *Forbes,* Feb. 23, 1998, p. 90.
7. Barrier, "Ties That Bind," p. 12.
8. Michael Price (general manager, Price Automotive, New Castle, Del.), interview conducted by Michael Lowenstein, Nov. 1999.
9. Barrier, "Ties That Bind," p. 15.
10. Pat Jameson, telephone interview conducted by Jill Griffin, Feb. 1999.

11. Patrick Asbra (advertising director, *Austin Business Journal*), telephone interview conducted by Jill Griffin, Oct. 1999.

12. D. Pruden, "How to Win Back Lost Customers," *Direct Marketing to Business Report*, Oct. 1995, p. 7.

13. Fernando Roman (director of revenue, Cellular One, San Francisco), telephone interview conducted by Jill Griffin, Sept. 1999.

14. S. Mahoney, "Customer Management: How to Minimize Buyer Fears," *Selling*, July 1, 1997, p. 12.

15. Stauss and Friege, "Regaining Service Customers."

16. Kathy O'Neal (senior vice president–marketing, ClubCorp), interview conducted by Jill Griffin, Apr. 1999.

17. Stauss and Friege, "Regaining Service Customers."

18. Joe Udell (CEO, Addressing Your Needs, Austin, Tex.), telephone interview conducted by Jill Griffin, Dec. 1999.

19. Bill Cone (president, Norwest Bank [now Wells Fargo], Wimberly, Tex.), telephone interview conducted by Jill Griffin, Aug. 1999.

20. Asbra, telephone interview conducted by Jill Griffin.

21. John Titus (director of circulation, *Inc.* magazine), telephone interview conducted by Jill Griffin, Oct. 1999.

22. Pete Wayman (president, Association Relocation Management Company), telephone interview conducted by Michael Lowenstein, July 1999.

23. Judy Kearney (director of sales, Holiday Inn, Florida Mall, Orlando, Fla.), telephone interview conducted by Jill Griffin, July 1999.

24. Christine Foschetti (vice president of Retail Resources, Lynhurst, N.J.), memorandum, "Reactivating Lost Customers," Aug. 6, 1999.

25. Titus, telephone interview conducted by Jill Griffin.

26. A. M. Hughes, "Reactivating Lost Cellular Phone Customers," [www.dbmarketing.com/articles/art103.htm], Sept. 10, 1998.

Chapter Four

1. Ruthie McDowell (save agent, Cellular One, San Francisco), telephone interview conducted by Jill Griffin, Jan. 2000.

2. Robert Paisner (CEO, ScrubaDub Car Wash), interview conducted by Michael Lowenstein, Mar. 22, 1999.

3. Fernando Roman (director of revenue, Cellular One, San Francisco), telephone interview conducted by Jill Griffin, Sept. 1999.

4. S. Johnson, "Home Furnishings Retailer IKEA Plans to Open Store in Emeryville, California," *San Jose Mercury News*, Mar. 30, 2000, p. 1-B.

5. S. Tax and S. Brown, "Recovering and Learning from Service Failures," *Sloan Management Review,* Fall 1998, *40*(1), 75–89.

6. David Pilgrim (account executive, Cambridge Technology Partners), telephone interview conducted by Jill Griffin, Nov. 1999.

7. John Hubich (senior vice president, Wachovia Bank), interview conducted by Michael Lowenstein, Feb. 2000.

8. S. Tax and S. Brown, "Recovering and Learning from Service Failures," *Sloan Management Review,* Fall 1998, *40*(1), 78.

9. L. Gill (Bancassurance customer development manager, Royal Bank of Scotland), "Linking Quality, Maintaining Customer Loyalty in the Retail Financial Services Industry," address presented at a meeting of the International Quality and Productivity Center, London, Mar. 1998.

10. Roger Taylor (executive vice president, PacifiCare Health Systems), interview conducted by Michael Lowenstein, July 1994.

11. B. Woolpert, "Granite Rock Story," keynote address presented at the *Inc.* Conference on Customer Service Strategies, San Francisco, June 1998.

12. S. Greco, "Real World Customer Service," [http://www.inc.com/incmagazine/archives/10940361], Aug. 11, 1998.

13. M. W. Lowenstein, *Customer Retention: An Integrated Process for Keeping Your Best Customers.* (Milwaukee, Wis.: ASQC Quality Press, 1995), p. 61.

14. "The Definitive Overview of the 1999 Internet Marketplace," *eOverview Report,* [http://www.emarketer.com/estats/sell_over.html], Feb. 2000.

15. The Jupiter/NFO Consumer Survey, Vol. 1, "Defining the Internet Shopper," [http://www.jupitercommunications.com], Oct. 1998. Accessed Mar. 3, 2000.

16. "eCRM: Forging a Path to Profitability," [http://www.atmckinsey.com/index.asp]. Accessed Aug. 29, 2000.

17. C. Zimmerman, "Sites Strive to Hold on to Buyers," *Internet Week,* Nov. 29, 1999, p. 1.

18. "Is Customer Service Getting Left Behind?" *eMarketer,* [http://www.emarketer.com/estats/022800_service.html], Feb. 28, 2000.

19. "Up Close and Sticky," *eMarketer,* [http://www.emarketer.com/estats/022900], Feb. 29, 2000.

Chapter Five

1. Bonnie Martinez (former president of retail banking, Norwest Bank, San Antonio, Tex.), telephone interview conducted by Jill Griffin, Mar. 2000.

2. Bill Cone (president, Norwest Bank [now Wells Fargo], Wimberly, Tex.), telephone interview conducted by Jill Griffin, Aug. 1999.

3. Martinez, telephone interview conducted by Jill Griffin.

4. Martinez, telephone interview conducted by Jill Griffin.

5. Fernando Roman (director of revenue, Cellular One, San Francisco), telephone interview conducted by Jill Griffin, Sept. 1999. All the information about Cellular One's win-back reps in this chapter is taken from this interview.

6. Catherine Sheeran (director of sales and program management, MCI Corporation), telephone interview conducted by Jill Griffin, Jan. 2000. All the information about MCI's win-back reps in this chapter is taken from this interview.

Chapter Six

1. N. Brodsky, "When the Price Isn't Right," *Inc.,* Oct. 1997, p. 31.

2. "The Definitive Overview of the 1999 Internet Marketplace," *eOverview Report,* [http://www.emarketer.com/estats/sell_over.html], Feb. 2000.

3. D. Peppers, "One-to-One Marketing," marketing keynote address presented at the *Inc.* Customer Service Conference, New Orleans, Apr. 2000.

4. K. Albrecht, *The Northbound Train* (New York: AMACOM, 1994).

5. K. Balog, "Starbucks Redefines Hill of Beans," *USA Today,* Oct. 1997, p. 4-B.

6. L. Arditi, "Service with a Smile Back in Style," *Providence Journal Bulletin,* June 12, 1996, p. A-1.

7. "RFM: The Next Generation." *Convenience Store News,* Jan. 11, 1999, p. 65.

8. M. W. Lowenstein, *Customer Retention: An Integrated Process for Keeping Your Best Customers* (Milwaukee, Wis.: ASQC Quality Press, 1995), pp. 7–9.

9. L. Grant, "Why FedEx Is Flying High," *Fortune,* Nov. 10, 1997, p. 158.

10. M. Breyer, "Marketplace of Ideas: At 3, Central Market Reflects Trends, Starts New Ones," *Austin American Statesman,* Jan. 19, 1997, p. B-1.

11. John Campbell (vice president, Central Market, Austin, Tex.), interview conducted by Jill Griffin, June 1998.

12. A. Slywotzky, "Guru of the New Economy," *CFO,* Sept. 1999, p. 79.

13. Slywotzky, "Guru of the New Economy," p. 79.

14. B. Woolpert, "The Granite Rock Story," keynote address presented at the *Inc.* Conference on Customer Service Strategies, San Francisco, June 1998.

15. Woolpert, "The Granite Rock Story."

16. Hepworth & Company, Ltd, "Profiting from Customer Dissatisfaction," *Customer Pulse Database,* Mar. 31, 1999.

17. Hepworth & Company, "Profiting from Customer Dissatisfaction."

18. Kathy O'Neal (senior vice president–marketing, ClubCorp), interview conducted by Jill Griffin, Apr. 1999.

19. J. Griffin, *Customer Loyalty: How to Earn It, How to Keep It* (San Francisco: Jossey-Bass, 1995), pp. 34–35.

20. Sara Bonner, telephone interview conducted by Jill Griffin, Feb. 1999.

21. Kathy O'Neal, interview conducted by Jill Griffin.

22. "Is Bigger Better?" an episode of *New Jersey, Inc.* (Show no. 320), New Jersey Public Television, Apr. 30, 1998.

23. Commerce One "Finance Highlights," [http://www.commercebank.com].

24. R. Rosenberg, "The Key Board to Success: Customer Support by E-mail and Chat Seen Crucial to Winning E-Commerce Customers," *Boston Globe,* Nov. 24, 1999, p. D-1.

25. Rosenberg, "The Key Board to Success."

26. Rosenberg, "The Key Board to Success."

27. Rosenberg, "The Key Board to Success."

28. Robert Paisner (president, ScrubaDub Car Wash, Natick, Mass.), interview conducted by Michael Lowenstein, Mar. 22, 1999.

29. G. Anders, "The View from the Top: The Past, Present and Future of the Internet Economy as Seen by Jeff Bezos, *Wall Street Journal,* July 12, 1999, p. R-52.

30. J. Sterne, "Every Click They Make," *Inc.,* [http://www.incmagazine.com], Sept. 15, 1999. Accessed Apr. 15, 2000.

Chapter Seven

1. S. Schafer, "Have It Your Way," *Inc.,* [http://www.inc.com], Dec. 15, 1997. Accessed Feb. 8, 2000.

2. Acxiom, "Case Study: Allstate Insurance Company/Data Warehouse Yields Market Gains," *Acxiom Case-in-Point,* [www.acxiom.com], 1996.

3. B. Rossello, "Customer Service Superstars: A Look at How Nonbank Companies Use Technology to Leverage Customer Information," *ABA Banking Journal,* Oct. 1997, *89*(10), 96–99.

4. Rossello, "Customer Service Superstars."

5. L. P. Ross Television, "High Rollers Vegas," Discovery Channel Video, Bethesda, Md., 1998.

6. "Setting Objectives Expands Horizons," *DCE's Data Warehouse Report,* [http://datawarehouse.dci.com/articles/1998], July 21, 1998.

7. N. Poulos, "Build a Knowledge Platform That Creates a Bond," *Strategic Edge* (white paper published by pmh cara manning inc.), Vol. Ed. 1, n.d., p. 2.

8. S. G. Thomas, "Getting to Know You.com," *U.S. News & World Report,* Nov. 15, 1999, p. 102.

9. P. B. Seybold, *Customers.com* (New York: Random House, 1998), pp. 227–230.

10. D. Peppers and M. Rogers, "Do You Really Know Four Customers?" *Sales & Marketing Management,* Jan. 1999, p. 26.

11. Acxiom, "Sales Data Integration: Bridging the Knowledge Gap," *Axciom Case-in-Point* [http://www.acxiom.com/caseinpoint/cip-rpt-ag.asp], Dec. 5, 1999. Accessed Jan. 12, 2000.

12. Acxiom, "Report: Sales Data Integration: Bridging the Knowledge Gap," *Acxiom Case-in-Point,* [www.acxiom.com].

13. Thomas, "Getting to Know You.com," p. 102.

14. R. J. Dalton Jr., "At New Web Site, Seniors Embark on Surfin' Safari," *Newsday* [www.grandmabetty.com]. Accessed May 21, 2000.

15. K. Ferrell, "Whose Data Is It Anyway," *Chief Executive,* Jan. 2000, p. 39.

16. Acxiom, "Case Study: Federal Express Corporation: Reaching the World on Time," *Acxiom Case-in-Point* [www.acxiom.com], 1998. Accessed Nov. 30, 1999.

17. Acxiom, "Case Study: Customer Relation Management in Channel Marketing." *Acxiom Case-in-Point* [http://www.acxiom.com], n.d. Accessed Mar. 15, 2000.

18. I. P. Schneiderman, "More Major Stores Offer Loyalty Programs," *Daily News Record,* Apr. 27, 1998, p. 2.

19. Acxiom, "Case Study: Customer Relationship Management in Channel Marketing."

20. Acxiom, "Case Study: Time, Inc. Captivates Advertisers." Acxiom Case-in-Point, [www.acxiom.com], n.d. Accessed Mar. 15, 2000.

21. H. Davis, "Next Steps in Knowledge Discovery," *Customer Loyalty Today,* Apr. 2000, p. 19.

22. E. Esterson, "A Shock to the System," *Inc.,* [www.inc.com/articles], Mar. 15, 1998. Accessed Nov. 4, 1999.

Chapter Eight

1. S. Bishop, "The Strategic Power of Saying No," *Harvard Business Review,* Nov.–Dec. 1999, pp. 50–61.

2. E. Ramsdell, "Streamline Delivers the Goods," *Fast Company,* Nov. 1998, p. 132; Frank Britt (vice president of marketing, Streamline, Inc.), telephone interview conducted by Michael Lowenstein, Apr. 1999.

3. G. Hallberg, *All Consumers Are Not Created Equal* (New York: Wiley, 1995), pp. 27–28.

4. Hallberg, *All Consumers Are Not Created Equal,* pp. 37–44.

5. A. Mitchell, "Preaching to the Converted," *Marketing Week,* June 5, 1997, pp. 24–25.

6. F. G. Thompson, "Connecting with Customers," *Construction Marketing Today,* Jan. 1995, pp. 17–18.

7. "Ten Guiding Principles for Market Segmentation," [http://www.agora-marketing.com/segmentation.html]. Accessed Dec. 19, 1999.

8. E. MacDonald, "More Accounting Firms Are Dumping Risky Clients," *Wall Street Journal,* Apr. 25, 1997, p. A-2.

9. C. Caggiano, "Seller, Beware! How to Spot the Customers You Don't Want," *Inc.,* May 1999, p. 99.

10. M. Schrage, "Honest, I Am Not a Boor," *Fortune,* Nov. 8, 1999, p. 324.

11. G. A. Patterson, "Target 'Micromarkets' Its Way to Success: No Two Stores Are Alike," *Wall Street Journal,* May 14, 1997, p. A-1.

12. Michael Kahn (vice president of marketing, Art.com), "Differences and Integration of Offline and Online One-to-One Marketing," IQPC One-to-One on the Internet Conference, Phoenix, Mar. 2000.

13. Bishop, "The Strategic Power of Saying No."

14. Ramsdell, "Streamline Delivers the Goods"; F. F. Britt, "Building a Lifestyle Solution Brand: The Unfolding Story of Streamline, Inc.," *Arthur Andersen Retailing Issues Letter,* 1998, *10*(4), pp. 1–4; Frank Britt, telephone interview conducted by Michael Lowenstein.

15. R. P. Barry, "Word of Mouth Can Be Your Best Marketing Tool," Graham Communications, Inc., [http://www.smartbiz.com]. Accessed Nov. 19, 1999.

16. K. Cheng, "eBay Best Viral Marketing," *Brandweek,* June 28, 1999, p. 42.

17. A. Beeler, "Virus Without a Cure," *Advertising Age,* Apr. 17, 2000, p. 54.

18. B. Barth, "Friendly Persuasion Online," *WWD,* Mar. 15, 2000, p. 15.

19. The Jupiter/NFO Consumer Survey, Vol. 1, "Defining the Internet Shopper," [http://www.jupitercommunications.com], Oct. 1998. Accessed Mar. 3, 2000; P. R. Hagen, "Must Search Stink?" Forrester Research, [http://www.forrester.com], June 2000. Accessed Mar. 3, 2000.

Chapter Nine

1. Elizabeth Haight (vice president of operations, The Math Works, Inc., Natick, Mass.), telephone interview conducted by Michael Lowenstein, Apr. 2000.

2. S. Nathan, "Hospital Mends Customer Service," *USA Today,* May 5, 2000, p. 7; Pam Bilbrey (vice president of marketing, Baptist Healthcare, Pensacola, Fla.), telephone interview conducted by Michael Lowenstein, May 2000.

3. E. Ramsdell, "IBM's Grassroots Revival," *Fast Company,* June 1998, p. 182.

4. D. Fenn, "Ask the Experts Where Teams Trip Up," *Inc.,* Nov. 1995, p. 94.

5. J. Griffiths, "Customer Service and Value-Added Teams," *Teams,* Nov. 1997, *3*(1), [www.legal-and-general.co.uk]; Clive Watkins (consultant, Morgan-Clarke, Ockley, Surrey, England), interview conducted by Michael Lowenstein, May 2000.

6. J. Sherriton and J. Stern, *Corporate Culture/Team Culture* (New York: AMACOM, 1996).

7. J. Sherriton and J. Stern, *Corporate Culture/Team Culture,* p. 160.

8. G. Hasek, "The Right Chemistry," *Industry Week,* Mar. 6, 2000, pp. 36–39; D. Anfuso, "W. L. Gore and Associates, Inc.: Optima Award Profile," *Workforce,* Mar. 1999, *78*(3), 48–53.

9. T. Petzinger Jr., "Bovis Team Helps Builders Construct a Solid Foundation," *Wall Street Journal,* Jan. 21, 1997, p. B-1.

10. G. Parker, *Cross-Functional Teams* (San Francisco: Jossey-Bass, 1994), pp. 112–115.

11. Haight, telephone interview conducted by Michael Lowenstein.

12. W. C. Taylor, "At VeriFone, It's a Dog's Life," In Handbook of the Business Revolution, a special pullout section of *Fast Company,* Nov. 1995, pp. 12–17. [http://www.fastcomopany.com/online/01/vfone.html]. Accessed July 15, 1999.

13. S. Solomon, "Now That We're Not a Start-up, How Do I Promote Teamwork? *Inc.,* [http://www.incmagazine.com/articles], Oct. 15, 1998. Accessed Apr. 4, 2000.

14. S. Caudron, "Tie Individual Pay to Team Success," *Personnel Journal,* Oct. 1994, *73*(10), 40–46.

15. "Measuring Team Performance," *Workforce Performance Newsletter,* Aug. 1994, p. 1.

16. "Performance Appraisal for Teams," *Workforce Performance Newsletter,* Aug. 1998, p. 1.

17. Parker, *Cross-Functional Teams,* p. 132.

18. "Attain Top Service Through Specialty Teamwork," *Customer Service Manager's Letter,* Apr. 1, 1999, 927, 1–3.

19. Kathy O'Neal (senior vice president–marketing, ClubCorp), interview conducted by Jill Griffin, Apr. 1999.

20. D. Jones, "GE Turns Decision-Making Art into Science," *USA Today,* May 1, 1998, p. 7-B.

Chapter Ten

1. "Make People Count," summary of D. G. McCarthy, *The Loyalty Lock* (Middlebury, Vt.: Soundview Executive Book Summaries, 1997), audiocassette.

2. S. Shellbarger, "It's a Touchy-Feely Kind of World," *Orange County Register,* Mar. 13, 2000, p. C-10.

3. Bruce Robertson (director, McKinsey & Company), interview conducted by Jill Griffin, Feb. 2000.

4. S. Branch, "You Hired 'Em. But Can You Keep 'Em?" *Fortune,* Nov. 9, 1998, p. 248.

5. T. A. Stewart, "Company Values That Add Value," *Fortune,* July 8, 1996, p. 146.

6. Shellbarger, "It's a Touchy-Feely Kind of World," p. C-10.

7. "Trust in Workplace Leaders Declining," *Customer Care Network News,* Oct. 17, 1997, *1*(2), p. 1.

8. C. Fishman, "The War for Talent," *Fast Company,* Issue 16, p. 104. [http://www.fastcompany.com/online/16/mckinsey.html], July 31, 1998. Accessed Feb. 3, 2000.

9. "Empower Reps to Make Financial Adjustments for More Efficient Service," *Customer Service Manager's Letter,* Aug. 10, 1997, p. 1.

10. "Retaining Employees a Top Concern," *AMA Research Reports,* [www.amanet.org], Apr. 20, 1999.

11. S. Bates, "Building Better Workers," *Nation's Business,* June 1998, p. 67.

12. M. W. Lowenstein, *The Customer Loyalty Pyramid,* (Westport, Conn.: Quorum Books, 1997), p. 186.

13. "Southwest Airlines' Herb Kelleher: Unorthodoxy at Work," *Management Review,* Jan. 1995, p. 9.

14. Judy Lowenstein (supervisor, State Farm Insurance Company), interview conducted by Michael Lowenstein, Sept. 1997.

15. C. Gaggiano, "How're You Gonna Keep 'Em Down on the Firm," *Inc.,* Jan. 1998, p. 70.

16. G. Imperato, "How to Give Good Feedback," *Fast Company,* Sept. 1998, pp. 144–154.

17. Imperato, "How to Give Good Feedback," p. 148.

18. C. Hymowitz, "Managers Often Miss the Promising Talent on Their Own Staffs," *Wall Street Journal,* May 9, 2000, p. B-1.

19. C. Olofson, "Meetings I Never Miss," *American Way,* Oct. 1998, p. 52.

20. B. Johnson, "Loyalty Lessons from the Pros," *Customer Support Management Newsletter,* July/Aug. 1999, p. 16.

21. S. Gross, "A Note from Steve," *Pinnacle,* May 1996, p. 1.

22. Michael Price (general manager, Price Automotive, Dover, Del.), interview conducted by Michael Lowenstein, Nov. 1999.

23. J. Stack, "Measuring Morale," *Inc.,* Jan. 1997, p. 29.

24. P. Kruger, "Jobs for Life," *Fast Company,* May 2000, p. 236.

25. C. Caggiano, "Perks You Can Afford," *Inc.,* Nov. 1997, p. 107.

26. J. Lublin, "Climbing Walls on Company Time," *Wall Street Journal,* Jan. 1, 1998, p. B-1.

27. N. L. Hutchin, "The Serious Business of Fun," Reengineering Resource Center, [www.reengineering.com].

28. Steve Gross (president and chief operating officer, Prudential Resource Management, Valhalla, N.Y.), interview conducted by Michael Lowenstein, Oct. 31, 1996.

29. Caggiano, "Perks You Can Afford," p. 107.

30. C. Salter, "People and Technology—MicroStrategy, Inc." *Fast Company,* Issue 33, Apr. 2000, p. 190.

31. "A Program to Reward and Recognize Good Workers," *The Motivational Manager,* Ragan Communications, Inc., [http://www.ragan.com]. Accessed Feb. 16, 2000.

32. D. Fenn, "The Right Fit," *Inc.,* Oct. 15, 1997.

33. C. Caggiano, "Recruiting Secrets of the Smartest Companies Around," *Inc.,* Oct. 1, 1998.

34. Caggiano, "Recruiting Secrets of the Smartest Companies Around."

35. Bruce Robertson, interview conducted by Jill Griffin.

36. T. A. Stewart, "The Cunning Plots of Leadership," *Fortune,* Sept. 7, 1998, p. 165.

37. "People Go, Knowledge Stays," *Fast Company,* Sept. 1998, p. 48A.

⟞⟞⟋⟍⟋ Subject Index

Company Index